Born in Sydney, Christine Osborne is a freelance writer and photographer with a special interest in developing nations. She has travelled extensively in South-east Asia, Africa, the Indian sub-continent and Africa. She has written and illustrated a dozen books, mainly on Islamic countries, and photographs from her stock library appear internationally. Based in London, Christine Osborne has a long association with Morocco, which she visited initially in 1964 and most recently to update this essential guide for visitors.

Other Independent Travellers Guides include:

MPC INDEPENDENT TRAVELLERS

Morocco

Christine Osborne

MPC

Jacket photographs:
Front: Blue Man near Merzouga (*Christine Osborne Pictures*)
Back/Spine: Boulmane du Dades (*Christine Osborne Pictures*)

Published by: Moorland Publishing Co Ltd,
Moor Farm Road West, Ashbourne, Derbyshire DE6 1HD, England

ISBN 0 86190 540 7

First published in English in 1990 by HarperCollins Publishers Ltd,
under the title *Collins Independent Travellers Guide: Morocco*
First revised edition 1994

© Christine Osborne 1990, 1994

British Library Cataloguing in Publication Data:
A catalogue record for this book is available from the British Library.

Typeset by Ace Filmsetting Ltd, Frome, Somerset.
Printed and bound in Great Britain by The Cromwell Press Ltd, Melksham, Wiltshire.

Contents

To the *marabout* of Taroudannt, my travelling companion on the
magical road to Zagora.

Preface

Each evening from my house in London I see a flight of racing pigeons circling the block, with one bird always flying higher, or lower, than the rest of the flock. I identify with this individual in my endeavours to write about Morocco. Since an initial visit in 1964, I have returned many times, the most memorable being in 1990, when I rented a Renault 4 and drove over 10,000 km to research this book. I have a deep affection for the country, but I always feel *in* society, rather than *of* it. Being a single, Christian woman is a disadvantage and, unlike Edith Wharton, who travelled 'around Morocco in thirty days', I had no hand-picked French military chauffeur and bodyguard to accompany me.

Many aspects of the research were stressful, and travel writing is by nature a solitary profession, but I never felt lonely in Morocco. Whether in Rabat or Marrakesh, there was always someone trying to sell me something, to be my guide, or, on finding the purpose of my visit, to be my friend. I am indebted to a number of Moroccans whom I will never see again. To those who littered my way with false promises, I have nothing to say except that tourism is a capricious commodity: take care of it.

Acknowledgements

I would like to thank in particular Clive Chandler MBE, long-time resident in Morocco, for his hospitality and interest in this book. Dr Ali Bouhajoub of the Maghreb Press Agency in London was never too busy to answer enquiries. Also Annie Austin, another loyal Morocco fan, whom I first met on the banks of the Bou Regreg in Salé.

Others helped me in various ways: Lakbir Aouam (unemployed) in Meknes; Michel Benisty (director Inter-Rent/Europcar), Casablanca; Redouan Ben Abdelouahab (ONMT Tetouan); Haji Abdullah and Madame Berrada (businessman and wife), Fez; Ahmed Brahim (guide), Kelaa des M'Gouna; Adenbi Bouayache (barman), Taliouine; Kacem el-Boukhary (boatman), Moulay Bousselham; Fouad Hajoui (ONMT), Agadir; Mohammed Haddouch (General Manager, Salam Hotel), Oujda; Hamid Laghouizi (unemployed), Azrou.

And friends . . .

CHRISTINE OSBORNE
London 1994

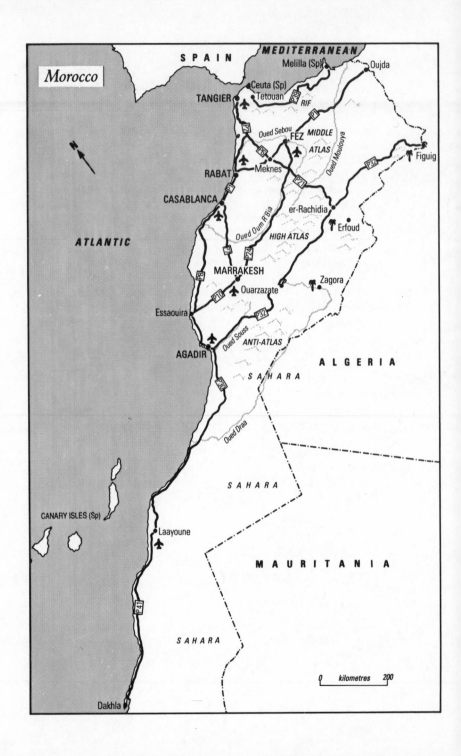

Introduction

The kingdom of Morocco is one of the most beautiful but least known countries within easy access of Europe. Spain, only forty minutes from Tangier by hydrofoil, receives more than 50 million tourists a year, while marginally more than 3 million, including many day-trippers from the Costa del Sol, visit Morocco.

The rewards for the curious traveller are infinite. Inland from the modern coastal towns is a rich medieval world that long ago disappeared from Europe. It is here, not in the Middle East, that you will encounter 'A Thousand and One Nights'.

Any day, somewhere in Morocco, the sun is shining, but because of the abrupt changes in landscape, within hours of feeling the sand between your toes in the Sahara, you can be skiing in the Atlas. This diversity is one of Morocco's fascinations: I have found no other country where you can experience desert, sea and mountain so effortlessly.

Morocco's excellent road and rail network is backed up by an efficient domestic airline service linking all but the most remote oases to important towns. Hotels and restaurants remain open throughout the year, and although some towns are short of accommodation, you will also find splendid hotels in the most unlikely places – the Auberge Derkaoua in the desert south of Erfoud, for example, is the last hotel between Morocco and Timbuktu.

You can live comfortably and very cheaply in Morocco compared to Europe in the 1990s: bed, meals and travel expenses need not exceed £10–12 a day. A bonus of a visit is the colourful regional folklore and a flourishing crafts industry specializing in attractive and unusual *objets d'art*. While you may find the custom of bargaining an unorthodox way of making a purchase, buying can be full of humour if you enter into the spirit of things. This is the East. There is no charge for mint-tea, even if you walk away without spending anything.

Beautiful, hospitable and cultured though it is, Morocco is not the place to go to relax on holiday (unless you wish to shut yourself in somewhere like the Gazelle d'Or in Taroudannt). Outside your hotel, it is a very demanding country, constantly tugging your sleeve for 'baksheesh'. Morocco is for the independent traveller who wants to confront it on its own terms, who is prepared to be knocked by loaded mules pattering through its ancient *souqs* and trailed by touts through every *medina*. You will never forget the mud-built *ksour* outlined like cardboard cut-outs against the desert sky, and the smell of the tenth-century tanneries in Fez will never leave your nose. Morocco will enchant and drive you mad, but it will not leave you unmoved.

There are many paradoxes. Muslim to its minarets, Morocco forbids infidels in its mosques, yet Christians and more than 30,000 Jews are allowed to practise their own religions freely. This *laissez-faire* policy extends to such things as homosexuality. But although easy-going in these ways, Morocco still requires a degree of decorum in the way you behave and dress. You cannot go to Morocco, nor indeed to any Muslim country, and behave as you do at home. If you flout certain restrictions and courtesies, you will do yourself an injustice. Until this century many Berbers in their mountain villages had never seen a European, and xenophobia still prevails in places such as the Rif.

Morocco has always fascinated travellers, but as statistics show, tourism has been slow to develop. It is difficult to say precisely why, but I believe there are several reasons. Although intrigued by writers' descriptions of its apparently unchanged, medieval world, potential visitors have also been frightened by the unfamiliar. Dubbed the 'Barbary Coast' by British seafarers, the name has stuck. In the nineteenth century Europeans used the word 'Moor' – 'blackamoor' was even worse – to frighten naughty children at bedtime. Morocco's great Kairouine University dates from the tenth century but in 1907 the French, arriving in Oujda, found the heads of captives impaled on the Bab Abd el-Wahab leading into the medina, and slave auctions were still being held in Marrakesh. Early adventurers had to take into account the hostility of the Berber population in what was known as the *Bled es-Siba*, or 'land of dissidents'. During the 1970s the occasional overland tourist expedition ran into problems with Polisario guerrillas, invariably highlighted by the international press. While Morocco sent a contingent to boost allied forces during the Gulf War, the Foreign Office decided to caution visitors, which resulted in massive holiday cancellations. Perhaps the current confrontation between Islamic Fundamentalists and the state in Algeria is seen by many travellers as being too close.

Morocco enters the 1990s with masses of unemployed who see every tourist as a target to earn a few dirhams. It took Turkey years to recover from the damage done by the film *Midnight Express*; today the *faux-guides* are giving Morocco a similar bad reputation. Incidents like marathon African walker, Fiona Campbell, being attacked near Rabat do not help the situation. The National Tourist Office (ONMT) has until now lacked a professional push in marketing Morocco overseas. Officials complain of a lack of government funding, but a professional approach is often wanting.

If you knew what Morocco offers, you would avoid the crowded, polluted resorts on the northern rim of the Mediterranean basin. Here is a beautiful and in many ways unique country that is also unspoilt. My advice is to let the *faux-guide* take the hindmost and visit Morocco while you are still a solitary sunbather on a magnificent Atlantic beach, or the only traveller to a fairy-tale *kasbah*. When the view of the ice-capped Atlas from the hot plains around Marrakesh is obscured by hotels, it will be too late.

The Land and Its People

'Morocco,' said the Minister of Culture in Rabat, more dramatic than accurate, I thought, 'is the last smell of donkeys and dirty streets before the West.' *Al Maghrib al-Aqsa*, as Arabs call this rugged, north-west shoulder of Africa, is the closest Muslim country to Europe, but despite keen European interest in its strategic position at the entrance to the Mediterranean, it was one of the last countries in the world to submit to colonial administration – by France in 1912. Throughout its history, avaricious visitors have left their mark on Morocco: Phoenician cisterns, Roman baths, Portuguese forts, Spanish cathedrals; and during the French Protectorate, a series of new towns was built.

In 1888, the *Larousse* dictionary estimated Morocco to have a total land area of 812,000 square kilometres; by 1914, this had been chipped away by the European powers to roughly half. Today Spain continues to occupy the Mediterranean enclaves of Ceuta and Melilla, but the recuperation of the Western Sahara in 1976 has given the kingdom around 703,000 square kilometres of North Africa alongside Mauritania, Algeria, Tunisia and Libya, its new partners in the Union of the Maghreb.

What makes Morocco different to the other desert states is the snow-capped central core of mountains, named the Atlas by Europeans who believed it was the home of the Greek god. Known to Berbers as *Idraren Draren*, or the 'mountains of mountains', it is the highest range in North Africa and the most complex on the African continent. Three ranges form the Atlas massif: the High Atlas, a backbone nearly 700 km long extending from the Algerian border to the coast north of Agadir; the Middle Atlas, a parallel but shorter chain rising near Taza and terminating at Beni-Mellal; and a branch of the High Atlas known as the Anti-Atlas, like a buffer on the edge of the Sahara, which ends at Sidi Ifni. A separate fourth range, the Rif, runs like a furrowed brow along the Mediterranean coast for 300 km between Ceuta and Melilla.

The High Atlas   The High Atlas is a formidable barrier between the grasslands and towns on the Atlantic coast and the sand and nomadic societies of the Sahara. The first known European to cross the mountains was a

Spaniard, disguised as a Moroccan, in 1804. The highest peak, Djebel Toukbal (4,167 m), was first climbed by a French party in 1923, although it had almost certainly been scaled by Berbers on hunting expeditions. A considerable Berber population lives in glorious isolation in the valleys of the High Atlas. Their citadels, or *kasbahs*, are a feature of travelling in this region. You can cross the Atlas at two major points south of Marrakesh: the Tizi N'Tishka (2,260 m), a high pasture pass, and the Tizi N'Test (2,092 m), a caravan route since time immemorial.

The Middle Atlas North of the High Atlas and separated from the Rif by deep, limestone river gorges, is the cool alpine area of the Middle Atlas. Known as 'Little Switzerland', it is a lovely area of forests, lakes and streams teeming with trout. There is at present insufficient infrastructure to support large tour-groups, so it is ideal for the independent traveller. The Middle Atlas is also peopled by Berbers, industrious craftsmen as well as farmers practising transhumance between the higher slopes and the plains.

The Anti-Atlas The Anti-Atlas is like a platform between the High Atlas and the part-cultivated, part-wilderness Berbers call the *bled*. Long river gorges lined with date-palms extend from the eastern flank into the desert. The mixed population of Berbers and Arabs are mainly farmers who live in *ksour*, fantastic fortified villages built of *pisé*.

The Rif The Rif rises abruptly off the Mediterranean coast to the peak of Djebel Tidirhine (2,496 m). Cedars, pine and oak dominate the mountains, peopled by historically xenophobic, protective and strong-willed Rifians; their resistance to the Spanish Protectorate is legendary. *Kif*, or marijuana, is the main crop grown in the western Rif, with olives and wheat. Cereals and vegetables are cultivated under irrigation where the mountains peter out into the plains near Oujda.

The Souss The fertile Souss Valley extends inland from Agadir. A beautiful, self-contained area, it is protected to the north by the High Atlas and from scorching desert winds by the Anti-Atlas. Well watered, historically it has been a 'bread basket' for Morocco, growing vegetables, fruit and olives, and sugar-cane, which was exported to Europe until the sixteenth century. The Berber population is dominated by the Chleuh tribe, who are proud, hard-working farmers and merchants.

The desert The western edge of the Sahara, the vast sand-sea stretching from Morocco across North Africa to the Sudan, laps the foothills of the Anti-Atlas. Huge dunes, or *ergs*, are a feature of the desert near Merzouga and in the Western Sahara. Sandstorms are common: the silence is suddenly broken by wildly thrashing date-palms and the sun becomes obscured by dust; Western travellers call it the *sirocco*, local nomads know it as the dreaded *chagi*. Most of the population are peripatetic tribes, with at least one member of each family dabbling in trading or date farming. Rainfall is negligible; local oases are fed by rivers draining the Anti-Atlas and by subterranean springs.

Flora and fauna

Growth in the desert after even the slightest drop of rain is miraculous. Elsewhere in Morocco the countryside in spring is awash with wild flowers. I was forever stopping to walk through carpets of crimson adonis, iris, lupins, broom and chrysanthemums; botanists from Kew Gardens in London list over 375 different species from a single valley. The *maquis* covering the rugged plains and the gorges of pink Persian roses near Kelaa des M'Gouna are unforgettable. At the sight of a traveller, children, quick as a wink, like musicians passing round a hat, pick posies to sell. The Renault ashtray was always filled with blooms – until I started smoking again.

The occasional smell of burning gum-leaves filled me with a haunting nostalgia for Australia. You will pass forests of silver gums on the Atlantic coast, there is a stunning wood of red-tipped eucalypts outside Taliouine and a shady avenue of gums welcomes you to Oujda after the barren drive from Taza. The lower mountain slopes in the Atlas are covered in rosemary, acacia, wormwood and cypress, while oak, cedar, juniper and fir flourish above 1,000 m. I found the dark Atlas forests intimidating after the tamarisks, date-palms and desert cacti of the south.

Fleshy succulents and dark green euphorbia grow on the Atlantic coastal ridge, especially around Tan-Tan and Sidi Ifni. Remarkably similar to vegetation in the Canary Islands, they add credence to the theory of a sunken land-bridge to Morocco. Elsewhere you often find a curious juxtaposition of alpine and hot-weather flora, as if nature does not know what to do in the ever-changing climate. For example, the road from Marrakesh along the Ourika Valley is lined with eucalypts on one side and conifers on the other.

Two interesting native trees are the gum-sanderac, or *thuya*, and *Argania sideroxlon*, or *argan*. Growing on the slopes of the Atlas, the *thuya* has rich wine-coloured wood with handsome roots prized by carpenters. A cross between a thorn-tree and an olive, the argan is indigenous to the Souss. Berbers extract oil from the small nuts for use in *tajines* and salads. Goats adore *argan* nuts and climb the topmost branches for them. The goatherd will not understand your enthusiasm for his hairy Christmas-tree decorations, but is quick to ask money for a photograph.

As well as beautiful wild flowers and curious trees, Morocco has a colourful variety of birdlife. The best time for bird-watching is during the European migratory season, from October to March, but lagoons and estuaries generally offer some interest throughout the year. Flamingoes are found in several areas along the Atlantic: the most accessible flock is in the Merja Zerqa Nature Reserve at Moulay Bousselham. Storks nesting in the *kasbahs* are a photographer's delight, but you must not frighten them as it is considered an evil omen if they fly away. In Merenid Fez a special bird hospital was built to care for sick storks, which have holy status in Morocco. Eagles planing on the air currents are a common sight in the Atlas, where I also passed a rare griffon vulture reluctant to leave a rabbit on the road. Other rare birds are kingfishers, electric-blue roller bee-eaters, lapwings and the jolly hoopoe, which, sadly, is hunted for its heart, believed to guard against the 'evil eye'.

A Carthaginian general in 5 BC records sightings of elephant along the Mediterranean coast of Morocco. The forests of the Middle Atlas were an important source of lions for Roman arenas, but the last panther was shot in Azrou in 1969 (the hunter was fined 1,000 dirham). Jackals are still fairly common: the Berber custom of placing a sharp stone on a grave dates from the Great Barbary Plague in the eighteenth century, when wolves and hyenas as well as jackals were frequent visitors to cemeteries. Wild boar flourish in the Rif and only 10 km outside Fez I passed a boar which had been struck by a car.

The only animal I killed on my travels was a tortoise which should not have been crossing the road near Moulay Bousselham. The Saharan land tortoise, thought to be extinct in the wild, grows to several hundredweight. Snakes are particularly common in the Souss, where they are caught for the snake-charmers performing on the Djemaa el Fna in Marrakesh. The poor chameleon is hunted ruthlessly; alive, it acts as a fly-catcher, dead as an antidote to various ills. You will also see children swinging choking lizards to sell to Berber apothecaries. Scorpions are common in the *bled* – the French used to stand the legs of their beds in tins of kerosene during an invasion of these poisonous creatures. Grasshoppers were considered a great delicacy by the Moors – stripped of wings and heads, boiled and sprinkled with salt and vinegar, they were said to taste like prawns. Today grasshoppers are viewed with revulsion, and many farmers went bankrupt during the devastating plague in 1988.

The people

Since recorded history began Morocco has been washed by the ebb and flow of different civilizations – Phoenician, Carthaginian, Roman, Arab, Jewish, Portuguese, Spanish, English and French – as well as tides from the Sahara – nomad traders from the Hoggar and Mauritania. As a result there are Arabs or Moors who may be of Semitic extraction, have Spanish blood, or be the descendants of negro slaves. In addition the indigenous Berber tribes each have its own customs, which means that it is as difficult to generalize about Moroccans as it is about the changing landscape.

The Berbers

Many theories are advanced about the origins of the Berbers, who inhabited Morocco before the great Arab invasion of the eighth century. Wyndham Lewis writes of a sunken land-bridge between Morocco and Mexico and the ancient Guanche language of the Canary Islands was also spoken by early Berber tribes, but their pale skin and often blue eyes makes a European link more likely.

Proud, self-reliant and extremely hard-working, Berbers account for Morocco's expatriate population in Europe. Their reputation for being energetic has been somewhat undermined by the Arab reputation for indolence, but you can see it everywhere in the tiny, intensively cultivated farms and the veritable explosion of energy that has gone into building the immense fortified villages, or *ksour*. Travelling in Morocco, you will see Berbers striding along the road in their hooded burnous and sandals, covering considerable distances to go to market, or to visit the *caid*. Now there are schools they expect their children to do the same.

As well as being home-loving, generous and loyal, Berbers can be suspicious by nature, are fiercely defensive and quite ruthless when it comes to settling any dispute. Spanish soldiers, confronted by an attack in the Rif in the 1920s, were said to have hurled themselves off the parapets rather than face capture. Feuds are still settled by the gun in many areas, but the freedom to resolve their own destiny is now also acknowledged by a political party, the Mouvement Populaire.

You will come across Berbers driven to the cities in search of work, but your true-blue Berber is a man of the *bled*. Most speak Arabic as a second language after one of the three main Berber dialects: Taselhait, spoken in the High Atlas, the Anti-Atlas and the Souss; Tamazizght in the Middle Atlas and Tarift in the Rif.

Urban Moroccans

No matter how poor, hospitality is second nature to every Moroccan. Often you may scarcely know someone, like your hotel waiter, or a student, who will invite you home to meet his family. It will not be merely for coffee, but for a vast dinner that his mother and aunts have spent all day preparing. He is immensely loyal to his family and the Western habit of placing elderly parents in a rest home is considered repugnant.

And kindness is not reserved for family and friends. Stopping to ask directions in the rain in Fez, I had a total stranger come more than 5 kilometres out of his own way to show me. I offered to return him to where we had met. 'No, I'll catch a bus,' he said, and, hoisting his *djellabah* clear of the puddles, he disappeared into the gathering night.

The Moroccan you are likely to meet in a town like Tangier, or Tetouan, is a mixed bag of tricks who takes himself very seriously. Expatriates with an intimate knowledge of the local character swear he has a sense of humour – unfortunately, it is not usually apparent. He will look after you royally if he respects you, but he will fleece you if he does not care for your looks. Arrogance is often a cover for the stigma of being unemployed – around 50 per cent of adult males are illiterate. He may also be nervous at being confronted by a foreigner, and prickly towards anything interpreted as a slur on national pride. French colonial administration remains a bitter pill for the citizens of the oldest surviving monarchy in the Muslim world.

History

Chronology

10,000–5,000 BC	Neolithic culture. Rock drawings.
1000 BC	Phoenician settlements on the Mediterranean coast.
500 BC	Carthage dominates Phoenician ports.
146 BC	Collapse of Carthage. Roman influence spreads through Berber kingdoms in North Africa.
25 BC–AD	Juba II rules from Volubilis.
AD 24	Direct Roman rule imposed.
253–429	Roman withdrawal to Tangier. Tangier and Ceuta remain under Rome.
682	Oqba Ibn Nafi conquers Morocco from Kairouan, in Tunisia.
705–11	Moussa Ibn Nasr establishes Arab rule.
711	Moorish invasion of Andalusia.
788–91	Moulay Idriss establishes the **Idrissid dynasty** in Volubilis and Moulay Idriss.
791–804	Rule of Rachid, the regent-servant.
804–28	Moulay Idriss II. Establishes Fez.
1062–1107	Youssef Ibn Tachfine. Establishes the **Almoravid dynasty** in Marrakesh. Almoravid invasion of Spain.
1121	Ibn Tumert establishes a *r'bat* at Tinmal.

1145–47	Abd el-Moumen. Establishes the **Almohad dynasty** in Fez and Marrakesh.
1184–99	Yaccoub el-Mansour. Extends Almohad rule in Spain. Extensive building programmes in Marrakesh and Rabat.
1213	Almohad defeat at the Battle of Las Navas de Tolosa in Spain.
1248–1465	**Merenid dynasty**.
1465	**Wattasids** (Merenid viziers) usurp power.
1471	Portuguese seize Tangier.
1492	Fall of Granada.
1520	Saadians establish rule in Taroudannt.
1541–2	Mohammed ech Sheikh establishes **Saadian dynasty** in Marrakesh and forces the Portuguese to retreat from Agadir, Azemmour and Salé.
1578	Battle of the Three Kings at Ksar el-Kebir.
1578–1603	Ahmed el-Mansour. Extends Moroccan frontier to Timbuktu.
1627	Moorish settlers from Andalusia declare the independent Republic of Bou Regreg in Rabat.
1630–40	Alaouite family establishes itself in the Tafilalet.
1662–82	British rule in Tangier.
1666–72	Moulay Rachid. Establishes rule of **Alaouite Dynasty** throughout Morocco.
1672–1727	Moulay Ismail. Declares a new capital in Meknes. Evicts British and Spanish from coastal towns.
1757–90	Sidi Mohammed Ibn Abdullah. Plans a new town in Essaouira.
1856	Morocco and Britain sign the Treaty of Peace in Perpetuity.

1860–2	First Spanish occupation of Tetouan.
1873–94	Moulay Hassan rules from Rabat and Fez.
1880	Madrid Conference establishes European control of Tangier.
1884	Dakhla, or Villa Cisneros, in the Western Sahara founded by Spain.
1890s	Saharan resistance to French and Spanish penetration from the south led by Sheikh Ma el-Ainin in Smara.
1907	French troops land at Casablanca and Oujda.
1912	Treaty of Fez ratifies a French Protectorate of Morocco. At the same time a Spanish Protectorate of Northern Morocco is agreed by France and Spain. El Hiba, son of Sheikh Ma el-Ainin declares himself sultan in Tiznit.
1914	Zaian Berbers massacre the French garrison at Khenifra.
1916	Spanish colonization of Tarfaya.
1923	Tangier declared an International Zone.
1934	Spain unilaterally declares a Spanish Protectorate of the Western Sahara. Spanish occupation of Sidi Ifni.
1930–40	Opposition to French administration increases. French conniving with Thami el-Glaoui, who becomes pasha of Marrakesh.
1943	Istiqlal, the nationalist party, formed in Fez.
1947	Sultan Mohammed V (1927–61) calls for independence in a speech in Tangier.
1953	French exile Alaouite royal family to Réunion.
1956	Independence from France.

1958	Spain withdraws from Tarfaya.
1961	King Hassan II accedes to the throne.
1969	Spain withdraws from Sidi Ifni.
1975	Green March into the Western Sahara.
1976	Spain withdraws from the Western Sahara.
1970–88	Guerilla war fought between Polisario, the Saharan independence movement, and the Moroccan army in the Western Sahara.
1989	Declaration in Marrakesh of the Union of the Maghreb between Morocco, Algeria, Tunisia, Libya and Mauritania.
1990	Ceasefire in Western Sahara.

Early history

The discovery of remarkable fish and shell fossils in a marble ridge in the Tafilalet, near Erfoud, indicates that an ocean must have covered Morocco during the Devonian period, more than 350 million years ago. Around 10,000–5,000 BC Neolithic Man scratched rock drawings of animals and hunting scenes at Oukaimeden in the High Atlas above Marrakesh, and in the region of Tafraoute. Other examples are on rocks around the Figuig Oasis, at Foum el-Hassan and Tazzerine, places rarely visited by Western travellers no matter how independent.

Recorded history in Morocco starts around 1,000 BC, with the establishment of Phoenician trading settlements at Melilla and Tangier and, later, on islands in Essaouira Bay. The Carthaginians, from Carthage in present-day Tunisia, took over their trading routes and developed some of the ports, notably Lixus, near Larache, Chellah, near Rabat, and Tingis.

When Carthage was defeated in the Punic Wars (146 BC) the region came under Roman influence, although people were still conversing in Punic as late as the sixth century. Before full Roman rule was imposed in AD 24, local Berbers were appointed to govern the Berber kingdoms of Numidia, in Algeria, and Mauritania-Tingitana, in Morocco. The most notable Berber ruler was Juba II (25 BC–AD 23), who had been educated at the court of the Emperor Augustus. Married to Cleopatra-Silene, love-child of Antony and Cleopatra, Juba ruled from the prosperous Roman city of Volubilis. His son Ptolemy (ruled AD 23–4) was summoned to Lyons, where he was murdered by Caligula – story says for daring to appear in a robe more brilliant than the emperor's own. Faced with mounting opposition from the *Bled es-Siba*, or land of dissidents, Rome lost its grip on its troublesome colony in North Africa. When Berbers blocked further advances, the Roman legions withdrew from Chellah to Volubilis and finally to Tangier.

The Islamization of Morocco

Evangelizing Arab armies spreading the word of the Prophet Muhammad brought the Berbers a religion as well as a social code. In AD 682, Oqba Ibn Nafi, the Arab governor of Kairouan, in present-day Tunisia, led a huge army across Morocco to the Atlantic, where, according to legend, he spurred his horse round in the surf and declared that this distant western outpost of Islam would henceforth be known as *al-Maghrib al-Aqsa*. With no god of their own, the Berbers were fired by the Arab zealots, and many were persuaded to embrace Muhammad as their Prophet, although they continued to maintain allegiance to their *caids*. Tribes in the western lowlands quickly became 'Arabized', but the mountain tribes resisted; when they did finally adopt Islam, they retained many of their animistic rituals, some of which survive today.

Moorish Spain

With Morocco relatively secure, the Moors launched their invasion of Spain. In 711 Tariq Ibn Zayed, the governor of Tangier, led an army of 7,000 into Andalusia, where they were welcomed by both Christians and Jews, glad to be saved from the German Visigoths. Within a decade the Moors had conquered the whole of Spain except for Asturias in the north. The Islamic conquest of Europe was checked by Charles Martel at the Battle of Poitiers in 732, but Moorish rule in Spain lasted for some 700 years. Agriculture, trades and the arts flourished, and Cordoba, the capital of Moorish Spain in the tenth century, was one of the most learned and sophisticated cities in the world. As well as the mighty *mezquita*, there were some 700 mosques and seventy public libraries. Seville, Toledo and Granada all blossomed under Moorish administration, but the fragmentation of the Western Caliphate led to defeats at the hands of the Christian forces. Jews as well as Moors sought refuge in Morocco and after Granada finally fell to Isabella and Ferdinand in 1492, the Spanish Inquisition forced the Moors to convert. Thousands who refused were either executed or expelled to

Morocco. Many aspects of their Andalusian culture are still evident today.

The Moroccan dynasties

The succession of sultans who have ruled Morocco since 788 may seem confusing, but it is useful to know where the main dynasties fit into local history and what they contributed towards Morocco's heritage, as the main monuments on every sightseeing tour were built by them.

Idrissid dynasty

The Idrissid dynasty was founded by Moulay Idriss (ruled 788–91), who travelled to Morocco to escape the schisms between Sunni and Shi'ite Muslims in Iraq. A great-grandson of the Prophet, he was welcomed as an *imam*, or leader, by Berber tribes in the Middle Atlas. After ruling briefly from Volubilis, he later transferred his court to Moulay Idriss. He was poisoned on the orders of the Abbassid caliph in Baghdad, Harun al-Rachid. The grand vizier, Rachid, ruled as regent until the boy-king Moulay Idriss II established a new kingdom in Fez c. 804. In the ninth century, many Moorish refugees from Spain and Arabs from Kairouan settled in Fez and their combined talents helped it to grow into one of the great cities of the time.

Almoravid dynasty

Family disputes eventually weakened Idrissid rule, and a new dynasty of tough reformers emerged from the southern oases. Islamic puritans, the Almoravids were nomadic tribesmen who had converted to Islam in the ninth century. In 1054 they set out to preach against the lax morals introduced by refugees from Spain. In 1062 Youssef Ibn Tachfine captured Marrakesh and his son, Ali Ibn Youssef (1107–44), pushed Morocco's frontiers out to the Niger. The Almoravids completed the great Kairouine Mosque in Fez and the Grand Mosque in Tlemcen, in Algeria. The only Almoravid structure to have survived intact is the *koubba* in Marrakesh.

Almohad dynasty

The Almohads, who succeeded the Almoravids in the twelfth century, had much in common with them. Berbers from the High Atlas, they were intensely puritanical and their leader, Ibn Tumert, a learned scholar who had visited Mecca, disapproved of anything contrary to the Qur'an. He outlawed wine and song and ordered desert women, who had never covered their faces, to wear a veil. Banished from Marrakesh, he established a *r'bat*, or fortified mosque, at Tinmal in the High Atlas, in 1121. His successor, Abd el-Moumen (1130–62) conquered Marrakesh in 1147 and adopted the title Commander of the Faithful, used by all subsequent monarchs including King Hassan II. The Almohads, in particular Abou Yaccoub Yussef (1163–84) and Yaccoub el-Mansour (1184–99) were great builders. Some of Morocco's finest monuments date from this period: the Koutoubia

Mosque in Marrakesh and the ramparts, Oudaia Gate and Hassan Tower in Rabat. The great Giralda in Seville was also built by Almohad architects. In attempting to extend Morocco's Spanish empire, Almohad armies suffered a terrible defeat at the Battle of Las Navas de Tolosa in 1213 and by 1269 family disputes had destroyed the dynasty.

Merenid dynasty

The Merenids, desert nomads trained in combat, seized control and established a new power base, Fez el-Jdid, beside the old *medina* in Fez. Their rule is very much a postscript to the other dynasties, as Morocco became more embroiled in domestic squabbles and disunity. Consumed by bureaucracy, the Merenids failed to prevent Portuguese incursions along the coast, but the sultans Abou Hassan (1331–51) and Abou Inan (1351–58) were responsible for building the great *medressa*, or religious colleges, seen in Fez, Meknes, Salé, Taza and Ksar el-Kebir, as well as mosques, fountains and *funduqs*, or hostels for travellers and visiting merchants. They also established special quarters known as *mellahs* where Jews could live and work in peace.

Wattsid dynasty

A branch of the Merenids, the Wattasids (1465–1554), allowed the Atlantic ports to slip away and Granada, the last Moorish stronghold in Spain, fell in 1492. The Portuguese seized Tangier in 1471, Larache in 1473, Azemmour in 1486, Essaouira in 1506 and Safi in 1508. Discontent increased and powerful *marabouts* joined ranks with the Berber population to undermine the Wattasids.

Saadian dynasty

In the 1520s the Saadians, a dynasty of *sherifs* from the Draa Valley, began a power struggle based in Taroudannt in the Souss. In 1541 Mohammed ech Sheikh established rule from Marrakesh and in the same year routed the Portuguese from Agadir. One of the great glories of Moroccan history is the Battle of the Three Kings in 1578, fought against the Portuguese at Ksar el-Kebir, which left the fifth Saadian sultan, Ahmed el-Mansour, triumphant. Morocco's fortunes soared during his reign. He extended the Moroccan frontier to Timbuktu and profits from the rich African sub-kingdoms filled the state coffers. Warrior-economists, the Saadians built the incomparable el-Badi Palace in Marrakesh, which was desecrated by the Alaouite sultan Moulay Ismail. They restored the mosques and *medressa* in Marrakesh and are best remembered for their own family tombs.

Several petty states emerged from the chaos that terminated the illustrious Saadian era. One of the most colourful was the Republic of Bou Regreg, created by refugees from Andalusia in 1627. They ran their tiny state, within the present-day capital of Rabat, on profits from piracy and hostage-taking on the high seas. Elsewhere power was held by various desert sheikhs and the powerful Tazeroualt *caids* of the Middle Atlas.

Alaouite dynasty

Meanwhile a new dynasty was gaining strength in the Tafilalet region of southern Morocco. *Shorfas*, like the Saadians, the Alaouites were a wealthy merchant family from Yenbo, in Saudi Arabia, who had migrated to Morocco in the thirteenth century. Moulay Ali Cherif was the first to be recognized as sultan, and by 1668 his son, Moulay Rachid, had established Alaouite rule throughout Morocco. His successor, Moulay Ismail (1672–1727) governed from his new capital in Meknes. Cruel and tyrannical, he maintained an imperial army of 140,000 negroes on constant standby. Infamous though he is, throughout Morocco you will find constructive aspects of his reign – roads, bridges, mosques and citadels. If a guide does not know who built something, he attributes it to Moulay Ismail and is not often wrong. Some writers say Moulay Ismail had 800 children, but only two sons emerged as reasonable successors: Sidi Mohammed Ibn Abdullah (1757–90) maintained resistance to the Spanish and Moulay Sliman (1792–1822) banned piracy and continued to press for a centrally recognized government.

In 1830 the French invaded Algeria. After inflicting a punishing defeat on a Moroccan force sent to Algeria's aid, they then bombarded Tangier. A Spanish garrison from Ceuta occupied Tetouan briefly in 1860–2 until Britain paid off a massive indemnity demanded by Madrid in return for increased administrative powers. Foreign consuls, especially in Tangier and Casablanca, began to interfere increasingly in Morocco's domestic affairs. Morocco's value for Europe was strategic, but France also coveted it to complement its Algerian and Tunisian colonies. Only jealousies among the European nations saved Morocco from being taken over like every other country in Africa during the scramble for colonies in the 1880s.

When Moulay Hassan acceded to the Alaouite throne in 1873, he attempted courageous reforms to prop up Morocco. Students were sent abroad to learn about Western technology, Western contractors were employed to upgrade local infrastructure and the sultan personally led many of the great *harkas*, or military expeditions, in an attempt to subdue dissenting *caids*. He died on one such expedition in the Atlas in 1894, and in *Morocco That Was* Walter Harris, the *Times* correspondent, describes how his death was kept a secret until his decomposing body was brought back to Rabat.

When news of his demise reached the *Bled es-Siba*, the *caids* took up arms. The sultan's successors, Moulay Abd el-Aziz (1894–1907) and Moulay Hafid (1907–12) inherited an impossible situation of debt, disunity, rebellion and European encroachment. According to Walter Harris, it was 'a pitiful period and one best forgotten'. The murder of French railway workers building port facilities in Casablanca was the catalyst which led to Morocco being declared a French Protectorate on 30 March 1912.

The Protectorate 1912–56

Under the terms of the Protectorate, responsibility for virtually every important ministry, except Islamic education, was transferred to French bureaucrats who knew nothing of the land which they governed, although the first resident general, Louis Hubert Gonzalve Lyautey, did seek to preserve Morocco's traditional culture. The sultan's role was reduced to approving new decrees and administering local endowments through the *habbous*. The *caids* were left responsible for the Berber tribal areas and it was they who benefited most from French occupation.

Apart from establishing military supremacy and supervising the day-to-day running of the country (three times as many French bureaucrats were deployed to govern Morocco as Englishmen were used to rule British India), the Protectorate's main concern was to develop agriculture and exploit mineral wealth. Laying an infrastructure to link the remote east with the more developed cities in the west was also a priority. Education was reserved for a hand-picked Berber élite, whom France hoped would become allies, but in fact the first educated Moroccans began agitating for independence.

Independence struggle 1927–56

Morocco's independence struggle was exacerbated by a lack of unity and by having to deal with two foreign powers instead of one. Tribal resistance was crushed in the 1920s when France and Spain joined forces against the Berber rebellion in the Rif, led by Abd el-Karim, but the movement gathered strength when the Istiqlal, or nationalist party, formed in 1943, rallied behind Sultan Mohammed V to rid the country of partisan settler politics. France tried to whip up opposition among powerful men like the *sherif* of Ouezzane and Thami el-Glaoui, pasha of Marrakesh, while the Spanish attempted to connive with er-Raisuli, the *caid* of Asilah, but by exiling the Alaouite royal family to the tropical island of R<ac>eunion, in what is now the Malagasy Republic, the French effectively made a martyr of Sultan Mohammed V. The Protectorate was further undermined by separate Rifian and Saharan resistance movements, and France, embroiled in a bloody civil war in Algeria, allowed Mohammed V to return in 1955. Morocco was accorded full independence on 18 November 1956. Spain relinquished Tarfaya in 1958, Sidi Ifni in 1969 and the Western Sahara in 1976. Ceuta and Melilla remain occupied.

Lost property

Controversy over the status of the Western Sahara dates from long before Spain declared a protectorate over the region in 1934. In the twelfth century, the kingdom of Morocco under the Almoravids extended from the river Niger to the Guadalquivir in Spain. For centuries traders had passed freely along the caravan routes. There were no borders and the local people, the Saharoui spoke a common language, Arabic. In the sixteenth century a Saharoui force attacked the Spanish garrison in Sidi Ifni; Saharouis also supported Sheikh Ma el-Ainin's Saharan resistance movement in the 1890s, but the question of self-determination arose only with the discovery of rich phosphate deposits at Bou Craa in the 1960s. This prompted a new nationalist movement, the Polisario (Frente Popular para la Liberación de Saguia el-Hamra y el Rio de Oro) to begin a war of attrition in the 1970s.

Rather than spend its phosphate profits on desert warfare, Spain announced it would hold a referendum giving the Saharoui a choice between integrating with Morocco and self-determination. King Hassan took the case of the Western Sahara to the United Nations. In October 1975 the International Court of Justice pronounced that while an allegiance existed between the Saharoui and the sultan, there was no evidence of any actual territorial ties, either with Morocco or its neighbour, Mauritania. It recommended that a referendum decide the status of the region, but this has still not been held.

Green March Determined to retrieve his lost property, on 6 November 1975 the king led 350,000 patriots carrying copies of the Qur'an into the Spanish Sahara, rousing vivid memories of Rifian successes against Madrid some fifty years earlier. As they moved south, Spain evacuated its citizens to Laayoune. But with Franco dying, the Spanish government sought to surrender sovereignty quickly to save face. His point made, King Hassan ordered his marchers back to Tarfaya, where a huge convoy of vehicles took them home.

On 26 February 1976 Spain withdrew from the Western Sahara, which was divided between Morocco and Mauritania, and on behalf of the Saharouis, Algeria proclaimed a Saharoui Arab Democratic Republic. Surprisingly, this was ratified by the Organization of African Unity, which until then had always opposed tribal separatist movements.

Desert warfare Following the partition of the Western Sahara, some 50,000 Saharouis fled to refugee camps in Tindouf, Algeria. The camps were a base for the Polisario's hit-and-run campaigns, which forced Mauritania to relinquish its half of the Western Sahara. Rabat then found itself alone in a costly desert war. Accustomed to the cooler northern climate, Moroccan soldiers proved no match for the nomads, and by

Hassan's Wall

1979 the Polisario had even struck as far north as Tan-Tan.

Morocco's solution was to build a line of defensive sand-walls, mined and monitored by radar. Some 3,000 km long – longer than the Great Wall of China – it protects south-west Morocco like a *cordon sanitaire*. King Hassan and Polisario leaders met for the first time in February 1989 in Marrakesh. They agreed in principle that no one could win the war, and a ceasefire was declared in 1990.

In 1991, the UN recommended a free referendum in Western Sahara. Since then Morocco has transferred thousands of settlers into the region and has demanded the registration of some 120,000 supplementary voters on the electoral roll in order to boost the pro-Moroccan vote. The UN now proposes to register voters on the basis of tribal factions and by reference to the Spanish population census in Western Sahara in 1974. With the unstable situation in Algeria growing daily more serious, many see the dispute as a conservative monarchy opposing radical socialism which supports the Polisario.

Morocco Today

The French legacy

'Everyone is filibuster of some sort who is installed upon a territory of a race that is not his own,' observes Wyndham Lewis in *Journey into Barbary*, an account of his travels in Morocco in the 1930s.

The French administration, based on military power and conniving with the *caids*, was basically self-serving, but has left an indelible impression on present-day Morocco. You will meet Moroccans who attribute all the country's problems to French colonialism, but after a long drive from Erfoud to Sefrou, I was not having the French blamed because the hot-water system in my hotel had broken down, particularly when I reflected that the road which had brought me up from the Sahara, like many others, is part of the well-integrated domestic transport system built during the Protectorate.

The French also built some of the most efficient and architecturally pleasing modern towns in North Africa. Thanks to the enlightened General Lyautey, instead of demolishing the old *medinas* to make way for essential services (as they did in Algeria), *nouvelle villes*, or new towns, were built outside the walls, thus preserving Morocco's incalculably valuable national heritage.

The country France took over in 1912 was fertile, but the constant feuds between the various tribes meant that very little land was under cultivation. With the imposition of peace the French developed agriculture to such an extent that by the mid-1950s a staggering 350,000 settlers, or *pieds-noirs*, were farming prime land, mainly around Meknes, Oujda and Marrakesh.

Industry took second place to agriculture, although French investment financed the beginnings of tourism and some industrial projects, mainly on the Atlantic coastal plain close to the major ports. The less accessible Atlas and the south were neglected, and the French policy of developing some towns at the expense of others (Kenitra and Khemisset are creations of the Protectorate) resulted in a lasting imbalance in living standards.

In the field of general education France failed miserably: by 1940 only 3 per cent of children were attending school, and when it gained independence in 1956 Morocco had only a dozen graduates – all from French universities. Education was one of the means by which the French sought to exploit ethnic and religious divisions. In 1914 the

Berber-speaking mountain regions, where roughly 40 per cent of the population lived, were divided from the Arabic-speaking communities on the coast and in the south; in French schools set up in Berber areas Arabic was banned, and an officers' academy was established at Azrou to educate an élite. However, policies intended to 'divide and rule' proved ineffective, as the independence struggle showed.

Since 1956 Morocco has made schooling a priority. Education is based on Western curricula with emphasis on preserving the country's cultural and spiritual identity. Technically education is free and compulsory for children aged seven to seventeen. The plea from children in the country for biros is a poignant indication of a desire to learn. Some children walk up to 15–20 km a day to school. You will pass them clamouring for a lift by the roadside. The number of primary school pupils has risen dramatically from under half a million post-Independence to nearly 3 million today. Secondary school students increased from 27,000 in 1957 to approximately 2 million today, and higher education has experienced a boom, especially in the past decade. Morocco now has six universities – in Fez, Rabat, Casablanca, Tetouan, Marrakesh and Oujda – and twenty-five technical schools and polytechnics. More than 30,000 students are enroled overseas.

Ironically, the French *can* be blamed for one of Morocco's worst problems: a soaring birthrate has led to 50 per cent of the population being under 20. Peace among the warring Berber tribes meant that the men no longer went away for months on the great *harkas* but stayed at home fathering children – after thirty years of French rule the population had increased by 5 million.

Some educated Moroccans show a certain nostalgia for France. You will hear many people, especially in the large towns, conversing in French, not Arabic, and French fashions and cuisine are in vogue among the well-off. Whether the next generation of educated but jobless students will share the same sentiments is a moot question.

King Hassan II

A monarchy since the eighth century, Morocco wears a crown with apparent ease and you are unlikely to hear any criticism of King Moulay Hassan II, twelfth sultan of the Alaouite dynasty. Mumblings about the exorbitant cost of the Grand Mosque in Casablanca, yes; complaints about the mounting cost of living, certainly; but no overt resentment about the thirty-ninth descendant of the Prophet, whose name is said in every mosque throughout Morocco at Friday prayers.

Born in Rabat on 9 July 1929, King Hassan is a graduate in law from the University of Bordeaux. Since inheriting the monarchy in 1961, he has concentrated on improving the living standard of the poor – roughly half of his 23 million subjects. A priority is bringing traditional agriculture into the machine age. His greatest domestic coup is the now legendary Green March (green is the colour of Islam) in 1975, when he led 350,000 Moroccan tribesmen into the Spanish Sahara to justify their historic claim to the region.

Following a policy of non-alignment, he enjoys warm relations with many Western countries, especially France and America. Anglo-Moroccan relations date back to the Saadian empire, when Sultan Moulay Abd el-Malek exchanged letters with Queen Elizabeth I, but the British tabloid press harassed King Hassan for keeping Queen Elizabeth II waiting for more than half an hour during her state visit in 1980.

At times King Hassan's views have upset radical Arab states. He flew in the face of Islam in allowing the first ever International Congress of Jews to be held on Moroccan soil – a reminder, said the king, that the two great religions once peacefully co-existed. Significantly, the Israeli prime minister Yitzhak Rabin made Rabat his first call *en route* home following the signing of the peace accord with the PLO in 1993. The visit to Morocco by Pope John Paul II in 1985 was his first to an Islamic country. King Hassan's support for the western alliance against Iraq is seen as a courageous move against general domestic opinion.

On a personal level, King Hassan is an intelligent statesman and shrewd diplomat. While Morocco enjoys more liberty than many other Muslim countries he has been the target of two assassination attempts: the second, in 1971, was part of an unsuccessful military *coup*. Many poorer people now believe he has the *baraka*, an Arab word meaning blessing, or is just extremely lucky. Fit, despite being a chain-smoker, he rises early, works hard and plays golf, rides, shoots, sails and swims. His Berber wife, Lalla Latifa, has given him three children and he is also the father of two children by unknown women presented by the *caids*. It is a tradition in Morocco for the sultan to father children of different tribes in an endeavour to strengthen bonds between potential enemies, and although resolutely Western in outlook, at the time, King Hassan did not wish to upset the *ulema*, a wise decision in view of Morocco's turbulent past.

Politics

From 1965 to 1970 King Hassan governed Morocco by direct rule, without the democratically elected institutions he had set up under the constitution of 1962. This state of emergency was brought to an end in 1970 with a new constitution that left him considerable control over Parliament.

Morocco's House of Representatives is composed of 306 members. Two-thirds are elected by universal suffrage (women obtained the right to vote in 1962) and a third by indirect electoral college. Members of the college are elected by municipal and rural councils, chambers of professions and trade unions. The House may be called to extraordinary session by absolute majority vote or by royal decree. Meetings are held in public and proceedings are published in full. MPs are elected for six years.

The fragmentation of political parties since Independence means that there has been no concerted opposition to the power of the king. The main parties (in order of the number of seats won in the 1984 election) are: Union Constitutional (Loyalists), RNI (Independent), Mouvement Populaire (right of centre, comprising many Berbers), Istiqlal (Nationalist with conservative leanings), USFP (Socialist), PND (Democrats), PPS (Communist). In 1993, the opposition won the elections but the victory was insufficient to form a government.

Human rights

While Morocco's human rights record cannot compare with the appalling situation in neighbouring Algeria, Amnesty International declares there is much to improve if Morocco is to consider itself a civilised nation and potential member of the EC. In 1991, after a worldwide campaign, Morocco released 300 'disappeared'. But more than 100 Moroccans are still detained in secret centres in Rabat as well as the Atlas mountains. The Dades valley is also named. Prisoners include opposition trade unionists and members of the armed forces implicated in the 1970s for attempted *coups*. Former guards of the 'disappeared' who helped smuggle out letters have also 'disappeared', as have hundreds of Sahrawis arrested in Western Sahara and southern Morocco since 1991. The rule of law is still denied in the disputed Saharan area with cases of severe torture reported.

In an effort to improve Morocco's reputation, a Consultative Council for Human Rights was established by royal decree in 1990. There is now also a special Minister for Human Rights, which indicates that the situation is ameliorating, while the list of 'disappeared' still includes 150 prisoners of conscience and more than 500 political detainees.

Economy

The Moroccan economy seemed to have reached its nadir in 1989 with the costly war in Western Sahara, serious debts and domestic riots. Signs now are very good, with the World Bank noting that Morocco is on its way to becoming an important industrial client for Western

Europe. Exports to the EC comprise 65 per cent of the kingdom's total exports, and it is believed that integration with Europe will increase in the long term.

Since Independence the economy has rested on several large, state-run enterprises – phosphates, railways and tobacco. Privatisation of some 112 state entities is planned by 1995, including 75 companies and 37 hotels. Migrant workers' overseas remittances amount to £1.43 billion, with tourism earnings £0.7 billion and rising. Phosphates, fruit and fish, together with textiles and manufactured clothing, represent the main visible exports. Agriculture continues to employ around 40 per cent.

While the local growth rate stands at 7 per cent, the annual GDP per capita is only $700. Foreign investment finally attracted to Morocco's manufacturing potential will also reduce the numbers of unemployed – currently some 3 million.

The down side of the economy is that 20 per cent of the urban workforce, roughly 6 million people, are permanently unemployed. This is why you and every Western visitor to Morocco is seen as a potential meal-ticket.

Unity of the Maghreb

In 1989, after some thirty years of disagreements, the five countries of the Maghreb – Morocco, Algeria, Mauritania, Tunisia and Libya – signed an agreement in Marrakesh proclaiming political and social co-operation through unity. Ideally the union was seen as an exchange of goods between the 'haves' and the 'have nots': foodstuffs to Algeria, manufactured goods from Algeria to Morocco and everyone exporting sardines. Nothing has come of the union, which is seen as moribund. Algeria's domestic problems and Libya's involvement in the Lockerbie tragedy are largely to blame. Tunisia tends to carry on regardless, while Mauritania shows no sign of shedding its maverick image.

Agriculture and fishing

You will not travel far in Morocco without noticing the intense cultivation, using the simplest methods, of the tiniest patch of soil. Despite government efforts to upgrade techniques, productivity remains low. A camel-drawn plough or a fisherman casting his net makes a pretty picture, but they are part of a string of problems confronting agriculture. Farmers south of the Atlas are at the mercy of a precarious climate and extreme conditions such as drought and grasshopper plagues. I recall the anguish when I drove into Goulimine with my car radiator bristling with the large, orange insects. Plucking them out, the farmers demanded to know where I had been: 'How far south?' I had passed farmers coaxing tiny shoots from the *wadis* as I drove south, but my return coincided with a cloud of grasshoppers estimated to be 60 km long, 30 km wide and 3 km deep: eating, mating and laying their eggs on the wing.

Morocco farms a variety of crops: cereals, especially wheat, barley and corn; citrus fruits, a major export; vegetables, in particular potatoes, tomatoes, cotton, sugar-beet and sugar-cane, which was a major crop in the Souss from the fourteenth to the sixteenth centuries. Beans, lentils, chick peas and other pulses are grown on small-holdings, while olives, almonds and dates are cultivated on large co-operative estates.

New irrigation works, especially in the Gharb region, have greatly boosted productivity. King Hassan's programme has so far created forty new dams and it is hoped Morocco will become self-sufficient in basic foodstuffs by the year 2000. But at present 82 per cent of agricultural production consists of only four crops: wheat, barley, beans and sugar-beet, and land ownership traditions are an impediment to agricultural output. In 1973 1,800 foreign-owned farms were distributed among the landless, co-operatives and state-run corporations, but after generations of sub-division, the average holding is no more than 4.8 hectares. At least half the peasant farmers live at subsistence level. The handful of tomatoes, or onions, spread out in the *souq* is often all a man has to sell after feeding his wife and children. Where a farmer has an under-productive plot, he is forced to work a share-cropping system, or to seek seasonal labour. At harvest time, you will see hundreds of men waiting to be assigned to some of the country's estimated 28 million olive trees. The scene is repeated when the dates are ripe; such work pays about £1 a day net.

Land ownership

Fishing

Fishing, too, remains entangled in archaic methods. Three ports – Safi, Agadir and Tan-Tan – account for most of the catch. Sardines comprise 40 per cent of Morocco's gross food exports. Tuna and shellfish, especially lobster, are also important. The Western Saharan ports of Boujdour and Dakhla are being upgraded but the biggest investment is in Tan-Tan, where trawlers, ice-works and canneries are likely to turn it into one of the biggest operations in the Maghreb. The government has declared a 200-km exclusion zone to protect its fisheries, in particular the bountiful banks of fish and squid off the Western Sahara.

Industry

Morocco is the world's major exporter of phosphates, producing a third of all world trade. Phosphate is mined at Khouribga and Bou Craa in the Western Sahara, which has reserves estimated at 1.7 billion tonnes. While phosphate production is stable, the mining of other minerals is suffering from depressed international markets. Iron ore is mined in the Rif, cobalt at Bou Azzer, and copper near Bleida. There are significant shale oil deposits around Timahdit and Tarfaya, but only small quantities of natural oil have been discovered. Morocco imports its oil requirement mainly from Russia in exchange for citrus fruits and phosphates, and from Saudi Arabia. Some oil is also supplied by the United Arab Emirates.

Light industry in Casablanca, Fez, Tangier, Agadir, Rabat and Safi produces leatherware, various building materials, chemicals, drinks and tobacco, rubber, plastic, paper products and textiles. Some 50 per cent of goods manufactured in the textile industry is exported – 80 per cent to France. Food processing – mainly canned fish and fruits and sugar refining – is also important.

A Muslim Society

Islam

Wherever you travel in Morocco, you are aware of the pervading influence of Islam. Moroccans follow the Sunni, or orthodox, teachings of the Qur'an. In the *medina* you will often hear children chanting some of its 6,200 verses, which are learned by heart, often with no clear understanding. A rough equivalent of the New Testament, the Qur'an consists of the collected pronouncements of the Prophet Muhammad. Muslims do not hold him to be a medium but the source of the revelations of God spoken through the Angel Gabriel. His recitations were transcribed by ghost-writers – faithful disciples in early seventh-century Mecca. In AD 613 Muhammad began preaching the duty of man to worship only one God, Allah. The word 'Islam' translates roughly as 'submission to God'. He enjoined Muslims to observe the five 'Pillars of Faith': prayer, fasting, charitable acts, the *haj*, or pilgrimage, and submission.

Prayer   The Qur'an requires Muslims to pray five times a day: at dawn, just after noon, in the mid-afternoon, four minutes after sunset and before sleeping. They do not pray at the precise moment of sunrise or sunset lest this have pagan connotations.

In former times a *muezzin* called Muslims to prayer from the minaret of the mosque; today the call is tape-recorded. *'Allahu Akhbar.* God is most great! I testify there is no God but Allah, and that Muhammad is his prophet. Come to prayer. Prayer is better than sleep . . .' implores the dawn prayer-call. In Fez to hear *muezzin* after *muezzin* calling in mosque after mosque is a moving experience, except in the wee small hours outside your hotel.

Muslims will pray anywhere – in a shop, a field, or the aisle of a jumbo jet – but where possible, they prefer the sanctity of a mosque. Friday's noon prayers are always well-attended.

Ablutions   Ablutions must be performed before prayers: sluicing the hands in running water up to the wrists, rinsing the nostrils and mouth and washing the face, forearms, scalp, ears and finally the feet. Each action is performed three times in a tap-room or tank in the mosque. A saying attributed to the Prophet, 'cleanliness is half the Faith', resembles the Calvinist 'cleanliness is next to godliness', except that when prostrating themselves before the Almighty, Muslims are better scrubbed. While Islam is an open religion, some men may object if you stare or try to photograph them performing their ablutions.

Ramadan

Fasting once a year during Ramadan, the ninth lunar month, is required of all Muslims. In seventeenth-century Morocco those who failed to observe the *saum* were stoned; today anyone who flouts the fast in public may be liable to arrest. Fasting is seen as an expression of submission to the divine will and involves abstinence not only from eating and drinking, but also from what are held to be evil tendencies. For thirty days, between dawn and sunset every Muslim must refrain from taking nourishment, from smoking, wearing perfume and engaging in sexual contact. The ill and elderly, children under the age of puberty, pregnant women and travellers are exempt. Fasting is accompanied by frequent readings of the Qur'an, which was revealed to Muhammad during Ramadan.

The *muezzins* begin calling about one hour before dawn and the fast begins after prayers. Most people get up for a light meal, and, believing it will help water retention and stave off the terrible thirst, take more salt than usual with their food. In a cool month, Ramadan is endurable without too much discomfort, but during summer it becomes an extreme test of physical and spiritual endurance. As sunset approaches, you see people scanning the sky, ears alert for the sound of the siren which signals the end of the fast.

Starved of liquid, most people break the fast with water or milky coffee; at least 1.5 litres of fluid is necessary to restabilize the metabolism properly. This is followed by *harira*, a traditional soup eaten in every household. It is also essential to eat fruits and sweetmeats which provide a rapid source of sugar. Around 10–11 p.m., the women serve a large *tajine*, or stew, accompanied by vegetables and salads. The table is very animated, with everyone talking and enjoying what can only be described as a *grande bouffe*. After eating, older men go to the mosque for *il-ichaa*, or evening prayer, younger ones go out, and the women clear away. Before long they are busy preparing *shor*, a type of crêpe, and other things for the morning; but no matter how much people eat, they will still suffer during the long hours of abstinence.

Fasting rigidly for a month is not a quick way to lose weight, as the calories go on again at dusk. What happens is that the biological rhythm is interrupted, causing a drastic fall in blood sugar. Deprived of fluids, the kidneys have to work overtime: urine becomes concentrated, vertigo and headaches are common. The person feels tired and unproductive, which is why Moroccans sleep a lot more during Ramadan. Many businesses and factories close for annual leave at this time, and people obliged to work are often unshaven and ill-humoured. A survey reveals that many wars in the Middle East break out during Ramadan.

Ramadan and the tourist

While there is no doubt about the effort needed to fast for 12–14 hours, the meaning of Ramadan is often lost in an orgy of eating and entertainment. Young men use it as an excuse to promenade all night in the streets or to watch videos, while older men play interminable games of cards. Some towns in the Deep South take on a veritable carnival atmosphere, with side-shows and dance troupes, and if your room overlooks the street, you are unlikely to get any sleep. It is also rare for staff to appear on time for work. Wanting to leave Sefrou at 8.30 a.m., I found no one in reception, but the hotel had been cunningly locked. Determined not to miss an early start, I opened a window, threw my luggage out and jumped out after it. A few shops open before noon in towns such as Rabat and Casablanca, but *café-terraces* remain shut until waiters begin washing the pavement and putting out chairs around 5 p.m. Northern Morocco is very strict, with everything except petrol stations closed. Between Fez and Oujda I could not even obtain a sustaining *café-cassé*. In Guercif I announced that I was a Christian, a traveller, and finally a pregnant traveller, but to no avail. In Taourit the owner of the Café Mauritania took pity on me and made me tea, but his colleague told me not to smoke (the stress of it all had started me smoking again) in front of Believers. Eating or smoking in front of Muslims is especially offensive during the fast.

Unless you are willing to do as the Moors do, Morocco is best avoided at this time. Believers are involved in religious obeisances, the idle use it as an excuse not to work. Never good, the standard of hotel cooking drops to an all-time low. Surprisingly, no one seems to have estimated how much the economy – and the tourist industry in particular – loses during the fast. If Morocco is to take tourism seriously, provisions must be made for visitors.

Charity | 'And perform the prayer, and pay the alms and lend to God a good loan . . .' says the Qur'an, 73:19. The act of giving is a natural gesture to Muslims and second nature to Moroccans. Unseen by tourists is *zakat*, a religious tax payable at the end of Ramadan. Parting with wealth is seen as an act of worship, the word *zakat* meaning to cleanse or to purify. It also underlines an acceptance that wealth really belongs to God, its owner being merely a trustee. The amount a person pays – a portion of income, jewellery or herds – is subject to complex rules, but *zakat* is not compulsory – it is left to an individual's conscience. Ideally *zakat* should narrow the economic gap between rich and poor, thus avoiding social tensions. It should also prevent hoarding, but the reverse is often true.

Pilgrimage | The ultimate act of submission is the pilgrimage to Mecca, which all fit Muslims are enjoined to undertake in their lifetime. The *haj* is performed during the second week of *Dhull-Hijja*, the twelfth lunar month. It involves considerable sacrifice and physical as well as spiritual strength to complete the complex rituals. Central to the *haj* is the sevenfold circumambulation of the sacred *ka'aba* in a human whirlpool. Given the number of pilgrims (now over 2 million) and the tensions arising from possible fanatic elements, the *haj* today is more stressful than it was when people sailed, or even walked to Mecca.

More than 150 planes a day arrive at Jeddah Airport, among them a Royal Air Maroc flight bringing pilgrims from Morocco. When pilgrims complete the journey to Mecca they may assume the honorific title of *Haj*, women being known as *Haja*, although they may not participate in prayers if they are menstruating. Moroccans who are too old or too poor to make the arduous journey to Saudi Arabia travel to important local shrines such as Moulay Idriss and Tamegroute.

Mosques and medersa

A major disappointment in Morocco is that you cannot go into the mosques, which are unquestionably the finest examples of Islamic art and the purest expression of Hispano-Moorish craftsmanship. They have been forbidden to infidels since the beginning of the French Protectorate, apparently at the behest of Resident-General Lyautey, because French soldiers trying to evade the military police sought sanctuary in the mosques.

Most mosques in Morocco follow the Syrian layout, with a wide congregational hall leading off a courtyard flanked by minarets. Prayers are said in unison, with the congregation performing genuflections towards the *quibla*, the niche indicating the direction of Mecca. The largest mosque is the ninth-century Kairouine Mosque in Fez, which can hold 20,000 worshippers.

Happily, you *can* visit most *medersa*. A *medrassa* originally complemented every important mosque in Morocco. Broadly speaking, it was like a medieval seminary, where students were lodged. The first great *medrassa* was built by the Merenids in Fez, the centre of religious and scientific studies during the tenth to fifteenth centuries. Fez and Meknes have the greatest number of *medersa* in Morocco. The basic design consists of the prayer and studies' halls built around a courtyard. Upstairs, the students' cells were separated by intricately carved wooden screens. As well as wood-carving – in particular the sumptuously carved ceilings – they are noted for rich stucco-work, tiles and mosaics, decorative arts at which Moroccan craftsmen excel. Some of the *medersa* in Fez are still in use by theological students, and their ceremonies and traditions rival those of Oxford or Cambridge.

Maraboutism

Prior to Islam, the Berbers followed various cults based on the worship of an ascetic holy man, or *marabout*. Rooted in ancient superstition, maraboutism, which resembles sufism, is the darker side of Islam in

Morocco, more akin to Shi'ite than orthodox Sunni doctrine. Brotherhoods arose around a *marabout* who was often well-educated in religious science. Some were lecturers at university, others mystical hermits. Naturally personal charisma also attracted disciples, in particular from illiterate rural communities. Veneration after death centres on *koubbas*, the white, domed tombs of ancient saints which are dotted all over Morocco. *Zaouias* are rural equivalents of the *medersa*: a seminary where the *marabout* preached his particular doctrine. Among more extreme brotherhoods, fetishes were practised: flagellation, music-induced trances and scorpion-eating. The government has outlawed the more orgiastic rituals of certain cults but saint-worship still flourishes.

Moussems

Originally a *moussem* was a pilgrimage to a *koubba*, which, because of its holiness, is a propitious spot to pray. Today, a *moussem* remains a fundamental act of homage, but it is also a commercial event, attracting traders, artisans and entertainers who often travel miles to get there in time, as well as pilgrims. There are two types of *moussem*. The urban *moussem* honours the *marabout*, who is usually the patron saint of the town – for example, Sidi Belout, patron saint of Casablanca. There are processions led by the *wali*, or governor, and other notables, with artisans bearing examples of their craft and the disciples leading an animal for sacrifice on the *koubba*. The event usually ends with a spectacular *fantasia*, or display of riding.

The jiggery-pokery of a rural *moussem* brings diversion in the mundane lives of country folk. Apart from a wedding or a birth, it is the most important event of the year. Hundreds of tents will be erected round the *koubba*, decorated with ribbons and pieces of cloth tied by pilgrims. Such an occasion sees Morocco at its colourful best, with markets, feasting, dancers and acrobats and towards evening the deafening volleys of Berber rifles fired during the *fantasia*. Rural *moussems* marking the end of the harvest are common.

In all there are 650 *moussems* in Morocco. Three of the most important are Moulay Idriss, attended by the king, Moulay Abdullah held near el-Jadida, and Setti Fatma in the Ourika Valley, outside Marrakesh.

Fête des Fiancés

One of the most unusual *moussems* is the *Fête des Fiancés* held by the Ait Haddidou Berbers at Imilchil in the Middle Atlas. Staged in September, it draws young people together to choose their own fiancé. Today the *moussem* is a tourist attraction, but because it is relatively inaccessible, it remains typical. The girls wear long white dresses secured at the waist with tasselled belts, a striped cape and masses of heavy silver jewellery. Cheeks painted scarlet with cochineal and eyes ringed with *kohl*, they circle the boys, seeking a partner. An ancient Berber rite which ignores the restrictions of Islam, it bears a startling similarity to *chowmas*, an uninhibited celebration among the pagan Kalash tribe in the Hindu Kush.

Islamic fundamentalism

Seeing the apparently liberal lifestyle of cities such as Casablanca, you may feel Morocco is ripe for a backlash against decadent Western trends. There is an Islamic movement which feeds off social problems and over-cordial relations with Western nations, but until now fundamentalist opposition has centred around one man, Abdessalam Yassine, a teacher who preaches the reconciliation of Islam with certain aspects of Marxist dogma and who has cooled his heels in prison.

Morocco's multi-party politics, the relatively free press and the monarch's active promotion of Islamic education makes the issue complex. Unlike the sweeping modernizations of the Shah of Iran, reforms proposed by King Hassan and passed by the *ulema* follow Islamic mores. His title of Commander of the Faithful is respected by every Moroccan, and in 1987 a French magazine reported him as saying, 'I received this title at birth, without asking for it, or desiring it. It is a title which brings with it a great deal of humility, and certain responsibilities.'

Moroccan-style fundamentalism, while nothing like the fanatical movement in Algeria, is growing. The unsmiling, hirsute gentleman selling Islamic literature near the harbour steps in Tangier is a fundamentalist. You will pass another, turning away from your camera, at a bookstall near the Kairouine Mosque in Fez. It is claimed that, with more than half the population living on the poverty line, one young member of every family is ripe for conversion. Remember this aspect when you unwittingly flaunt your Western wealth – money, cameras, jewellery – which they have no possibility of sharing. The seeds of fundamentalism are like a cicada biding its time in the ground. Only the king himself, as Morocco's temporal sovereign and religious head of state, stands in the way.

Women in Muslim society

Moroccan society is dominated by men, a bias beginning at birth when women give three shrill ululations for a boy, and one, or perhaps none, for a girl. Popular belief even decrees that a boy baby should be kept longer on the breast. Aided and abetted by his mother, the young boy soon knows his status: his sisters are there to serve and he begins bossing them as soon as he can talk. Girls must help in the kitchen after school but boys can go out to play; boys may have friends, but sisters are allowed to socialise only with brothers or first cousins. The male ego grows as a young man enjoys his first sexual experience while his sister is guarding her hymen as closely as the Crown Jewels.

Virginity   The blood-stained nuptial rag remains of paramount importance in Moroccan society. Without her virginity intact on the night of her marriage, a Moroccan girl is condemned. Blood from an authentic virgin is said to be pink and stays so even when it dries; some old women place the rag on their eyes to prevent blindness.

Muslim society is complex everywhere, but in Morocco it is entangled with Berber superstitions. And while it is clear a bride must be a virgin, this is not to say a modern girl cannot have pre-marital sex. Increasingly popular in cities such as Casablanca, where the world's first trans-sexual operation took place, is a simple operation known as *l'hymeneorraphie*, or the surgical sewing of a broken hymen. The method saves not only the girl, but also her mother, as some families will demand a medical certificate to ensure that their son is not marrying 'second-hand goods'.

Male superstars   The male superstar role reaches a climax on the nuptial night. The moment must be horrible for a young virgin who has probably never seen a naked man. Also, in arranged marriages the husband is frequently older – I met a twenty-one-year-old betrothed to a wizened creature of eighty-three. There is usually no fore-play. Often not a word is spoken before the girl is abruptly penetrated and the rag flourished among the wedding guests. Many women never recover from this devastating experience, and love among older people is rare. The majority, women included, believe a woman's place is in the home.

Times are changing in the university cities, where the modern generation aspires to marry for love. Exposed to Western TV programmes, even a girl cloistered in a traditional household hopes to choose her husband. In a survey conducted in Casablanca, 65.3 per cent of unmarried girls aged nineteen and over had experienced sexual contact (*Au delà de toute Pudeur*, Soumaya Naamane-Guessous, 1988). Some courting couples contrive to have an affair, although a girl always sees her boyfriend, or *régulier*, as her future husband. Intercourse is difficult in watchful Moroccan society where *zina*, the act of fornication outside marriage, is rigorously forbidden by the Qur'an. It may take place behind a classroom door, in a lavatory, or a discothèque. When the couple marry, the girl will have a *hymeneorraphie*.

One sees more and more young couples in Rabat, or Casablanca, strolling hand in hand; I also met several boys enjoying relationships with older, usually divorced, women. In Fez I lunched with a young couple living in defiance of society: the girl, who had been beaten by an older, former husband, expected to marry her twenty-seven-year-old lover. Although he was obviously caring in many ways, it did not stop him bossing her around. 'Moroccan women love to wait on men,' he told me.

Moroccan society is slowly emerging from its chrysalis, but the carapace is tight. Not this generation, but hopefully both partners of the next, will believe in love and equal rights.

Hammams

Every town has at least one *hammam*, or public-bath. Some are a series of tiled, vaulted rooms, others are simple. Most are centuries old. If there is only one *hammam*, it is shared: men in the morning and women in the afternoon, or vice versa. Tourists are welcome. The entrance fee ranges from 1 to 2 dirhams. Some *hammams* supply a threadbare towel and a nugget of soap, but it is better to bring your own. It is usual to leave your knickers on while washing, as Moroccan women cling to this last vestige of modesty. Otherwise the *hammam* is relaxed, even jolly. An attendant keeps up a supply of buckets of hot water and may offer to wash your back.

For Moroccan women, the *hammam* is much more than a place to wash. Men can meet in the *souq*, or the *café-terrace*, but the *hammam* is the only place where women can gossip out of male earshot. Many women treat bath-day like a holiday, getting up at dawn to prepare the *ghassoul*, or black shampoo, and a quantity of food. Sometimes they stay all day.

Rites of passage

The *hammam* plays a central role in various rites of passage. One is the obligation to wash immediately after intercourse. This means that a woman without a bathroom must go to the *hammam* on a day which is not her official bath-day and everyone – family members, neighbours and traders – knows what she and her spouse have been up to. More forceful women may even refuse to have relations except on bath-day – for many, a welcome excuse.

A bride will spend days purifying herself in the *hammam*, seated on the tiled floor with relatives and friends scrubbing her vigorously and washing her hair. She will also shave or pluck her pubic hair, a custom considered to be more hygienic. She is rubbed with orange-blossom water, her hands and feet are decorated with henna, her cheeks with carmine and her eyes encircled with *kohl*. A week after her wedding, she returns to the *hammam* again for post-nuptial rites. Accompanied by the same retinue, she completes another long purifying process; the baths will be packed, conversation about the cost of her wedding gifts taking precedence over washing.

The *hammam* is important during pregnancy, its hot vapour being considered good to facilitate cervical dilation. A week after delivery she returns again to relax and allow her pelvic girdle to settle, everyone listening to her experience of giving birth and recounting their own. The widow also visits the *hammam* once her official mourning period is over and she can dress normally and wear make-up.

For women living in the crowded *medinas* of Fez and other old towns, life without the *hammam* is unthinkable, but for the younger set of Casablanca, the Thalassothérapie Clinic and Lido swimming-pools have largely replaced the *hammam*. Many scorn the idea of a public bath-house, claiming, with some reason, that the humid rooms which are never disinfected are a breeding ground for disease.

Homosexuality

While any sexual act outside marriage is considered illegal by Islam, the Moroccan authorities resemble the Dutch in their *laissez-faire* attitude towards gay expatriates and tourists. Tangier and Marrakesh are favourite destinations for gay tourists – not the young clones from Western gay discos, but ageing homosexuals searching for elusive happiness.

The Djeballa tribe in the western Rif may have started the rush when it was learned of their preferences for men. Certainly Tangier had attracted many notable homosexuals by the time it became an International Zone. It was equally well known as a paedophile centre. By the early 1960s most of the boy brothels in the *medina* had been closed, but you could still see lissome boy dancers in old tea-rooms overlooking the sea-walls.

Tangier's expatriate community today includes some rich elderly men who enjoy dressing up behind the closed doors of their fabulous homes. Rivalry is bitter between two bitchy circles from different social backgrounds: it is the kiss of death for someone not invited to the reigning Queen of Tangier's birthday party. Marrakesh has a small homosexual group, while any single man is automatically dubbed 'gay' by the god-fearing British heterosexual communities of Rabat and Casablanca.

The Weather and When to Go

Morocco is very hot in summer and exceedingly cold in winter, but there is always somewhere enjoying an equable climate. Spring (April and May) is superb throughout the country, but it coincides with the start of the holiday period.

If they can, Moroccans take a break during the hot months of June to August, so hill resorts are crowded and accommodation is hard to find by the sea. Humidity is high on the coast during the summer; Casablanca, in particular, drips with moisture, while blustery winds make life unpleasant in Tangier and Restinga-Smir. Inland, it is too hot to travel comfortably. Visiting Marrakesh in July, I washed my jeans out and was wearing them within the hour. Temperatures of 45°C (107°F) are not uncommon in the Deep South, where even mad dogs and Englishmen do not go sightseeing between 10 a.m. and 4 p.m. But summer *is* the ideal time for trekking in the Atlas.

Marrakesh is a traditional winter resort, with the sunny days and cool nights also characteristic of the Tafilalet and the Western Sahara from December to March. You can ski on the peaks of Oukaimeden, just two hours' drive from Marrakesh, during these months. Northern Morocco has a cool, Mediterranean-type winter. It is too chilly to swim north of Casablanca and to sunbathe you must travel south – to Agadir, or ideally Tan-Tan. Dakhla enjoys the mildest winters of all, but it is subject to cold Atlantic breezes and temperatures may plummet at night.

Average temperatures (°F)

	Jan	Feb	Mar	Apr	May	Jun	Jul	Aug	Sep	Oct	Nov	Dec
Agadir	69	70	72	75	76	78	80	79	79	78	76	69
Al-Hoceima	61	62	65	67	72	78	83	85	81	74	69	63
Casablanca	63	63	66	68	72	75	81	81	80	77	68	64
Essaouira	64	64	64	66	68	68	72	70	70	70	68	66
Fez	61	63	66	72	79	88	97	97	90	81	66	61
Marrakesh	66	66	73	79	84	91	102	101	91	82	70	66
Meknes	59	61	64	70	74	84	93	93	86	79	66	61
Ouarzazate	63	67	73	80	86	96	102	100	91	80	70	62
Rabat	63	64	66	70	73	77	82	82	81	77	68	64
Tangier	59	61	62	66	72	77	80	82	79	73	64	61
Taroudannt	72	73	79	81	86	90	99	100	95	90	77	72
Zagora	69	73	78	86	93	102	108	106	97	86	78	70

Distance Chart

The chart is a triangular road-distance matrix. Cities run along the diagonal (Dakhla at the top to Tiznit at the bottom). Each row gives the distance from that city to every city listed above it in the column headings.

To \ From	Dakhla	Agadir	Al-Hoceima	Beni-Mellal	Casablanca	El-Jadida	Er-Rachidia	Essaouira	Fez	Figuig	Khouribga	Laayoune	Marrakesh	Meknes	Nador	Ouarzazate	Oujda	Rabat	Safi	Es-Semara	Tangier	Tan-Tan	Tarfaya	Tetouan
Agadir	1173																							
Al-Hoceima	2246	1091																						
Beni-Mellal	1640	467	564																					
Casablanca	1684	511	536	210																				
El-Jadida	1590	417	632	271	99																			
Er-Rachidia	1854	681	616	375	545	506																		
Essaouira	1346	173	887	370	351	252	745																	
Fez	1920	756	275	289	289	388	364	640																
Figuig	2249	1076	669	920	1160	1066	1330	822	719															
Khouribga	1680	507	614	90	181	425	410	176	483	820														
Laayoune	524	649	1740	1116	1066	727	510	701	905	1725	922													
Marrakesh	1448	273	758	194	238	197	510	380	741	234	672	1156												
Meknes	1913	740	335	120	328	346	580	60	741	322	672	1736	467											
Nador	2260	1095	175	628	920	727	510	979	339	516	672	1024	826	399										
Ouarzazate	1548	375	992	398	442	399	306	380	687	701	438	1024	204	403	884									
Oujda	2272	1099	293	632	545	731	514	983	326	676	1748	652	816	104	361	652								
Rabat	1775	602	445	256	91	190	482	198	343	877	205	1251	321	138	535	528	541							
Safi	1467	294	351	256	157	683	129	545	1078	328	943	321	138	287	486	403	609	347						
Es-Semara	746	551	1635	1018	1062	1265	1232	724	1307	1627	1058	222	1251	1284	884	816	1650	1153	845					
Tangier	2053	880	323	538	369	468	608	720	303	988	483	1529	287	287	361	926	278	625	625	1431				
Tan-Tan	633	331	1011	961	1055	961	1225	517	1300	1620	1051	109	1284	1639	1188	437	919	1146	838	331	1443			
Tarfaya	842	544	278	536	385	484	604	736	281	931	499	1541	258	437	820	641	331	294	641	331	57	213		
Tetouan	2065	892	536	1018	1055	510	604	266	849	1169	600	586	675	833	1188	468	1192	699	387	458	973	1223	1436	
Tiznit	1080	93	1011	560	604	510	774	266	849	1169	600	586	366	833	1188	468	1192	699	387	458	985	213	451	985

Travelling Around

Thanks to the French, Morocco has one of the best-integrated domestic transport systems in Africa. Boosted by private bus and taxi services, it is comparable to anything in the West. A traveller stranded without a bus in the *bled* may disagree, but you would wait an equally long time in the Australian bush or mid-west America. The French infrastructure has been well maintained and new bitumen roads are slowly licking their way into the desert. All major towns are now linked by highways – you can travel on tarmac from Tangier to Dakhla, a distance of 2,230 kilometres. Road and rail transport is backed up by Royal Air Maroc's efficient domestic airline service.

By air

British Airways
Gatwick–Marrakesh 2/weekly winter, and 1/weekly summer.
Heathrow–Casablanca 4/weekly winter, and 5/weekly summer.
Heathrow–Tangier 2/weekly winter, and 1/weekly summer.

All flights by Boeing 737–200 with high-standard Club and Economy class service. Enquiries: British Airways Sales tel. (081) 897 4000; Linkline tel. (0345) 222111.

Royal Air Maroc
From Heathrow to:
Casablanca daily.
Tangier 4/weekly.
Agadir 7/weekly.
Fez 5/weekly.
Marrakesh daily.
Ouarzazate 2/weekly.

RAM domestic service is highly rated for internal travel further afield, to Laayoune and Dakhla. The airports are good and groundstaff helpful. Enquiries: Royal Air Maroc, 205 Regent Street, London W1, tel. (071) 439 4361.

Flight Only
Travel operators such as **Inspirations** sell flight-only on charter flights operating from Gatwick, Manchester, Birmingham and Newcastle. For last-minute bargains, tel. (0293) 822244.

By train

Train travel is limited to about 2,000 km of track, with four main lines:

Casablanca–Rabat–Kenitra–Meknes–Fez–Oujda–Algerian frontier
Rabat–Casablanca–Azemour–el-Jadida
Casablanca–Tangier
Casablanca–Marrakesh

The Marrakesh–Laayoune extension is possible if there is a permanent peace settlement in the Western Sahara.

Moroccan trains have three classes. First class is comfortable and inexpensive (e.g. Tangier–Rabat, single, 130 dirham). Trains travel at a pleasant pace for sightseeing – not very fast (e.g. Tangier–Rabat about 4½ hours, compared to 2–2½ hours by road). Information from the **Office National des Chemins de Fer**, Avenue Al Mansour Ad Dabhi, Rabat. Porters are available at stations, usually rather old to be carrying suitcases but in good voice, demanding 5 dirham per piece; a tip of 3 dirham is adequate. Most railway stations are in the town centre, near an ONCF hotel. Muzak is an irritant on all trains. Sexes are not segregated. Refreshments are available, but take mineral water on long journeys. If you are under twenty-six, you can use an InterRail card.

By bus

Many young, independent travellers in Morocco go by bus. Provided you are patient, you will reach your destination at some stage on the same day, or night. Moroccan buses – a combination of CTM (national), ONCF (government-rail) and private lines – operate to 90 per cent of towns. The service offered by CTM and ONCF buses is fast and efficient, and you pay about 50 per cent more. On popular routes buying a ticket in advance from the bus station avoids hassle on the day. National buses run to fixed departure times; private buses often do not leave until they are full, which may include a flock of sheep tied on the roof. It is also not uncommon to break down in the middle of nowhere.

By taxi

Grands-taxis | Usually Mercedes or big Peugeots, *grands-taxis* are a boon for independent travellers. About 30 per cent more expensive than buses, they travel twice as fast. Departures are more frequent – any time, provided they are full (six passengers). If you find this means of travel too cramped (two passengers in front and four in the rear), you can pay for space. Buying an extra place is a shrewd move in summer: the cost is still economical compared to renting a car. You can also rent an entire *grand-taxi*. To discover the true fare, ask a local out of earshot of the *grand-taxi* rank. Most ranks are found on the town perimeter, usually near the *souq*. At the time of writing, the fares to the airports were Casablanca 150 dirham, Tangier and Agadir 50 dirham. Do not travel by *grand-taxi* if you have a weak heart. The occasional accident in Morocco invariably involves a red-plate *grand-taxi*, which never travels at less than 100 kph and frequently more.

Petits-taxis

Petits-taxis are small Renaults or Fiats, for inner-city use. Few meters are functional, so agree on a fare before getting in. If sharing with other passengers, try to see what they pay. Needing a *petit-taxi* to take me from the Casablanca Hyatt Regency to Anfa, I was quoted 50 dirham by the hotel concierge, 100 dirham by a taxi on the rank, 30 dirham by a policeman (who also invited me out) and 20 dirham by a cruising taxi.

Hitch-hiking

It should not be necessary for a Western visitor to hitch-hike in Morocco, given the range of cheap transport. (The situation was different in the 1960s, when there were fewer buses and no *grands-taxis* – and with another girl I hitch-hiked all over the country.)

Many Moroccans hitch out of economic necessity and, remembering past kindness, I could not – despite warnings – drive past someone on the road. In the Deep South I constantly picked up hitch-hikers – students walking 20 km a day to school; people going to market, to the doctor, to visit relatives; a policeman hitching to work; and Habiba Ibn Radi, a toothless woman who wheeled a heavy bag up to the car in a barrow. Flushed with excitement – she had evidently been waiting for two hours – she kissed my cheek and all the way down my arm while crying in high-pitched Arabic. Still shouting when I dropped her near Oualidia, she attracted a small crowd of men, one of whom explained in French that she wanted me to take her address so I could send her a postcard (which I did).

There are some rules if you plan to stop for hitch-hikers. Except for old men and tired young boys, I never took male passengers. Berber hitch-hikers may offer you money towards the petrol, which Moroccan drivers accept, but you can graciously refuse. Do not stop for foreign backpackers. Remember that involvement with drugs risks imprisonment without a trial.

By car

Taking your car

Morocco is ideal for a leisurely self-drive holiday; four-wheel drive is recommended. Note customs regulations, however. Your car must not exceed ten years old. Apart from a Green Card, your insurance policy is only valid if issued by an insurance company with a local office. Enquiries: **Bureau Central Marocain d'Assurances**, Rue Mostafa el-Maani, Casablanca.

The closest access is by Brittany Ferries, 2/weekly sailing Plymouth–Santander (or Portsmouth–Santander November to March). The 32,000 ton *Val de Loire* takes 600 cars and has cabin accommodation for 1,700 passengers; the crossing takes 24 hours. Car ferries from Algeciras sail to Tangier, Ceuta and Melilla. Enquiries: **Brittany Ferries**, Millbay Docks, Plymouth PL1 3EW, tel. (0752) 263388.

Car-hire

Hiring a car is an excellent, but costly, way to see Morocco, unless you find people to share costs. At last count there were some fifty rent-a-car companies, at least half unreliable, so go for a big name like InterRent-Europcar. InterRent's fleet of 800 vehicles ranges from Renault 4s to Landrovers. The cheapest car – the remarkably reliable Renault 4 – is ideal in rough conditions, for sandy tracks, rocky pistes, flooded fords and other travel adventures. The best plan is to hire a car for three to seven days with unlimited mileage. Documentation required is a British or American licence, or an International Driving Licence.

Driving

Moroccans are not bad drivers compared to those in other Muslim countries. I passed only three accidents, all on the Tetouan–Ceuta road, all involving *grands-taxis*. Bus and truck drivers pull over to let you pass. *Grands-taxis* are likely to break your wing mirrors. But the biggest threat is posed by camper-vans driven by mustard-coloured Germans in white hats.

Pedestrians are a major worry. At least half of all urban victims of car accidents are on foot. Treat anyone – child, adult or donkey – as potentially insane. They all walk on the road but you cannot predict when they will dash across it. Shepherds also suddenly drive their flocks from one side to another – I think it is a game. And avoid the *souq*. Oh, the *souq*! If you drive into the *souq* on market day, you will never forget it. Also avoid taking your car into a *kasbah*. In Tinerhir I jammed mine between two houses; unable to move, I needed a team of date-pickers to lift me out.

Driving is on the right with *priorité à droite*. The urban speed limit of 40 kph rises to 100 kph in the country and 120 kph on an autoroute. Traffic roundabouts are frequently off-centre and traffic lights set too high are difficult to discern.

Traffic police

There are frequent check-points on rural roads but the police generally wave you on. Outside Ksar el-Kebir was the only place I was stopped. 'Are you carrying any pistols, or hashish?' asked the police-man. 'What, me?' I replied, and we laughed. I was, however, halted on a dozen occasions for not circumnavigating the off-centre roundabouts and driving through red lights. If this happens, it is best to smile and feign no knowledge of French. They appear tough, but with tourists Moroccan policemen are generally helpful; locals may get a ticket for merely sneezing at the lights, but then locals give the police a hard time: in Rabat some parking-meters have been dug up, others have been decapitated.

Parking

Parking is easy but avoid the red-and-white striped kerb, the equivalent of double yellow lines. There is always a *gardien des voitures* to help you park and to watch the car: cost 1 dirham. Check he wears the official badge, as there are dozens of hopeful *gardiens*. They perform an invaluable service when you have to leave your car in a remote town. Often you return to find it washed, in which case give him 5 dirham. On the one occasion I did not have a *gardien* in Tetouan, two youths tried unsuccessfully to break into the car in broad daylight outside the Artisanal Centre. Be warned.

Where to Stay

There is a shortage of good, middle-priced hotels in Morocco. During popular months, the most desirable accommodation may be full, and in cheaper hotels it is very difficult to obtain a single room. Non-classified hotels abound, but they often have three or four beds to a room and cater more for local travellers and truck-drivers. Remember, however, that a hotel of any sort is a miracle in many towns. Fez, which had some 200 *funduqs*, or inns, in the sixteenth century, is now particularly short of accommodation. Unable to find a hotel on one visit, I was loaned a flat owned by a local businessman. He forgot to warn his partner and mistress that I was there so they joined me in bed (there was no electricity) in the middle of the night. An advance reservation is essential in a popular resort. It will not always be confirmed. Beneath ***A, nothing is necessarily confirmed – not heating, light, nor flushing WC. In one **A hotel I had to sleep on a mattress on the floor.

Morocco boasts some beautiful camp sites, though they are not always well maintained. I can only describe as dazzling the glorious lagoon-site of Moulay Bousselham, but it had neither water nor electricity. I also found a horse in the nightclub. Camping rough is recommended if you are completely self-sufficient. In official camp sites, the price varies, from 5 dirham per tent.

Much of my time in Morocco was spent checking hotels. In one I opened the window to assess the street noise and the window fell out into the courtyard; in another the bed collapsed when I lay on it; and in testing the sound-proofing of a room in Beni-Mellal I punched a hole in the dividing wall. So, if you try a hotel not listed in the Gazetteer, I suggest you check the room before booking in.

The Moroccan Tourist Board classifies hotels on a scale from *B to *****A and the government sets the price for categories *B to ****A. A 17–19 per cent government tax is usually payable on top. The table opposite gives prices for 1993.

Prices for five-star hotels are not fixed by the government and vary enormously, from a little more than the price of a ****A hotel to 14,000 dirham for a deluxe suite. Unclassified hotels charge less than a *B establishment but, as with five-star hotels, the tariff will depend on the management, demand and the time of year. I found some basic hotels where a bed cost only 50 dirham, rising to 80 dirham in the summer. In the Gazetteer, if a hotel is unclassified I have given an indication of the price.

1993 Hotel Rates (in dirham)†

Category	Single room	Double room	Tax‡	Category	Single room	Double room	Tax‡
Fez, Oujda & Rabat regions				*Casablanca region*			
****A	345	440	5	****A	500	600	5
****B	288	360	5	****B	300	370	5
***A	216	261	3	***A	220	260	3
***B	186	229	3	***B	190	230	3
**A	146	171	2	**A	145	170	2
**B	113	138	2	**B	110	135	2
*A	105	121	2	*A	100	120	2
*B	83	106	2	*B	85	100	2
Marrakesh & Meknes region				*Ouarzazate region*			
****A	362	460	5	****A	350	450	5
****B	302	377	5	****B	288	360	5
***A	226	273	3	***A	216	261	3
***B	195	240	3	***B	186	229	3
**A	153	179	2	**A	146	176	2
**B	119	144	2	**B	113	138	2
*A	110	127	2	*A	105	121	2
*B	87	111	2	*B	83	106	2

Category	Single room		Double room		Tax‡
Agadir region					
****A	LS 362/HS	377	LS 460/HS	480	5
****B	LS 302/HS	315	LS 377/HS	393	5
***A	LS 226/HS	236	LS 273/HS	285	3
***B	LS 195/HS	203	LS 240/HS	250	3
**A	LS 153/HS	160	LS 179/HS	186	2
**B	LS 119/HS	124	LS 144/HS	150	2
*A	LS 110/HS	114	LS 127/HS	132	2
*B	LS 87/HS	90	LS 111/HS	116	2
Tangier region					
****A	LS 345/HS	362	LS 440/HS	460	5
****B	LS 288/HS	302	LS 360/HS	377	5
***A	LS 216/HS	226	LS 261/HS	273	3
***B	LS 186/HS	195	LS 229/HS	240	3
**A	LS 146/HS	153	LS 171/HS	179	2
**B	LS 113/HS	119	LS 138/HS	144	2
*A	LS 105/HS	110	LS 121/HS	127	2
*B	LS 83/HS	87	LS 106/HS	111	2

*Deluxe & ***** hotels*

City	LS/HS	LS/HS
Agadir	650	800
Casablanca	832/2300	964/2300
Fez	850/1350	1050/1550
Laayoune	450	500
Marrakesh	900/3000	1100/3200
Meknes	520	750
Ouarzazate	850	1080
Rabat	900/1900	1050/1900
Tangier	600/800	800/1030

† £1 = 13 to 14 dirham
‡ Additional local tax varies from 1 to 30 dirham depending on hotel category and region
LS = low season, HS = high season

Eating and Drinking

Classic Moroccan cooking includes nomad food, Berber food and imperial food, a vestige of Abbassid court cuisine from Baghdad. Together they form a uniquely Moroccan rather than *Maghrebi*, repertoire.

Nomad food

Nomad food consists of simple items suited to a peripatetic lifestyle: dates chewed by a herdsman, *brochettes* seared quickly on a camp-fire. Southerners prefer camel-meat to beef; if young, it is tender, milder and less fatty. *Ejben*, or salty white camel-milk cheese, is excellent.

Berber food

Chemical-free, Berber food consists mainly of warm, nourishing meals, especially soups and oily *tajines*, or stews. The *argan* nut is made into a peanut-butter-type paste in the Souss. Used on salads, its taste is rather bitter. Almonds are widely eaten and wild mountain honey is delicious. A typical Berber meal begins with bread and *smen*, or rancid butter, and honey, followed by a *tajine*, with vegetables or salad.

Imperial food

There are surprising similarities between the cuisine of Mesopotamia and *al-Maghrib al-Aqsa*. They can be traced back to the arrival in Morocco of Moulay Idriss and his retinue, which included several chefs. Cleverly matched spices, in particular cinnamon and cumin, are liberally used. *Ras al-hanout*, translated as 'top of the shop', is a *mélange* of as many as two dozen spices. Moroccans share the Persian penchant for blending sweet with savoury, a classic example being *bstilla*, a filo-pastry pie made with pigeon flesh and almonds and dusted with icing-sugar. *Tajines* frequently mix poultry and meat with raisins, nuts and prunes. Fez is considered the gastronomic centre of Morocco. Diluted by Berber cooking over the centuries, imperial food is also eaten by old families in Rabat, Meknes and Marrakesh.

Where to eat

Having whetted your appetite, I must now disappoint by saying you are unlikely to get more than a *soupçon* of truly grand Moroccan food. The standard of hotel cooking is poor and you will find the same menu everywhere: *harira* soup, *brochettes*, *tajine*, couscous and, if you are fortunate, a *poulet au citron*, or lemon chicken. Why this should be is not clear, when there are dozens of regional dishes with many variations. I suspect it is laziness on the part of hotel chefs combined with Western travel agents cutting costs by ordering the cheapest meals for tour groups.

In the *Nouvelles Villes* you have a choice of hotel food, usually French or Spanish, but also German in Agadir. Café-grills serve fresh, cheap Moroccan meals in the *medina*. There are also excellent street stalls which char-grill snacks while you wait. The cost of a meal varies from 30 dirham in a café-grill to more than 300 dirham in an up-market restaurant. Should a Moroccan invite you home for dinner, accept with alacrity; your chance to eat home-cooking should not disappoint.

Moroccan food

Entrées

Kebabs, or *brochettes*, are common starters, usually of lamb or beef, although street stalls also cook offal such as kidneys and liver, and in Sefrou I ate 'fries' or 'prairie oysters'. Salads of raw or cooked vegetables are popular. *M'riquat hzina*, made with sliced oranges, garlic and pepper, is a speciality of Rabat. There are endless soups, but you will eat *harira* in Morocco until it comes out your ears. It is commonly made using a light vegetable stock with morsels of meat and spices. Minted *harira* is a speciality in Tangier. There are more than thirty variations of the standard, dull *harira* served in tourist hotels. You can also eat local *fois-gras* from a farm near Casablanca run by an enterprising Moroccan woman.

Main courses

A small, steaming volcano of couscous, or semolina, served with meat, poultry or fish, is the national dish. Camel-meat couscous is eaten by the Blue Men of the south. *Couscous bidaoui*, made with seven vegetables, is a speciality of Casablanca. Sweet couscous cooked with milk, raisins or dates and almonds is popular in the Tafilalet. Many families eat couscous daily or as a ritual Friday lunch. It is good for the digestion, but you usually feel hungry a few hours later. Endeavouring to eat it like Moroccans do is as awkward as learning how to eat with chopsticks: using their thumb and first finger, they pick up a portion, flick it into their palm, roll it into a ball and pop it in their mouth without dropping a grain.

Tajine, a stew or casserole, is almost as popular as couscous. There are hundreds of recipes, mostly for meat or poultry, but also fish. It is served in a dish with a conical lid – thousands are sold along the roadsides. *Tajine m'rouzia*, made of mutton, prunes and almonds, is a Marrakshi speciality. Veal *tajine* with prunes and sesame seeds is popular in Casablanca. Beef *tajine* garnished with oranges and potatoes is famous in Tafraoute. Seafood *tajines* are renowned in Essaouira and often all you can find in Dakhla. Chicken with lemon, and *meslalla*, olives, garlic and chicken stewed in honey and prunes, are favourite poultry *tajines*.

Bstilla is a poultry dish fit for a king, for whom it is made on state occasions; it is served at any important event, as is roast lamb, or *mechoui*. A big *bstilla* for a society wedding may contain up to one hundred pigeons. Casablanca's Royal Mansour Hotel, which has one of the most extensive menus in Morocco, is known for its *bstilla*. Many items require advance notice.

Seafood
Inland there is a conspicuous absence of seafood and the commercial sale of trout in the Middle Atlas is banned. The old Portuguese ports of Safi and Essaouira are the best spots for seafood, where sardines are grilled straight out of the ocean. Other popular local fish are tuna, bream, bass, *loup*, or grouper, and sole. Nador has the best seafood on the Mediterranean, while Oualidia on the central Atlantic coast is the centre of a thriving oyster cultivation industry. Local lobsters, prawns, mussels and crabs are excellent. Driving south of el-Jadida, you will see fishermen holding up gangling spider crabs for sale, but avoid these as they are as skinny as they look.

Bread
The staff of life has sacred status in Morocco. No matter how stale it is, bread is never thrown out and should a passer-by find a piece in the street, he will pick it up and bless it. Subtle variations exist between urban and rural bread, but whether made from wheat or barley flour, it is always unleavened, round, flat and quite delicious.

Hotel restaurants do not serve Moroccan bread, but you can buy some in the *souq* and take it in to dinner – the waiter will be flattered you prefer it to the French *baguette*. Poor families send their dough to the public oven, stamped with their symbol to avoid confusion. Bread is eaten with every meal and different sorts of fried dough, crêpes and beignets are popular at breakfast.

Fruit
Morocco is renowned for its excellent fruit, especially citrus fruits, peaches, grapes, bananas, melons and strawberries from Larache. A dish of fresh fruits, including dates, usually ends a meal. Thirty-five different types of date are grown in the southern oases; most are eaten fresh, or used in cooking couscous. Bread spread with date-jam is eaten in the Deep South. Figs are popular in northern Morocco. *Tighliki*, a dessert of figs and raisins soaked in oil, is a tradition in al-Hoceima.

Sweetmeats
Like most Arabs, Moroccans have a sweet tooth, but choose your pastries carefully; mass-produced at Ramadan, many are sticky bangles of sugar and water crawling with insects. Popular sweetmeats are *briouats au miel* (pastry cases stuffed with almond paste and dripping with honey); *m'hencha*, a coiled pastry also filled with almond pâté (*hench* means serpent in Arabic); and *kaab el-ghzal* (pastry horns

stuffed with marzipan spiked with cinnamon and orange-blossom water). *Feqqas* are sweet aniseed biscuits. Tetouan is said to make the best sweetmeats in Morocco. An excellent shop is the Pâtisserie Bennis in the Habbous in Casablanca.

Drinks

Wines

That the local wine industry established by the French is doomed will please Islamic fundamentalists, although Morocco has never encouraged wine-making and production is suspended during Ramadan. As vines die off, they are not replaced and many have been supplanted by sunflowers. You will see great gaps in the vineyards of the former wine-producing areas around Mohammadia–Meknes, Oujda and Marrakesh–Casablanca. Production has dropped from 1 million to around 400,000 hectolitres.

The main wine-makers and distributors are Sincomal, who produce 80 per cent of *gros rouge* table wine, and Meknes Vines, who produce 18 per cent. The balance concentrate on better types of wines, which come from the Ben Sliman region near Casablanca. In general, Moroccan wines should be drunk young, but there is usually no option. One of the best wines, a rosé called Gris de Boulaouane – similar to Listel Gris de Gris – is hard to find. So, too, is the crisp, dry, white Spécial Coquillages, which complements seafood perfectly. Common reds are Toulal, Ksar and Les Trois Domaines. Two good reds from Domaine des Ouled Thaleb are Cabernet President and Cabernet Medaillon (1984). A Ma Bretagne in Casablanca has an excellent cellar of Moroccan wines. French brands are sold in up-market hotels. Off-licences are very few and far between. Outside major towns such as Tangier, Fez, Meknes or Casablanca there are none, although enquiries may elicit a supply of black-market spirits, usually Scotch.

Beer

Moroccan beer lacks the bite of a good bitter, but it swills down well after a hot day's travels. The best beer, Flag Special, costs from 12 dirham in a bar. Imported brands cost from 25 dirham; five-star hotels charge from 50 dirham for spirits.

Mineral water

Tap-water is generally safe to drink in urban areas such as Rabat, or Casablanca. In the mountains an apparently clear stream may well be polluted by villagers living higher up. You can never be sure, so in Morocco I only drink the superb local mineral water. Oulmes, a sparkling natural water, ranks with the world's best. Sidi Ali and Sidi Harazem are good brands of still water – from 6 dirham in grocers' shops.

Mint-tea

Moroccan society would probably collapse without traditional mint-tea – an increase in sugar prices was the cause of the Casablanca riots in 1984. Tea is made with fresh mint leaves and green tea, preferably Gunpowder, which was introduced by British merchants in the nineteenth century. It is drunk in a tall glass with lots of sugar – the waiter will ask whether you like it sweet, very sweet or sickeningly sweet. It may be spiked with tuber-rose in Tangier, orange blossom in Marrakesh, or saffron in Taliouine. Meknes is noted for highly fragrant mint-tea.

Café society

The most popular coffee is *café-cassé*, literally coffee 'broken' with milk, served hot and strong in a small glass for 2.50 dirham. I survived Morocco on *café-cassé*, but every time I drank it I had to smash a social barrier to enter the *café-terrace*, a pillar of male chauvinism throughout Morocco, and especially in Tangier. Persevere, however, for the *café-cassé* is worth it. If you are a woman, the first time you enter the waiter will not see you and you may have to fetch your own coffee from the bar. On the second occasion he will say *'bonjour'* and take your order; on your third visit, he will put your coffee down and ask you out. By now you will also be on nodding terms with the unemployed sitting over empty glasses. When a tout bothered me in Marrakesh, the entire *café-terrace* rose to my defence. In Tangier the least intimidating coffee-lounge for women is the Vienne, owned by a member of the notorious *kif* syndicate from Bab Bered. During the day Spanish women friends from Tetouan meet there, but at night it becomes exclusively male. I had a coffee there at 10 p.m. surrounded by ninety men and a table of four prostitutes. Not unnaturally, I got propositioned with my bill.

Independent Sightseeing

Guides

Faux-guides

Sightseeing on your own in towns which are frequented by tour groups is unfortunately impossible in Morocco. As soon as you leave your hotel, you are besieged by young men waiting in the shade. I counted twenty dotted around the Palais Jamai in Fez, like lions around a kill. It is the *faux-guide* – not the child, or the beggar, or the man with the *djellabahs* on his arm – which is spoiling tourism. The false guide is not the least interested in showing you his beautiful country, but in encouraging you to spend so he can earn a commission. The patter is predictable. '*Soyez bienvenue*. English? German? French? You are welcome in my father's, uncle's, brother's shop.' 'Hello, my friend, don't you know me? I am your hotel waiter.' In Tangier I was approached outside El Minzah Hotel by a man, a little older and somewhat greyer than thirteen years ago, but still saying he was a student of English.

Refusing the service of a *faux-guide* usually elicits verbal abuse. The way to outwit the *faux-guide* brigade is to employ an official guide who also hopes to earn a cut from what you buy, but at least the others will leave you be. Local Tourist Offices have a list of official guides, who must speak at least one foreign language apart from Arabic and French. They wear a brass badge and cost £5 per half-day and £10 for a full day. If you are pestered by a *faux-guide*, ask to see his credentials. An ID card or a school report is not an accreditation – nor is a doctor's prescription, given to me by a man who suspected I did not read French.

The Moroccan view-point

For a poor Moroccan, the tourist from affluent Western society is guilty of abstract aggression. An approaching group is a horrible sight as, dressed in a variety of shorts, T-shirts and terry-towelling hats, it moves en masse through the *medina*. The temptation to pick on a straggler is almost overwhelming. 'They call us hustlers. I call us hard workers,' said a boy-runner for a string of carpet-shops in Marrakesh. What he and others do not realise is that the poor, sunburned creature who looked forward to his holiday in Morocco has never had a moment's peace. He wants to buy something but the group is carrying on and, terrified of becoming lost, he starts to panic. Did it turn left for the spice market, or right for the mosque? Calling to each other in foreign tongues, the hustlers move in. 'No charge for looking,' says one. 'I make you good price, Mister,' says another. Once four-letter words are exchanged they are repeated like a litany through the *medina*.

If you are not part of a group and dress sensibly, you are less likely to be bothered, but the wise traveller will still employ a guide, either an official guide or a pleasant boy from among the crowd. 'I wouldn't dream of taking money,' said a poor boy in Meknes, his hand lightly brushing his heart, an endearing gesture, oft-repeated in Morocco.

Beggars

You do not have to go to Morocco to find beggars, but the increasing numbers indicate the rising problem of making ends meet. Clad in a ragged *djellabah* and with a tin, or a palm held out for alms, beggars are a fact of life in Morocco. Do not over-react to them. Drop them a few centimes, not more – they might suffer a heart attack.

Who to help and who to ignore is difficult. In Fez, where a row of blind men stands near the Kairouine Mosque, I slipped one man a dirham. This was passed from hand to hand, each man feeling what it was, until the last man slipped it inside his robe. Fine, cream cotton, his djellabah was beautifully ironed and I mentioned this to my guide who told me a remarkable story. Every day for twenty years, a beggar woman had sat in his street and his family and neighbours had always given her money as they passed. When the old lady died, his family went to pay their respects and the boy learned that she owned two houses in the *medina*. Female relatives in one of them were counting thousands of silver dirhams.

Syndicates of beggars are also part of life in Morocco, as they are in Manila and Bombay. Each member has his or her spot which, like that of the butcher and the shoe-maker in the *souq*, never varies. Walking down behind the Law Courts in Casablanca, I used to see the same faces, day after day: a woman with three children sitting with her back to the gutter, a blind man, his head tilted against the sky, and another woman perpetually feeding a baby. One day I squatted beside her and asked in broken Arabic where she came from. Sidi Bou-Abid, she whispered, a horrible little village out in the *bled*. Too many mouths is one reason why you will see so many women beggars in Morocco. If employed at all, their husbands, former farmers, cannot earn enough.

Morocco and the woman traveller

When I first went to Morocco less than a decade after Independence, I was a naïve, young blonde fresh out of Sydney, but in spite of my vulnerability, I was everywhere treated with respect. Boys were as keen then as now to invite me home for couscous with their family, but their approach was shy and the word 'sex' was never mentioned. Over the years Morocco has developed a bad reputation among lone women travellers. Sensible Moroccans know that all Western women are not like the tarts portrayed in American videos, but plenty of cocksure youths today consider any young woman to be fair game. You only have to see the camel-drivers waving goodbye to a charter flight to know they are not solely responsible.

While researching this book I was hassled by *faux-guides* and pestered by touts, but the only improper suggestion was made by a boy who was so young he was allowed into the woman's *hammam*. 'Fucky-fucky,' he whispered when his mother was performing her ablutions and I was dabbing at myself with a sponge.

You are better off with a companion in Morocco – not another woman, as two girls are seen as an invitation, but a male friend (who may be equally glad of female company). If you do travel alone, there are simple precautions: walk tall and purposefully even though you may be hopelessly lost; if needing directions, check with several people, as a Muslim, anywhere, will only tell you what he thinks you want to hear. Do not ask 'Is that the road to . . .?' because he will answer in the affirmative. Instead enquire, 'Where is the road to . . .?' and look in the opposite direction. Always spend more, not less, on accommodation – one of the penalties of being a woman. Morocco is infinitely safer than most Western countries, but you tempt fate to travel after dark. Avoid the Ketama region (see pp. 111–12) and learn some French, or Arabic.

Entertainment and Sport

Folklore

Morocco's colourful folklore is rooted in Berber traditions. When least expected, you may come upon an explosion of tribal dancing at a wedding or a thrilling *fantasia* at a rural *moussem*. Many tourist hotels have a *Soirée Folklorique*, tourism having encouraged rather than spoilt regional local culture. The summer *fantasia* in Marrakesh is a wonderful spectacle.

Music

Andalusia has influenced classical Moroccan music, as the haunting *ala* shows; a lament similar to the flamenco, but essentially religious, complements the music. A social occasion among aristocracy in Fez, Tetouan or Rabat always features an Andalus orchestra. Ask the Tourist Office, or your hotel concierge, whether your visit coincides with a performance in the theatre or concert-hall.

Popular music is not the 'rock-pop' of the West (although you do hear this in discos) but a type of country-folk sung in Arabic and performed on typical instruments: the *houd*, or lute, the *rebab*, similar to a violin, drums, flute, zither and *kemania*, resembling a viola but played on the knee. Popular music continues to evolve. One type is influenced by the great classic artists of the Middle East – Oum Kaltoum, Fairouz, Abdul Halem Hafid and others.

Dances

Moroccan folkdances vary between tribes as well as regions. Whether sedentary, or nomadic, each tribe has a traditional repertoire. While exotic to watch, the steps are symbolic and largely incomprehensible to a foreigner, even to a Moroccan brought up in Rabat or Casablanca.

The ***ahwash*** is danced round the campfire in the *kasbahs* of the High Atlas. A circle of women stands motionless around a group of men clutching drums. Following a strangled cry, the dance begins. Men sing, women respond and, merging together, they sway back and forth, faster and faster until the finale. One of Morocco's most exciting regional dances, it may be staged by one of the big tourist hotels in Marrakesh.

The ***guedra***, from the Deep South, is rooted in ancient symbolism with music supplied by drums. A veiled woman swirls in the centre of chanting, clapping dancers, faster and faster, flinging off her veils as the singing changes to short, erotic grunts and she collapses in a heap.

The *ait haddidou* from the Atlas stars women in spectacular striped kaftans. The robed men, wearing huge turbans, coax a rustic rhythm from their goat-skin drums; a second group is led by a man chanting tribal poems. Fascinating, if complex, it is a slow dance, based on local folklore known only to the tribal elders. The dance speeds up in the area of el-Hejjab and Khenifra in the Middle Atlas.

The *gnaouar*, said to originate from Guinea, can be seen on the Djemaa el Fna in Marrakesh. An urgent, foot-tapping rhythm is played on large drums and iron castanets. The dancers, usually young boys, perform acrobatic leaps.

Dancers of the *houara* come from Inezgane, near Agadir, and are seen in the tourist hotels. Dervish-like whirling is the key-note with virtuosi executing spectacular solo performances.

Dances such as the *taskioune* and the *ait bodar* have origins in ancient feuds. Frank, powerful and virile, they are a feature of towns in the Rif Mountains.

Sports

Golf King Hassan II likes golf, and since he has residential palaces all over Morocco there is an equal array of golf courses where visitors are welcome. Of note is Les Dunes, a 27-hole course built on rolling terrain outside Agadir; the three nines are reported to be challenging. Designed by Trent Jones, Les Jardins de la Palmerie in Marrakesh weaves around seven lakes within the vast villa estate. Sir Winston Churchill used to play golf at the original 18-hole Royal Marrakesh; King Hassan II, an 8-handicap, is a regular in winter.

Morocco's most famous course, however, is the 45-hole Royal Dar-Es-Salaam, fifteen minutes' drive from Rabat. Venue of the Moroccan Open, it is highly recommended. Other golf courses are: Agadir Royal (9 holes), Anfa Royal Casablanca (9 holes), Benslimane Royal (9 holes), Cabo-Negro Royal (9 holes), El-Jadida Royal (18 holes), Fez Royal (9 holes), Meknes Royal (9 holes), Mohammedia Royal (18 holes), Ouarzazate (9 holes), Tangier Royal (18 holes).

Fishing Few countries offer as much scope for fishing as Morocco, which has some of the world's best ocean and freshwater angling. There are snags, however. Most fishermen like to be independent, but some fishing spots are very inaccessible. Tortuous tracks lead to isolated trout streams in the Atlas, but fishing south of Tan-Tan requires four-wheel drive, as the bitumen road is often inland from the ocean. Take all your gear, as few shops sell fishing tackle. As a result, Moroccan fishermen use the most rudimentary equipment, often only a length of line on a stick. A nice way to reward your guide or boatman is to bequeath him some gear.

Ocean fishing

The Dakhla peninsula – 1,339 km south of Agadir – deserves to rank with places like Cuba, Cairns and the Pemba Channel for legendary fishing. A day's fishing is likely to yield half a dozen fish weighing 20–30 kilos each while local *corberone* reach 100 kilos. **Sochatour**, a tour operator in Casablanca specializing in hunting and fishing, organizes trips by jeep to within 100 km of the Mauritanian border. Local boats can be hired for fishing in Dakhla Bay but take everything you need for survival, as Dakhla is the end of the road. There are some excellent fishing spots between Tan-Tan and Tarfaya, but you will have to camp out in the desert.

Freshwater angling

Inland fishing for trout and pike offers a variety of potential water varying in altitude and accessibility, but always in beautiful surroundings. Trout occur throughout the Atlas: thirty minutes south of Azrou, off the road to Marrakesh three lakes known as Amghas I, II and III are renowned for excellent fishing. The Middle Atlas region east of Beni-Méllal is also reported to be good. Zerrouka, 20 km from Ifrane, has excellent trout water. Such places are within easy reach of comfortable accommodation; elsewhere camping-out and wading along the stream is the only way to reach water often teeming with trout. The trout season opens on 31 March; lakes may only be fished from 6 a.m. to 12 noon. Permits cost 3 dirham a day. Worms and wet flies are the most common fishing techniques.

The local term 'pike lake' distinguishes such a lake from one stocked exclusively with trout. Huge pike are said to lurk in Aguelmane Azizga near Khenifra. Most lakes are also inhabited by perch, carp, roach, walleye, barbel and bass. Big bass are fished in the Moulay Yussef dam, 80 km east of Marrakesh, and in Bin el-Ouidane, 50 km from Beni-Méllal; the average size is about 750 grams. The Hotel Salam in Khenifra and the Panorama in Azrou are well-located for popular fishing water.

Hunting

The hunting season in Morocco lasts nine months a year. The main areas are:

Arbaoua: marshes, wetlands and woodlands south of Tangier. Game includes wild boar and snipe, woodcock, duck, teal, quail and the Barbary partridge.

Ben Sliman: forest near Casablanca with partridge and pheasant and the occasional woodcock.

Marrakesh: an excellent base for hunting boar, red-legged partridge and turtle-doves.

Kabila: a forested hill region behind the Mediterranean offering good boar shooting, also duck, snipe and red-legged partridge.

Agadir: the Souss Valley offers excellent shooting, mainly turtle-dove and quail.

For further details of hunting and fishing in Morocco contact

Sochatour, 72 Boulevard Zerktouni, Casablanca; tel. 277513/273195, telex 21767.

Skiing

Covered in good, packed snow for three to four months, the Atlas massif offers splendid skiing opportunities, but facilities remain underdeveloped. The two main centres are:

Oukaimeden in the High Atlas, with snow from the end of November until Easter. Slopes of 640 m starting from the Oukaimeden peak contain most obstacles usually encountered in international competitions. There is a good run from Djebel Attar (3,258 m), while eastern slopes range from the great descent of 630 m starting at the peak, to smaller ones serviced by ski-lifts. Oukaimeden has three ski-lifts and two ski jumps of 40–50 m. The resort has a training school, four hotels and is easily accessible from Marrakesh – a two-hour drive.

Mischlifen experiences snow on forty to sixty days a year. Accessible from either Marrakesh (424 km) or Ifrane (18 km). The premier ski resort in the Middle Atlas, it has two ski-lifts, of which one goes from the depth of the crater to an altitude of 2,000 m. There are shelters and mountain lodgings opposite the ski station.

Other rustic stations exist in the Middle Atlas near Azrou.

Trekking

Trekking in Morocco will likely one day be as popular as in Nepal. The Atlas massif offers the largest area for cross-country accessible all year, although the best time is from April to October. Ski-trekking, or the combination 'mule-ski', in the High Atlas can be carried out from April to October. The Middle Atlas and Rif chain offer fine forest walks, autumn and spring being the best times.

Canyon walks, rock climbing and ice-climbs (the latter in the Djebel Toukbal region) are also available to anyone reasonably fit – altitudes over 3,500 m are recommended only for experienced walkers. Beware of sudden summer storms if tackling canyon walks: within minutes of being dry, a wadi can become a raging torrent of rainwater pouring off the hills.

Buses and taxis serve the main villages in the High Atlas foothills. From here the central massif is further accessible by four-wheel drive, or mountain market lorries. Chauffeur-driven Land Rovers are available for hire in popular resorts.

Although the Moroccan mountains are safe and the people are friendly, you are advised to take a qualified CFAMM guide (*Centre de Formation aux Metiers de Montagne*).

Baggage mules are available for hire in every village. An animal is capable of carrying about 100 kilos, corresponding roughly to the needs of four trekkers. Porters are available for high-altitude sections who will carry 20–30 kilos according to the terrain.

Accommodation ranges from inns and *gîtes* at lower altitudes, to local homes and refuge huts. Camping is possible during summer months. Buy basic provisions before you leave. Simple groceries, vegetables, eggs, chickens and fruits are sold in the weekly mountain *souqs* – check the day.

Special trekking holidays are arranged by **Inspirations**, Saxley Court, Horley, Surrey RH6 7AS, tel. (0293) 822244.

Horse-riding

Special riding holidays in the Atlas are offered by leading Morocco tour operator **Inspirations** (see above). A special five-night riding package from Agadir is based at the charming Auberge des Cascades (see p. 215). A short-distance ride to allow you and your mount to become acquainted, is followed by a three-day hack up to 1,600 m. Accommodation is rustic farmhouse and open fires. Tack is provided, but bring a helmet. Riding is also a feature at the **Roseraie Hotel** at Ourigane. Enquiries at some Middle Atlas hotels may also bring on the horses.

Camel treks

Inspirations also specialise in short camel treks into the desert from the southern oasis town of Zagora. The way follows ancient caravan routes and offers encounters with the 'Blue Men' of the Sahara. Accommodation is hotel and camping. Highly recommended. Available from Agadir.

White-water rafting

White-water rafting is available on the Ourika river, near Marrakesh. The 27 km descent passes down the beautiful Ourika Valley, classified grade A with rapids class II and III. Seasonal.

Shopping

Souqs and bargaining

The *souq* is a major feature of every town in Morocco. Why tourists show such an interest in their market is a mystery to most Moroccans, who, if asked, would no doubt prefer a modern supermarket. A *souq* is much more than just a market, however; it is a thriving community of traders and craftsman.

Urban souqs

The concept of the *souq* is rooted in religion as well as commerce. It is always within walking distance of the mosque, for the convenience of traders and shoppers during prayer times. While apparently chaotic; the *souq* is in fact very well organized. Based on a commercial and social hierarchy, the various shops and crafts all have different allocated areas. There is the *souq es-sabat*, or shoe market, the *souq el-attarine*, or spice *souq*, a goldsmiths' quarter, a street for mats and basketware, and so on. The rope-makers have their place, the coppersmiths and knife-grinders theirs. Herbalists, potters, butchers and sweetmeat shops are all similarly grouped. Being together means the vendors or craftsmen have common links in conversation as well as materials. Some trades are considered more demeaning than others. A barber, for instance, is not held in such high esteem as a pastry-maker, a subtle pecking order that is not apparent unless you are familiar with Muslim society.

The fact that shops selling similar merchandise are grouped together is also helpful to the buyer. It enables you to compare prices and quality without having to traipse all over town. You can go from shop to shop and then retrace your steps. No one minds. It is a fairly safe bet, however, that you will finally make your purchases where you can browse in peace, something infinitely rare in Morocco.

Bargaining

When you decide to buy, you are expected to bargain. Accustomed to fixed prices in the West, many people find this embarrassing. Men, in particular, tend to scorn the custom as eroding their potential spending power, but most women find the practice less daunting. Pride sees many tourists foolishly pay the initial asking price, which will disappoint the merchant, who enjoys the cut and thrust of a good haggle. There are no rules to bargaining. That the merchant, alone, knows the true value of what you want is disconcerting, but you must bear in mind three criteria: do you really like it; what are you willing to pay; and remember that it was made in a poor country (this is being realistic rather than condescending). Most shop-keepers will cheat you a little, but you have no means of knowing. As no one knows in advance what you will end up paying, the whole bargaining process has an aura of pantomine. Prices are rarely displayed because the canny merchant has a different price for everyone: for the tourist off a coach, the backpacker, the servant of a foreign resident; a special price for multiple purchases, a price for rich locals, a price for poor locals, for the blind, the chief of police.

Seated in his web of paraphernalia, it seems the merchant has all day; it is you who are in a hurry. Remain cool, calm and determined, cracking the odd joke or discussing something completely different, or have your companion insist there is no room for such an object in your case. Replacing an article and pretending to walk away is my own favourite ploy. For his part, the trader may also break off bargaining if you make a silly proposition. Do not feel that accepting a mint-tea puts you under any obligation: this is a traditional courtesy and whether you buy or not, you are not expected to pay.

Finally, if you have discussed Morocco's initiative in the Maghreb, the cost of the great mosque in Casablanca, your family, his family and your job, and have reached a compromise, he will be as pleased as you are as he wraps it in last week's *L'Opinion* for a helper to carry as triumphantly as the Olympic torch to your hotel.

Rural souqs

The permanent urban market is supplemented by the rural *souq*, or farmers' market, which springs up once or twice a week on the outskirts of a town. It is worth enquiring about.

The real country *souq*, held in the *bled*, has evolved from xenophobia. Well-fortified, no *kasbah* would have consented to a weekly invasion of strangers, so the *caids* chose a spot where goods could be bought and sold on neutral ground, preferably in the open, in case of attack. Here a rudimentary compound, often nothing more than dividing walls, was erected. The place was simply called after the market day: *Souq el-Arba*, *Souq el-Tleta* – Wednesday, Thursday *souq*, and so on. This is why, when you are travelling about Morocco, you will see such *souqs* on open, often rocky ground way outside a village. The Saturday *souq* in Goulimine is a classic example. Traders often move to a different village each day. Any movement of people and animals on the road is an indication of a *souq* in the vicinity. Most begin early and by noon the crowd is trickling back towards the *bled*.

Main souqs

Agadir Province

Agadir	Saturday, Sunday
Inezgane	Tuesday
Bou Izacarn	Friday
Tafraoute	Wednesday
Goulimine	Saturday Camel Market
Taroudannt	Friday
Tiznit	Thursday, Friday

Ouarzazate Province

Ouarzazate	Sunday
Skoura	Monday, Thursday
Taliouine	Monday

Zagora area

Zagora	Wednesday, Thursday
Agdz	Thursday
Tagiounite	Thursday, Sunday
M'Hamide	Monday

Boumalne area

Boumalne	Wednesday
Tinerhir	Monday
Kelaa des M'Gouna	Wednesday

Tafilalet Province

Erfoud	Sunday
Er-Rachidia	Sunday, Tuesday, Thursday
Rissani	Sunday, Tuesday, Thursday

Kenitra Province

Khemisset	Tuesday
Tiflet	Wednesday
Kamouni	Sunday
Sidi Allal Bahraoui	Sunday
Souq Had Ouled Jelloul	Sunday
Souq Tleta	Tuesday
Souq Larbaa	Wednesday
Souq Khmis Rmila	Thursday
Jamaa Mograne	Friday
Jamaa Lala Mimouna	Friday
Had Kanouni	Sunday

Marrakesh Province

Marrakesh	Thursday Camel Market
Sidi Larbi	Thursday

Tetouan Province

Chechaouen	Thursday

Meknes Province

Midelt	Sunday

Moroccan handicrafts

Local arts and crafts reflect the diversity of Moroccan history and culture. Encouraged by the government and by tourist demand, the ancient trades are again flourishing. Some, like brassware and weaving, have tried to cater to package tourism, but others have strict standards passed from generation to generation, which preclude modern trends. The shape of a vase, the pattern of a brooch, have remained unchanged for centuries; the *souqs*, too, where handicrafts are made, have changed little since the Middle Ages.

Jewellery

Ancient Muslim superstition disdained gold. As a result, Arab women have traditionally worn silver jewellery – bracelets, anklets, pendants, earrings and rings worn on every finger. Silver remains the bank of poor rural women – you will see many women, especially in the Tafilalet, performing arduous chores under layers of silver and amber.

Berber jewellery has a rustic charm that is unmistakably Moroccan. Each tribe has a different geometric pattern made by craftsmen faithfully reproducing the ancient designs. Among common items seen in the *souq* are head-jewellery like the *lanech*, with tiny dangling discs set with semi-precious stones, and earrings such as the *ledjar*, huge silver loops strung with beads. Popular necklaces include the *medja*, set with precious gems, and the *chaira*, composed of small plaques with tiny gold balls. Breast-jewellery is frequently large and extravagantly decorated; the *tazra* are silver plates set with multi-coloured stones.

Two of the most unusual pieces of jewellery have Phoenician origins. The *fibula*, an ornate silver 'safety-pin' with which women secure their robes, also known as the *croix du sud*, is worn typically by women in the Zagora region. Tiznit and Taroudannt are two good places to buy beautiful old fibulas. The 'Hand of Fatima', usually of gold filigree, is the feminine symbol of ancient Carthage. Filigree work is a craft inherited from Jewish communities in the anti-Atlas and southern oases, and silversmiths working in Tiznit, Tata and other centres still use Jewish techniques. The finished items are polished with fine desert sand.

Pottery and ceramics

Morocco is renowned for its pottery and colourful ceramics. The terracotta-ware seen along the roads would be in huge demand among foreigners were it not so awkward to carry. Traditional Berber pottery is still fire using brush-wood kilns. Some of the best comes from the Anti-Atlas, the curve of a jar often resembling an ancient urn. Traces of Carthage, or Rome, are seen in the fine terracotta ware of the Rif. The art of glazing ceramic is an equally old tradition. Fez is the historic centre of the still flourishing ceramics industry, and produces beautiful tiles. Cobalt on white and yellow, blue and green are popular colour combinations. If you plan to buy ceramics, be guided in your choice by artefacts. If you plan to buy ceramics, be guided in your choice by artefacts in a museum, such as the Dar Batha Museum in Fez. Safi on the Atlantic coast also has a flourishing ceramics industry (see p. 145).

Leatherware

The leatherware industry continues to employ the largest number of artisans. You will no doubt visit the tanneries in Fez, Marrakesh or Tetouan, where the skins are still treated by the archaic method of immersing them in urine. Fez specializes in gold-leaf designs on red and green, in particularly for items such as folders, book binders and document holders. Pouffes, belts, bags, coats and cases are popular buys.

Babouche

The *babouche*, or *belgha*, the traditional flat, soft-leather slipper of Morocco, may be plain or decorated. They may vary slightly in shape between the main *babouche*-making centres – Fez, Marrakesh, and Taroudannt – and come in many colours. *Babouches* are sold in all *medinas*, but two important markets are the Middle Atlas towns of Khenifra and Azrou. Light to carry, *babouches* make attractive presents, but they are not easy to wear, as your feet tire with the effort of keeping them on. The idea of *babouches* is that they can be slipped off to enter a mosque, or to avoid bringing the *'poussière ignoble de la rue'* into a house (as a nineteenth-century French traveller put it).

Woodwork

Woodwork and marquetry reach a high standard in Morocco. Essaouira is the best place to buy beautiful wooden artefacts and to see the craftsmen at work. They use the sweet-scented *thuya*, which polishes up like antique rosewood but it is frequently too green and artefacts, especially boxes, tend to fall to pieces. Damascene is a speciality of Meknes – coffee tables, trays, chess sets and boxes set with mother-of-pearl and camel-bone are especially attractive. In any old building in Morocco look up at its richly carved cedar ceiling. A superb example is the Bou Inania *medersa* in Fez. Craftsmen still turn out this fine work and one wonders what the great carved *minbar* in the Hassan II Mosque will look like. Furniture-makers in Marrakesh and Fez use cedar and olive wood to make coffers and musical instruments. The carved grill, or *musharabia*, which covered windows to prevent women being seen from the street is an unusual interior decoration. Such work is now rare, but it is made by craftsmen in the Artisan Centre in Marrakesh.

Metalwork

Many silver and brass objects are now mass produced, but the main handicraft centres are Marrakesh, Fez, Tetouan and Casablanca. Brass lanterns and candelabra and silverware trays and teapots are a speciality of Casablanca – look for them in the Habbous, or new *medina*. Brass objects are found in every shop in Morocco – finely chiselled trays, candlestick-holders, incense-burners, bells and door-knockers. You can also buy rifles, powder-horns and daggers engraved and decorated with silver and camel-bone. Old ones may be found in Tiznit, Taroudannt and the pre-Saharan towns of Goulimine and Rissani. Attractive reproductions are made for the tourist market. Moroccan wrought iron – tables, lamp-stands and pot-plant stands – reflect an Andalusian influence.

Basketware

Countless practical and decorative objects are woven by Morocco's talented basket-makers – many of them women working at home. RAM flights from Tangier and Agadir are always filled with passengers carrying baskets on board. A medium-sized one sells for 8–12 dirhams in the *souq*. There is a good wickerware market as you come off the Casablanca roundabout into Marrakesh, or try Fez, Taroudannt and the weekly rural markets.

Carpets

Morocco is famous for hand-woven carpets. Generally they come with a thick pile, or with the pile cut neatly like a lawn. There are considerable differences between urban and rural carpets. The urban carpet has a central medallion and is rather Oriental looking: Rabat carpets have seven different colours with three borders around a dusky pink, blood red, sky blue or 'Granny-Smith' green background. Rural carpets tend to have geometric patterns: beige, brown and cream are popular colours in the Atlas. Marrakesh, Midelt and Rissani are some of the best carpet centres in Morocco. A measure of quality is the number of knots to the square centimetre – an average carpet has about twenty-five. Young girls are preferred for weaving as their slim fingers can tighten more knots. Some carpets have as many as 110,000 knots to the square metre. All orthodox hand-woven carpets have the Regional Handicrafts seal attached to the back on a piece of green cloth. The price is fixed by the government, but you will have to bargain with the carpet merchant, watched by the tout who brought you sitting avariciously in a corner.

Other hand-woven textiles are the red and white striped *futas*, or shawls, worn by the Rif women – sold in Tetouan and Tangier – and lightweight wool blankets.

Other souvenirs

Other crafts include embroidery from Marrakesh, Fez and Tetouan and hand-twisted belts. Ornate candles are sold outside the Kairouine Mosque in Fez. Strange objects sculpted in crystal, or left as natural rock, are sold everywhere in the Atlas mountains and in nearby towns such as Midelt. Mined near Erfoud, fossils set in polished marble are unusual souvenirs. I bought a 350-million-year-old nautilus from the Devonian period for £20. Roadside vendors are everywhere in Morocco. At various points I was offered oranges, eggs, potatoes, asparagus, flowers, Barbary figs, baskets of dates, figs, chameleons, puppies, straw mats, hats, pottery, marijuana, blankets, spider crabs, fish, rocks, marble eggs, olives, jewellery, strawberries and carpets.

General Basics

Communications

Letters

The time letters take to reach their destination in Morocco, or to depart for the exterior, is remarkably consistent: between seven and ten days. It does not seem to matter whether the article is posted in Rabat Central Post Office or in the back of beyond. A problem may arise over post office employees confusing Western names. When enquiring about your mail – and this also applies in hotels – ask under both your surname and given name. Then try the letters on either side. You will need your passport to collect mail at *poste restante*. Most post offices open 8.30 a.m. to 2 p.m. *Tabacs*, which sell cigarettes, newspapers and postcards, also sell stamps. Buy stamps from them to avoid the queue. In Tetouan PTT, where signs are in Arabic only (I spent forty minutes in a government pension queue).

Telephones

Telephones vary from direct dial to a 'bush service' via the operator and several stations. When I tried to call Madrid from Zagora, I was advised it would have to go via the post office as well as Ouarzazate, Marrakesh and Casablanca. (The operator then rang back to ask whether Madrid was the capital of Spain!) When the service is manual and you do manage to make an international call, it can be expensive. A reverse charge call also carries a loading: the best advice is to call someone briefly and have them call you back. If you are quick, this should not add more than 30 dirham to your bill.

An operator trick on a private line is to call your number and when you answer, to switch into your extension on behalf of another party wanting to make an international call. Make sure the operator hangs up before you do. Should you be offered the loan of a house in Morocco, keep the telephone locked, as the maid or cook will find it a splendid chance to call friends.

Local dialling codes

Casablanca	02
Marrakesh	04
Fez	05
Oujda	06
Rabat	07
Agadir	08
Tangier	09

Algeria	213	Netherlands	31
Australia	161	Portugal	351
Austria	43	Spain	34
Belgium	32	Switzerland	41
Canada	1	Tunisia	216
France	33	United Kingdom	44
Greece	30	United States	1
Italy	39	Germany	49

Customs

Customs regulations allow the import of a litre of spirits and 200 cigarettes. You are required to clear customs on entry, but tourists are usually waved through by courteous customs officers. Customs checks are encountered outside Ceuta and Melilla, but Moroccans are the target. Do not, however, attempt to sell your car.

Documentation and immigration

Holders of British, American, Canadian, Australian and New Zealand passports may enter Morocco for ninety days without a visa. Visas are valid for one month and normally take forty-eight hours to process. Renewing or extending a visa is tedious. Present regulations require a minimum 14,000 dirham deposit in a Moroccan bank account. Most people find it easier to make a day trip to Ceuta or Gibraltar every ninety days. Note that entry to Morocco is forbidden if your passport shows an Israeli or South African stamp. Temporary passports, including British visitor's passes, are not valid. If travelling with children, a photograph of them is required in one of the adult's passports.

Dress

Keep decorum in mind when you choose your holiday wardrobe. Hip Moroccan youth follows Western fashions, with a penchant for locally made denim, but in rural areas, the older generation still wears the traditional *djellabah*, an ample, ankle-length robe. Women did not cover their faces in pre-Islamic Morocco but, enjoined by the Qur'an to 'guard their modesty', they adopted the veil, or *haik*. Mohammed V tried to discourage the practice by allowing his daughter to appear unveiled in Tangier in 1943. Young Moroccan girls quickly copied, but from habit as much as anything older women prefer to remain incognito.

Favour long-sleeved shirts, and slacks rather than shorts. Figure-accentuating garments should not be worn in public. Acceptable at the hotel swimming-pool, a bikini may attract attention on the beach, while local people find women who sunbathe topless extremely offensive.

The dramatic changes in altitude make it important you also take something warm: a padded jacket is ideal for outdoors, while a cardigan or a sweater is sufficient protection against hotel air-conditioning. If you strike freak weather, as I did in Meknes, you can buy a very reasonable wool *djellabah*. Saharan temperatures fluctuate considerably, which is reflected in local dress. While I am not proposing you should dress like a Blue Man, you may find a *litham*, or turban, useful in a sandstorm. Even in Agadir, take a warm wrap for desert nights. Winter clothes are essential in the mountains between October and March. Casual wear is acceptable in most resort hotels, but up-market establishments require more elegant dress (a tie is *de rigueur* at the Gazelle d'Or in Taroudannt).

Drugs

Morocco does not have a Western-type drugs problem, but smoking *kif*, or cannabis, is a regular pastime like chewing *qat* in Yemen. As a tourist with money you are vulnerable: the possession, offer, purchase, distribution, sale, transportation and exportation of hashish – in whatever form – carries a prison sentence of between three months and five years, plus a stiff fine. Moreover the law may seize the means of transportation, usually a car. According to a British embassy spokesman, several Britons have been involved in drugs-related charges, genuine or otherwise. A favourite local trick involves hiding the drugs under your car and advising the *gendarmes*; the proceeds are then split. Alternatively a rich youngster is jailed and a private deal struck with his parents. If you want to see *kif* in safety, drive out of Tangier along the road to Ksar es-Seghir, but stay away from areas in the Rif where *kif* is grown. Plants are also seen on the approach to Chechaouen.

Electricity

Mainly 220 volts AC, using two-point, round-pin plugs. It is usually reliable, although it is not guaranteed in basic hotels.

Embassies

Canada: 13 bis, Rue Jaagar Assadik, Agdal, Rabat; tel. 771375.
United Kingdom: 17 Boulevard de la Tour Hassan, Rabat; tel. 720905.
United States: Avenue de Marrakesh, Rabat; tel. 762265.
Australia and New Zealand use the British embassy.

Etiquette

Introductions

Courtesies in Morocco are more or less the same as in other Muslim countries. Most families will say it is not necessary to remove your shoes at the door, but it is customary to do so. Do not display the soles of your feet. If invited to eat, begin by shaking hands with everyone, but do not start with your hostess. Begin with the person on your right and circle the room anti-clockwise. When a servant brings a kettle for washing, soap your hands over the dish while water is poured over them.

Table manners

At the table, Moroccans will say *'bismillah'* ('in the name of God') in appreciation of the meal, however humble. Use only your right hand if no cutlery is supplied (the left hand is used for ablutions in Muslim society). Accept choice pieces offered by your host, who will consider you an honoured guest. Do not display too much interest in any *objet d'art* – your host will probably give it to you. Do not hesitate to ask for more mint-tea, as you are expected to drink at least two glasses. Patting a child on the head is not considered very good manners. And on no account disturb or draw attention to someone offering prayer.

Hairdressers

Moroccan hairdressers are excellent. A shampoo and blow-dry costs from 40 to 100 dirham upwards in a fashionable salon in Rabat. A haircut and shave at a local barber's costs 30 dirham rising to 100 dirham in a smart hotel. In Oujda the hairdresser I picked turned out to be deaf and dumb, but gave me a good haircut none the less.

Health

You are not obliged to have vaccinations for Morocco, although a tetanus injection is advisable. Cholera and yellow fever are compulsory if you come from an infected zone. Mosquitoes are a nuisance in the southern oases, but there is little risk of malaria. Take a mosquito repellant. Swimming in inland streams is safe if unorthodox, but avoid still water which may harbour bilharzia, or fluke.

Morocco gets a good bill of health. The odd stomach upset is usually due to self-abuse such as drinking too much wine, or eating a large lunch and letting the sun cook it in your stomach. Eating at local cafés is safe provided the food is refrigerated and protected from flies. Never eat ice-cream or water ices, as you will almost certainly become ill with a bacterial infection causing diarrhoea. Ice is always suspect. Even small towns in Morocco have friendly, competent pharmacists selling familiar drugs, and either they or your hotel will know a French-speaking doctor. Tampons are sold in general stores and hotel boutiques, *not* pharmacies – and do not expect to find them in the *bled*. Contraceptives are sold in pharmacies in the major towns.

Avoiding sunburn

It is vital to take adequate precautions against sunburn in Morocco. Do not lie outside for more than thirty minutes on your first day. Cover exposed skin with a good protection lotion, but do not bake all day or you will look like a German mustard pot. Wear a hat and sunglasses and keep your shoes with you, as the sand and tiles round swimming-pools become red-hot. If driving, avoid sunburn through the wind-screen.

Avoiding colds

Many travellers fall foul of the common cold on holiday in a hot country. You are most vulnerable on arrival, before your body adjusts to the climatic change. The situation is aggravated by hotel air-conditioning, which is often too cold. To avoid a chill, never come in from the heat and lie down with nothing over your chest. Wear a jacket over your shoulders in restaurants and never sleep with the air-conditioning on.

Language

The majority of Moroccans speak French, so with some basic French you should be able to travel around. It is also a great help to have some knowledge of Arabic spoken Moroccan-style. Very occasionally, I picked up Berber hitch-hikers with no knowledge of either language.

Maghrebi or Moroccan Arabic is very different from the classic Arabic of Syria or Egypt. It is even more guttural, with hard conso-nants being formed far back in the throat.

kh   is sounded like a Gaelic 'och'.

gh   pulled from the back of the throat, this should purr like 'r' in French.

ai   should sound like 'i' as in 'ice-cream'.

ay   should sound like 'a' in 'able'.

mm   and other double consonants are usually pronounced shorter
      when final.

If you just learn: *wakha*! (OK), *labes* or *Salam aleykum* (hello, and
formal hello), and *flooss* (money) you will get by, smiling . . . In
restaurants most waiters will speak French.

Useful phrases in Arabic

Where?	*Feen*
Yes/No	*Naâm, Eeyeh I La*
OK, I Agree	*Wakha, Mootafik*
Good Morning	*Sabah El Khair*
Good Night	*Laila Saïda*
Good Bye	*Maâ Assalama*
Please	*Ila Jaâla Khatrek*
Thank You	*Shookran I Barak Allah Oufik*
I understand	*Fhamt I Araft*
I don't understand	*Ma Fhamtch I Maâraftch*
Here/There	*Hna/Temma*
On the Right	*Ala Limeen*
On the Left	*Ala Shmal I Ala Liassar*
Straight on	*Ala Tool*
Tall/Little	*Kbir/Sghir*
Cold/Hot	*Bred/Hamy*
Good/Bad	*Mazian/Khaib*
Authorized/Forbidden	*Moomkin/Mamnooa*
How much is it?	*Shhall Yisswa Hada*
Too Expensive	*Ghali Bezzef*
Cheap	*Rkhiss*
Much/Few	*Bezzef/Shweeya*
Yesterday/Tomorrow	*El Barah/Ghadda or Ghaddoua*
This Morning	*Had Sbah*
This Afternoon	*Had Laashia*
Tonight	*Had Laila*
In . . . Minutes	*F' . . . Dakika*
In . . . Hours	*F' . . . Saâ*
Day	*Yoom/Nhar*
I have no time	*Man deesh looakt*
I have time	*Andi looakt*
Money/Change	*Flooss/Serf*
Mr/Sir	*Sidi*
Mrs/Madam	*Lalla*
Miss	*Anissa*
There isn't/Aren't any	*Khasse*
Toilets	*Bait el Ma*
I should like	*Bgheet . . .*

The menu	*El Oujba/Makhlat el Yoom*
Sugar	*Sookar*
An aperitif	*Mashroob*
A soup	*Soba/Sharba*
Hors d'œvres/Starters	*Shlada/Dakhla*
Meat	*El Lham*
Beef	*Begri*
Mutton, Lamb	*Ghanmi*
Bread	*Khobzz*
Salt	*Melh*
Fish	*Hoot/Samak*
Chicken	*Djaj*
Eggs	*El Beyd*
Pepper	*Lebzar*
Mustard	*Mootar*
Potatoes	*Batata*
Vegetables	*El Khoodra*
Cheese	*El Froomage*
Dessert	*Fakia*
Fruit	*Froota*

Lavatories

Western-type lavatories have replaced squat holes in all but unclassified hotels and cafés. This does not mean they work. Two-thirds of WCs (as they are known throughout Morocco) also have only a tap or a tin of water to clean yourself. Local lavatory paper is rough, so take your own and keep it handy. The most stylish toilet in Morocco is the ladies in the Restaurant Yaccout in Marrakesh. At roadside cafés WCs are generally mixed. The best policy is to go to the loo whenever you have the chance, as you never know how far it is to the next one.

Laundry and shoeshine

There are laundry and shoeshine services in every town. Laundries in the *medina* are cheapest, places in the *Nouvelle Ville* are half the price of hotels. The service varies: if quick, it may not be first class. Most laundry receipts are only in Arabic, so check the address before you leave.

Shoeshine varies wildly from town to town, but pity the poor bootblack who has lost a lot of business because of the current trend for gym-shoes. The only boy with white shoe polish in Morocco operates on the Place Assareg in Taroudannt. Local women never have their shoes polished in public, but it is accepted for female tourists to do so. The cost is the famous 'Up to you, madame' – about 3–7 dirham.

Money matters

Morocco's unit of currency, the dirham (dh), is divided into 100 centimes. There are 100, 50 and 10 dirham notes. The tendency of older people to quote in *anciens* francs is confusing (100 francs = 1 dirham). In former Spanish zones they may also quote in pesetas.

Banks Service in Moroccan banks is courteous and efficient. Banking facilities are available on arrival and departure at major airports. The exchange rate is fixed by the Banque al-Maghrib (currently 13 dirham to the pound sterling and 9 dirham to the US dollar). There is no black market, so where you change money makes no difference to the rate. Banks open 8.15 to 11.30 a.m. and 2.15 to 4.30 p.m. In summer and during Ramadan some open 8.30 a.m. to 2 p.m. *Bureaux de change* operate more flexible hours. Travel agencies will usually change money for a small commission. If using travellers' cheques, choose a familiar name; Eurocheques are relatively new. Airport immigration is unlikely to ask to see bank receipts for currency transaction, but it is as well to keep them. The dirham is non-convertible outside Morocco and is not acceptable on Royal Air Maroc.

Plastic money Visa and American Express are the most widely accepted credit cards, but check before running up a bill. Several well-known hotels and restaurants do not accept cards.

Loose change Despite the risks of carrying cash, it brings instant action in Morocco, as in any developing country. Sterling, dollars and French francs are best. Keep loose change handy for paying the *gardien des voitures*, to put in a beggar's palm, or to pay for a small service such as carrying your basket in the *souq*, pedalling in front of the car to point out your hotel, or similar token efforts rendered by one of the thousands of unemployed.

National and religious holidays

The main secular holidays are: 1 January, New Year; 3 March, Coronation Day of King Hassan II; 1 May, Labour Day; 23 May, National Day; 9 July, Youth Day and King Hassan's birthday; 6 November, Anniversary of the Green March; 18 November, Independence Day.

Muslim holy days are based on the lunar calendar and vary with the seasons. Feasts move backwards against the Gregorian calendar by ten or eleven days each year. In 1994 Ramadan was observed from February to March.

Newspapers

Foreign Foreign newspapers arrive in Morocco the same day they are published in Europe. British tabloids are in abundance in Tangier and Agadir. The *Times*, *Daily Telegraph* and *International Herald Tribune* are available in all major cities, as are *Le Monde* and *Le Figaro*. The latter is printed in Casablanca, with an extra page for local news.

Local Although you are unlikely to read the local papers, they give an insight of sorts into local interests. In Morocco this means two pages of soccer, and several pages of *'Petits Annonces'*, none of which have the poetry of the *Times of India*. Occasionally you will find an article on the world outside the Maghreb. If so, it is a safe bet that it will concern events in the Arab World, although *L'Opinion* (the Conservative opposition newspaper) frequently carries an international snippet on the front page. Starved of news in Taliouine, I was riveted by news of a Uruguayan farmer who had grown a cucumber 1.10 metres long weighing 21 kilos. I was usually the only person reading the paper over coffee in the *café-terrace*. Curiosity getting the better of me in Meknes, I asked a man why everyone just sat staring into space. He explained that the local paper was so thin it was not worth buying. 'To get decent news, you must buy *Le Monde* and the price of *Le Monde* is equal to four Moroccan newspapers and a cup of coffee, or no Moroccan newspaper and lunch,' he told me. Of five French dailies, *Al-Bayanne* (Communist Party) is most gutsy. While far from liberal in a Western sense, the press in Morocco is free compared to other Arab countries. Ministers are not above criticism, but no one may criticise the king. *La Quinzaine du Maroc* is a comprehensive tourist guide published monthly – free.

Photography

Morocco is one of the most photogenic countries in the world, but ideally you need a variety of film to cope with ever-changing conditions: shadowy *souqs*, blinding snow scenes and dazzling deserts. Fuji Velvia 50 ASA gives good, deep colour. Panther 100 ASA is a good all-round film. Where scenery is cool – lakes and forests at higher altitudes – an 81 A filter gives a warm effect.

Film for colour prints and slides is sold in all major towns, but buy only where it is kept refrigerated. Elsewhere, even if the exposure date is within limits, the film is unlikely to give good results. Most large towns have automated printing facilities. The service takes two to six hours. Results vary from reasonable to good.

To keep your cameras free of dust on the *pistes* seal them in plastic bags, and make sure you do not leave your camera bag, or film, in the heat.

Remember that most Moroccans, especially rural people, dislike being photographed. Craftsmen in the *souqs* may react violently and never photograph women, as they believe you imprison their spirit. In one remote village I even had trouble with the children: instead of rushing at me demanding money, they fled screaming into the *kasbah*. Some Moroccans will pose in return for a copy of the photograph, which brings endless delight. Many people also expect to be paid. Water-sellers find posing for pictures more lucrative than selling water, and demand 10 dirham. Do not cheat, or you will get drenched!

Radio and television

Morocco has two local channels, which broadcast in Arabic but with a French news service. Some hotels receive satellite TV: Sky (English), Wordnet (American) and TV5 (French). In the north you can also receive Gibraltar, Portugal and Spain. The most popular radio station for news and music is MEDI-1 (Arabic and French). You can also pick up the BBC World Service on 17.705 mhz (8.00–16.156 m), 15.070 mhz (6–9.156 m) and 12.095 mhz (7–9.15 and 17–23.00 m).

Security

So far Morocco has no record of hijacking or terrorism, which is one reason why security is generally lax. On one visit, I left Agadir with no check at all.

Smoking

There are no smoking bans in Morocco, where, typical of a poor developing nation, locals smoke like chimneys. Most popular brands of foreign cigarettes are sold at *tabacs* and hotel bookshops. Foreign cigarettes cost from 16 dirham, local brands from 6 dirham. You can also buy loose cigarettes from people squatting in the *souq* or coming round the *café-terraces*: foreign 1 dirham, local 50 centimes. Beware of

Moroccan matches. You can strike a locally manufactured match anywhere – on the wall, the sole of your foot, the side of your head – and it will ignite, or the head will fly off and set you on fire.

Time

Morocco is in the same time zone as Britain, so GMT applies. For religious occasions, Morocco observes the *hegira*, or lunar calendar, which has 354 days in a year and eleven leap years in a cycle of thirty years. Businesses observe the secular calendar.

Tipping

Tipping is customary. There are baggage trolleys at airports, but if you use a porter, tip him 3 dirham per piece. Do not let him bamboozle you into paying more. Do not tip cab drivers. If the taxi meter is not working, agree on a fare before getting in. 5 dirham is fair for a bellboy in a big hotel, 7–10 per cent of your bill is generous in a restaurant. Small change is appreciated in *café-terraces*. A fixed touristic menu should include all taxes and service.

Tourist information

Overseas offices of the ONMT generally have an excellent range of free brochures dealing with all aspects of a holiday in Morocco.
Canada: 2 Carlton Street, Suite 1803, Toronto, M5B 1K2.
France: 161 Rue Saint Honoré, Place du Théâtre Français, Paris.
United Kingdom: 205 Regent Street, London W1.
United States: 20 East 46th Street, 5th floor, Suite 503, New York, NY 10017.

Apathy is commonly encountered in the Tourist Offices in Morocco. When I asked to see the director of the ONMT in Casablanca, I was told by yawning staff that he was in Mecca. Returning, I was told he was *'fatigué'*, and on a third occasion, that he was *'toujours fatigué'*. Elsewhere excuses were: sick, on holiday, run out of information, no information, or closed for lunch. The French-styled *Syndicats d'Initiatives* are found in many towns.

Travel agents While travel agents are a potential source of information, not unnaturally, they prefer to sell you a tour. Ultimately, the independent traveller in Morocco will find most facts in a guide-book.

UK tour operators

Abercrombie & Kent   tel. (071) 730 9600
Africa Explored   tel. (0633) 222250
Airtours   tel. (0706) 260000
Alecos Tours   tel. (071) 267 2092
American Express   tel. (071) 637 8600
Artscape Painting Holidays   tel. (0702) 435990
Best of Morocco   tel. (0380) 828533
Cadogan Travel   tel. (0703) 332661
CLM   tel. (071) 235 0123
Club Med   tel. (071) 581 1161
Cosmos Tourama   tel. (081) 464 3444
Cox & Kings   tel. (071) 931 9106
Dragoman   tel. (0728) 861133
EMS   tel. (0279) 421606
Encounter Overland   tel. (071) 370 6951
Exodus   tel. (081) 675 5550
Explore Worldwide   tel. (0252) 319448
Field Studies Council Overseas   tel. (0743) 850164
Forte Travel Services   tel. (0293) 824040
Goldenjoy Holidays   tel. (071) 794 9818
Golf International   tel. (081) 452 4263
Guerba Expeditions   tel. (0373) 826689
Hann Overland   tel. (0883) 744705
Hayes & Jarvis   tel. (081) 748 0088
Insight Holidays   tel. (081) 464 3444
Inspirations   tel. (0293) 822244
Intrepid Trips   tel. (0256) 893432
Jasmin Tours   tel. (0628) 531121
Kuoni Travel   tel. (0306) 743000
Michael D. Jones MSc, FGS   tel. (0533) 700837
Moroccan Sun   tel. (071) 437 3968
Morocco Bound   tel. (071) 734 5307
Naturetrek   tel. (0962) 733051
Nomadic Thoughts   tel. (071) 265 8196
OCA   tel. (0494) 729184
Pan World Holidays   tel. (071) 734 2562
Prestige Holidays   tel. (0425) 480400
Ramblers Holidays   tel. (0707) 333276
Saga Holidays   tel. (0303) 857000
Sherpa Expeditions   tel. (081) 577 2717
Solo's   tel. (081) 202 0855
Steppes East   tel. (0285) 810267
Sunway Travel   tel. (010) 3531 288 6828
Titan Hi Tours   tel. (0737) 760033
Trafalgar Travel   tel. (071) 235 7090
Travelscene   tel. (081) 427 4445
Worldwide Journeys & Expeditions   tel. (071) 381 6838

Glossary

Abbassids   Second dynasty of orthodox Islamic caliphs, who ruled from Baghdad (750–1258)

Agadir   Fortified communal hilltop granaries built by Berber tribes.

Aguelmane   Crater

Agdal   Enclosed garden, or park, that contains a water tank

Ain   Spring

Ait Aitta   Berber tribe from Djebel Saghro who dominated southern Morocco from the sixteenth century to 1934

Ali   Cousin and son-in-law of the Prophet through his marriage to Fatima, who became the fourth caliph in AD 656; his reign split Islam into Sunni and Sh'ite camps

Almohad   An Islamic reform movement founded by Ibn Tumert in the High Atlas, Almohad dynasty (1147–1248)

Almoravid   Crusading reform movement founded in the Sahara; Almoravid dynasty (1062–1147)

Alaouite   The present ruling dynasty of Morocco which replaced the Saadian sultans in 1666. Related to the Prophet through Ali

Andalusia   Moorish Spain

Argan   Hard, oil-producing tree indigenous to the Souss

Attarine   Spice market

Bab   Gate

Babouche   Traditional flat soft leather slipper

Baraka   Blessing, or saintly luck

Bstilla   Sweet and savoury filo-pastry pie based on pigeon

Bled   The bush, or semi-cultivated semi-wilderness

Bled es-Siba   Literally 'land of dissidents'; areas of Berber territory outside central control

Caid	Tribal chief recognized by the sultan, judge or administrator
Caliph	The successor of the Prophet; the Almohads were the first Moroccan dynasty to claim this title
Damascene	Decorative inlay work, usually metal or wood
Dar	House, building or palace; city quarters are often named after the most distinctive house there
Djemma	Mosque, Friday
Djebel/Jebel	Mountainous region
Djebella	Tribes that occupy the mountains but specifically the western Rif
Djellabah	Large cotton or wool outer garment with sleeves and a hood
Djedid/Jdid	New
Djinn	Geni or evil spirit
Draa	Arm; the river Draa flows south from Ouarzazate into the Sahara
Ejben	Camel-milk cheese, salty, white and pungent
Erg	Sand dunes
Fantasia	Display of horsemanship featuring small charges, dramatic halts and firing of muskets, performed on national holidays and at *moussems*
Fassi	Resident of Fez
Fatima	Wife of Ali, central cult figure; 'Hand of Fatima' symbols guard against the evil eye
Fibula	Silver costume jewellery worn by southern tribes; desert safety-pin used to secure robes
Filali	A resident of the Tafilalet; family name of the ruling Alaouite dynasty
Funduq	Inn, or hostelry with courtyard overlooked by rooms, now used as a warehouse or market site
Garum	Pungent food flavouring made from salt and fermented fish, made by the ancient Romans in coastal settlements
Gharb	West

Gnaoua	Religious brotherhood from West Africa; music and dance-steps
Habbous	Religious foundation; property bequeathed to the faith whose income finances the construction of mosques, schools and other community projects
Hadith	The collected sayings of the Prophet Muhammad
Haj	Pilgrimage to Mecca prescribed in the Qur'an – one of the 'Seven Pillars of Faith'
Hammada	Flat pebble plain or plateau, often of volcanic origin
Haram	Impure, forbidden by the Qur'an
Harka	Armed expedition of imperial forces through the *Bled es-Siba*
Hegira	Islamic era which began with the flight of the Prophet from Mecca to Medina (AD 622); the Muslim calendar
Ibn Battuta	Travel writer, born in Tangier in 1304, died Fez 1377
Ibn Khalboun	Historian and scholar, born Tunis 1332, whose family fled from Andalusia; died 1406
Idrissid	First Arab dynasty founded by Moulay Idriss I in AD 788
Islam	Submission to God, or Allah
Istiqlal	Independent political party formed in 1943 which played a leading role in resistance to the French Protectorate
Jihad	Holy war, conducted against infidels
Ka'aba	Portion of meteorite venerated in Mecca. Muslims circumambulate it seven times during the culmination of rites of passage during the *haj*
Kasbah	A citadel or fortress
Khoubz	Flat, wholemeal bread
Kif	Hashish
Kissaria	Covered central market in a *souq* selling textiles and jewellery
Koubba	A domed shrine, specifically the shrine or tomb of a *marabout*; central to prayers and an annual pilgrimage

Ksar (pl. *ksour*)	Fortified *pisé* village in southern Morocco
Kufic	Angular style of Arabic script used for stone-carving and plasterwork
Lalla	Lady, title of respect used for a woman of dignity; female saint
Leo Africanus	Born in Granada in 1494, El Hassan Ibn Mohammed Alwazzan was a Christian intellectual who wrote his famous description of North Africa and died, a Muslim, in Tunis in 1552
Lyautey, Louis Hubert	An officer of the French Colonial Army, who became Resident General (1912–26) of the French Protectorate; his foresight did much to shape modern Morocco
Maghreb	Lands of north-west Africa; in Arabic 'where the sun sets'; the fourth prayer at sunset
Marabout	Ascetic or saint who has won the respect of the people and whose tomb is venerated by devotees
Mechouar	Open square, used to be a parade ground
Medrassa	Residential school for the study of the Qur'an and religious law
Medina	Old walled city
Mellah	The Jewish quarter
Merenid	Dynasty which replaced the Almohads in 1248 and built a series of fine *medrassa* and other monuments
Minzah	A garden pavilion, usually with a view
Mihrab	Prayer niche in a mosque indicating the alignment with Mecca
Morisco	A Moorish settler in Andalusia
Mouloud	The Prophet Muhammad's birthday on the twelfth day of the Muslim month of *Rabi at-Tani*
Moussem	Annual pilgrimage to the tomb of a saint; festival
Muezzin	The prayer caller
Oued	River
Pasha	Governor of a city
Pisé	Packed wet clay, baked by the sun, used for building *kasbahs* and houses

Protectorate	Period of French colonial rule of Morocco from 1912 to 1956
Qur'an	Muslim holy testaments containing the orthodox doctrine of Islam
R'bat	A fortified monastery
Ramadan	Muslim month of fasting in the ninth lunar month of the year
Saadian	Moroccan dynasty established in 1541, originating in the Draa Valley and ruling from Taroudannt and Marrakesh
Sanhaja	One of the three Berber groups occupying the Sahara and parts of the Middle and High Atlas; their dialect is known as Tamazight
Saum	Fast required of Muslims during Ramadan
Seguia	Water channels, or canals, above ground
Sherif/shorfa	Descendant of the Prophet
Shi'ite	Unorthodox branch of Islam which recognizes a succession of prophets; founded in seventh-century Iraq
Sidi	Honorary male title
Souq	Market
Souss	Fertile valley extending inland from Agadir to Taroudannt
Sufi	Mystical Islamic brotherhood
Sunni	Orthodox Muslims; the prevalent Moroccan form of Islam
Tafilalet	Region of oases and desert around Rissani
Tajine	Traditional Berber casserole
Thuya	Gum sanderac; hard, worm-resistant wood used for carving
Tizi	A mountain pass
Tolba	Reciters of the Qur'an
Ulema	The council of professors of Islamic law consulted by the sultan
Vizier	Chief minister

BACKGROUND INFORMATION

Wadi	Dry river bed or valley
Zaouia	Sanctuary or college around the tomb or sanctuary of a *marabout*; a rural seminary
Zakat	A religious tax sanctioned by the Qur'an
Zellij	Geometrical mosaic pattern made from chipped glazed tiles

Gazetteer

Introduction

Morocco divides naturally into five main areas: the Rif mountains running behind the Mediterranean coast, the coastal plain of the Atlantic seaboard, the Middle Atlas, the High Atlas, and the Sahara. The gazetteer has been divided up in the same way. Each chapter covers one of the towns best-known to Western tourists and the starting point for most holidays in Morocco – Tangier, Casablanca, Fez, Marrakesh and Agadir – but also takes you to the remote corners in each region.

For convenience the itineraries assume that you have transport, but there are very few places that cannot be reached cheaply by bus, train or *grand-taxi*. Details of public transport are given in the Useful Information section at the end of each main town.

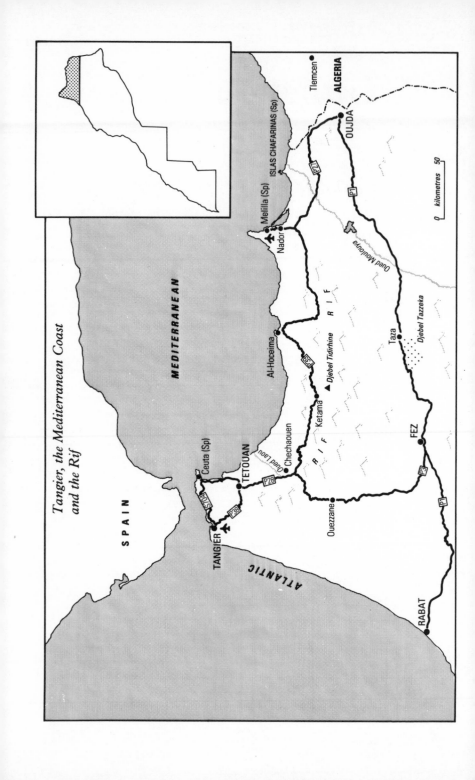

Tangier, the Mediterranean Coast and the Rif

Tangier, the Mediterranean Coast and the Rif

Introduction

The ruggedly beautiful Mediterranean coast of Morocco is within an hour's sail of the Costa del Sol in southern Spain. The tiny fishing villages of Mediterranean Morocco are reminiscent of Spain in the early 1960s. You are likely to be the only traveller, as often the only access to such places, cut off from the hinterland by the Rif mountains rising steeply off the beaches, is by boat. Few motorable roads cross this jagged ridge and, lacking other infrastructure to support a tourist industry, the Rif is one of the poorest, but one of the least spoiled, destinations in Morocco. Rifian Berbers, the inhabitants, remain isolated and xenophobic, speaking the Tarift dialect and following local traditions. Powerful syndicates which control the cultivation and sale of *kif* around Ketama further isolate the Rif from mainstream life.

Tangier is the best-known tourist resort in north-west Morocco. Its reputation as the gay capital of the Maghreb is rooted in the homosexual proclivities of the Djeballa tribesmen of the western Rif. A misjudged pass in the eastern Rif, on the other hand, invites a trouble from n'er-do-goods hustling drugs. Tangier is 57 km from Tetouan, the handsome, former capital of the Spanish Protectorate. Chechaouen and Ouezzane are rustic towns south of Tetouan, in Djeballa heartland. Easy-going Oujda on the Algerian border is a base for tourism in eastern, or Oriental, Morocco. Ceuta, Melilla and some tiny off-shore islets have been under Spanish occupation since the Middle Ages.

If you are crossing the border for lunch, remember they keep time with Madrid.

Tangier

Tangier is the front door to Morocco. Many people fly there, but slowly, on the car-ferry from Spain, is the most sensual way to arrive. From a distance the town looks like a saucepan of bouillon which has boiled over on the stove. Grey-stained walls enclose the *medina*, which long ago overflowed on to the surrounding hills. Nearer, you can see the minaret of the Grand Mosque and the sweeping, palm-lined corniche around the bay. The breeze carries a trace of jasmine and grilled brochettes: the smell of the much-maligned, greatly loved, quite unmistakable Tangier.

History

Ancient mariners spoke of setting a course for 'Tingis' by the stench of *garum*, a pungent food additive obtained from fermented fish, an important industry in Roman times. The sight of a sail in the Straits of Gibraltar must have prompted the same rush then as the ferry does now. Among the *garum*, skins and mats laid out for sale were shiny tangerines – not a native fruit, they were probably introduced from Andalusia. A considerable amount of southern Spain has rubbed off on Morocco, but Tangier's reputation as a cosmopolitan city was established when the port and surrounding countryside were declared an International Zone in 1923.

The Phoenicians were the first of many visitors to the sheltered anchorage at the entrance of the Mediterranean. In 1471 the town was captured by Portugal, but in 1662 it passed to Britain as part of Catherine de Braganza's dowry on her marriage to Charles II. The first action of the British governor was to destroy all traces of Catholic and Muslim worship, enraging Berber tribesmen, who laid siege to the town. Finding Tangier too costly, Britain spurned Lisbon's offer to buy it back, but withdrew in 1682. They pick-axed the mole and the last boat blitzed the *kasbah* with cannon-fire.

Tangier was subsequently rebuilt, but anarchy followed Moulay Ismail's reign and the town stagnated until a new flurry of commercial zeal in the nineteenth century. In the tense years before 1914, Tangier was a focus of frantic European rivalry for influence in the Maghreb. Concerned at German interest in Morocco, the Allies agreed to a French Protectorate in 1912. After the war the Statute of Tangier, signed by the United States, France, Spain, Portugal, Sweden, Holland, Belgium, Britain and Italy, made Tangier an International Zone between 1923 and 1956.

With its own rules, tax-laws and duty-free status, the International Zone was unique. But Tangier also had the most baffling bureaucracy. Each foreign legation had its own office, post office and currency. By 1945 there were eighty-four banks and more than 500 bars and brothels serving its free-wheeling lifestyle.

Into Tangier streamed tax-exiles, entrepreneurs, currency-dealers,

Tangier society spies and intelligence agents, speculators and smugglers, minor aristocrats on remittances, paedophiles and other social misfits. Anyone normal was considered an eccentric by an international community competing for social kudos. According to one old resident, the Americans mixed the best cocktails, the French hosted the smartest dinners, the Italians threw the wildest parties and, when not chasing boys, the British kept the most beautiful gardens. Millionaires, moviestars and princes (sheikhs were still vulgar in those days) dropped in for lunch. Other high-fliers popped in on Friday evening just for a dry martini at Madame Porte's *Salon du Thé*, reckoned to have made the crispest, driest martinis in the world.

Whatever else Tangier had, it had style. Rimsky-Korsakov, Saint Saëns, Delacroix and Matisse were early visitors. Sir Winston Churchill painted there, as well as in Marrakesh. Gertrude Stein and Edith Wharton were among many writers, mainly male, attracted to Tangier like bees to honey – Ian Fleming, Gore Vidal, Truman Capote, Evelyn Waugh, William Burroughs and Tennessee Williams, who occupied a flat in the Rue Pissaro. Joe Orton was battered to death by his boyfriend just thirty-nine days after returning from a holiday there. American Paul Bowles has largely created most people's perception of Tangier in his haunting novels – 'Tangier is to Bowles as Dublin to Joyce, as pre-war Berlin is to Isherwood, as Alexandria is to Durrell,' says writer Ian Finlayson in his rivetting retrospective *Tangier – City of the Dream*. Guy Burgess topped a long list of international agents. Among many filmstars were Douglas Fairbanks, Marlene Dietrich, Errol Flynn, Humphrey Bogart and Lauren Bacall, Margaret Leighton and Lawrence Harvey, and Prince Aly Khan and Rita Hayworth, who stayed at el-Minzah.

Moored off the Rif Hotel in the Bay of Tangier, Aristotle Onassis threw extravagant parties, but the best soirées were held by Barbara Hutton in her white palace beneath the *kasbah*. They are part of local legend. Camels were brought in from the Sahara, bands from New Orleans and the food from Maxim's in Paris. Barbara sat on a gold throne showering her guests with rose-petals.

For spectacle, Tangier had seen nothing like Hutton's 'happenings' until mega-rich American Malcolm Forbes held his seventieth birthday party in the Palais Mendoub in 1989. An estimated $2 million was spent bringing 700 guests to Tangier on a fleet of aircraft that included Concorde. They were welcomed by 274 royal guards of honour and entertained in six giant marquees lined with satin. King Hassan wisely stayed away, but he was represented by his sons Crown Prince Sidi Mohammed and Prince Moulay Rachid. The party-goers included ex-King Constantine of Greece, Mr and Mrs Henry Kissinger, three Rockefellers, Roger Moore, Julio Iglesias, Robert Maxwell, Betsy Bloomingdale and Elizabeth Taylor. They dined on *bstilla* and *mechoui* for which hundreds of pigeons and lambs were slaughtered. Six

Tourists and
faux-guides

hundred belly-dancers provided an exotic finale.

Nowhere so close to Europe – only 2¼ hours by air from London or Paris – feels so alien as Tangier. Expatriates who commute between Tangier and the West consider the sudden culture shock is part of the city's charm. Whether you find it charming, or loathsome, it personifies the beggar constantly tugging at your sleeve.

Arriving by ferry from Gibraltar (2 hours), Algeciras (2¼ hours), Malaga (5 hours) or Sète (38 hours) is an endurance test if you allow yourself to become upset by the *faux-guides*. Change money in the ferry terminal and engage a porter to carry your case, as the gate is a long walk. Outside the port be friendly but authoritative with the taxi-driver. Tell him, in French, that you are glad to be back, and insist he uses the meter. If he says it's broken, offer 15–20 dh just to get the hell out of it.

Hearing the name of your hotel, hustlers will say it is full, closed, burned down, or that they know somewhere cheaper. Pay no attention. Passengers arriving by hydrofoil have fewer problems, as locals know they are mainly day-trippers from Spain, but a favourite trick is to delay them so they miss the boat and have to spend the night. The hotels will pay the *faux-guides* commission, and they will also be tipped for looking after the visitors.

Tourists have a hard time in Tangier. You are bombarded by hard-sell as soon as you leave your hotel. Nowhere is sacred. You are approached in a *café-terrace*, the bank, walking in the *medina*, or lying on the beach; I was swimming when someone paddled up and asked whether I would like to buy some fish. The hustler's view is that he must earn a living in a town with 80 per cent unemployment. Oddly enough, your 'lager lout' is intimidated by this hard-sell in Tangier. After a quick conducted tour, he retreats to bingo, limbo and 'Mr Puniverse' contests in his hotel. On a sunny afternoon, I found the video-room in the Solazur full of British tourists.

An official guide solves the problem. With a companion who knows the way you will not get lost nor will you be overcharged by shop-keepers – or not much anyway. Pay him only at the end of the day; 50 dh is the fixed rate, regardless of whether or not he is looking after his widowed mother and five, eight or ten brothers and sisters.

What to see

Tangier has three areas of interest: the 5 km Bay of Tangier, the *Nouvelle Ville* built during the International Zone era, and the old Arab town tucked under the *kasbah*.

Beachfront

Clip-clopping along the beachfront by *calèche* was a great pleasure in the old days. Today it is overlooked by hotels and tacky shops. Unless you fancy a dip in the glacial Straits of Gibraltar, avoid it. Or, to evade hassles, rent a chair in one of the beach-bars. Saying which is popular will mean it is full of tourists. Avoid the port end at night. Single women should avoid it at all times unless catching a train, bus or the ferry back to Spain.

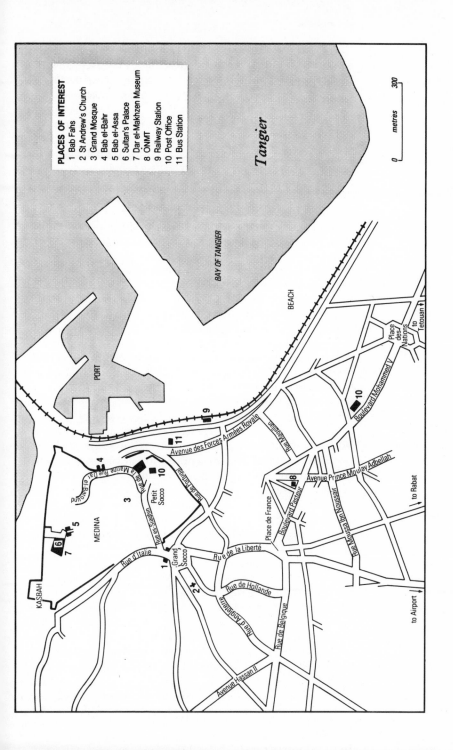

PLACES OF INTEREST

1 Bab Fahs
2 St Andrew's Church
3 Grand Mosque
4 Bab el-Bahr
5 Bab el-Assa
6 Sultan's Palace
7 Dar el-Makhzen Museum
8 ONMT
9 Railway Station
10 Post Office
11 Bus Station

Tangier

BAY OF TANGIER

PORT

BEACH

KASBAH

MEDINA

Petit Socco

Grand Socco

Rue es-Siaghin

Rue d'Italie

Rue de la Liberté

Rue de Hollande

Rue d'Angleterre

Rue de Belgique

Avenue Hassan II

Avenue des Forces Armées Royale

Avenue Prince Moulay Adbellah

Boulevard Pasteur

Place de France

Place des Nations

Boulevard Mohammed V

Rue Moussa Ibn Noussair

to Tetouan

to Rabat

to Airport

0 metres 300

Nouvelle Ville

The *Nouvelle Ville* is where tourists retreat when they have 'done the *medina*', and you will see them sitting outside the Metropole. The **Boulevard Pasteur** is the central shopping area. Near the Place de France a belvedere is where locals get a shoeshine while watching for the car-ferry. Opposite the Café de France is the French consulate. The Spanish consulate, near the hospital, is the showpiece of local legations.

The *Nouvelle Ville* effectively ends on the **Grand Socco** (the Spanish version of *souq*), where camels used to bring goods as late as the 1930s. Donkeys still do for the Thursday and Sunday *souqs*. You can watch water-sellers, beggars and life in general from the Café Orient (in front of the Spanish-style police station). Everyone coming in, or out, of the *medina* must cross the Grand Socco. Bab Fahs, the main gate into the *medina*, is named after a tribe from the Rif who settled there after the British left.

At the bottom of the Rue de l'Angleterre between the *Nouvelle Ville* and the Grand Socco is **St Andrew's Church**. The land was donated by Sultan Moulay Hassan in 1889 and it was consecrated in 1905 as part of the diocese of Gibraltar. Note the cedar ceiling carved by craftsmen from Fez, and the Gloria and the Lord's Prayer carved in Arabic above the chancel. The graveyard contains headstones of well-known Tangier figures such as the *Times* correspondent Walter Harris (1886–1933) and Sir Harry Maclean, the ebullient Scots instructor to the imperial guard of Sultan Moulay Hassan, who created him *caid*. But who was Henrietta Moodie Vickers, I wondered: artist, born Toronto, Canada, 1870; died Tangier, 20 September 1938.

In the Palais Mendoub on a corner of Marshan Square is the **Forbes Museum of Military Miniatures**, the creation of Malcolm Forbes. Among thousands of fascinating figures, mainly hand-made, are 600 models recreating the Battle of the Three Kings (see p. 26). Open daily 10 a.m. to 5 p.m., admission free.

Medina

A tour of the *medina* and *kasbah* takes three to four hours. The labyrinthine alleys are lined with tall, thick-walled houses; in the Rue Zeitouna they touch overhead. The main entry to the *medina* is the Rue es-Siaghin, leading off the Grand Socco. It is named after Jewish silversmiths long since gone from Tangier. The Spanish Cathedral on your right is an old Franciscan mission whose monks were slaughtered by Muslim fanatics. On learning of their fate, St Francis is said to have cried out: *'O Tingis! Tingis! O dementia Tingis, illusa civitas!'* – 'Oh Tangier! Tangier! Oh, demented Tangier, foolish citizens!' (Barnaby Rogerson, *Morocco*, Cadogan Guides, 1989).

The **Petit Socco**, a large square lined by *café-terraces* and old hotels, was the centre of male prostitution when Tangier was an International Zone. Following the Rue de la Marine to the Bab el-Bahr (Sea Gate) by the harbour takes you past the **Grand Mosque**, which stands on the site of the original mosque and a Portuguese cathedral, both in turn demolished. The white walls convey no impression of the grandeur that lies within; like all mosques in Morocco, it forbids entry to non-Muslims.

Straight up the Rue des Chrétiens and left into the Rue Ben Raisuli brings you near Bab el-Assa (Gate of Vigilance) leading to the *mechouar*, or parade ground, in the *kasbah*. You will pass a **Rifian market** en route. Note the herbalist seated slightly apart from the other women, dressed in traditional striped shawls and Mexican-style hats with pompoms dangling from the brim. She acts as a lookout for approaching tourists; at the sight of a camera, they all freeze. Somewhere on the walk up to the *kasbah* you pass a junction named after Ibn Khaldoun, the respected historian, and the famous traveller Ibn Battuta, who was born in Tangier in ¹304.

In the *kasbah* Roman graves indicate the existence of an early fort on the headland, with twin views of the Mediterranean and the Atlan-tic. The present structure dates from the seventeenth century. Its north ramparts have been breached to allow coaches onto the *mechouar*, where children, *faux-guides* and snake-charmers are a menace. At one end is the seventeenth-century palace built by Moulay Ismail, the Alaouite sultan who built so many of Morocco's notable buildings.

Where to stay

The **Dar el-Makhzen Museum** at the end of the *mechouar* displays various arts and crafts – wrought iron, embroidery, carpets and ceramics illustrating the various styles and colours of Moroccan potters. There is a room with works by Delacroix, who painted in Tangier in the 1830s. Open daily 9.30 a.m. to 12 noon and 3 to 6 p.m.

Tangier has a good range of accommodation, but you must book during May–August. Visitors drop to 30–40 per cent during winter, so you can – and should – bargain for your room. The star rating of some of the up-market hotels is dubious; once good, the majority now cater exclusively for package tours. The Intercontinental has no connection with the international hotel chain. Stay in town, as Tangier's town life is its main attraction, although hotels in the *medina* are strictly for backpackers. Some of the beach hotels, such as the Malabata, are a long walk from town. The following hotels are within fifteen minutes' walk of the *Nouvelle Ville*, the *medina* or the Mediterranean.

El Minzah (★★★★A), 85 Rue de la Liberté; tel. 938787. An elegant refuge built on land bought by Lord Bute in 1928. Comfortable and elegant rather than de-luxe. Rooms are rather small. The front rooms have a view (the meaning of *el minzah* in Arabic). Dress for dinner. Efficiently managed by Utell International, which also manages the venerable Rock Hotel in Gibraltar. Tangier's best hotel for discerning travellers, although some group tours stay here.

Tanjah Flandria (★★★★A), 6 Boulevard Mohammed V; tel. 93300. A comfortable, if not spectacular, hotel in a convenient position in the *Nouvelle Ville*. Good nightclub. Roof-top pool. Parking.

Hotel Rembrandt (****A), Boulevard Mohammed V; tel. 937870. Centre of the *Nouvelle Ville*. Rather small rooms, front ones have a sea view. Garage.

Hotel Continental (*A), 36 Rue Dar el-Baroud; tel. 931034. Built in 1888, this was Tangier's grand hotel, but it has failed to keep up appearances, and the location, above the port, is seedy. Front rooms have sea view. Old *hammam*. No lift.

Hotel el-Munira (*A), Rue Magellan. Spotless, British-owned hotel in a steep street between the *Nouvelle Ville* and the beach. Tables are provided for aspiring writers. William Burroughs penned *The Naked Lunch* in Room 9.

Pension Hollande, 139 Rue de Hollande; tel. 937838. Basic rooms.

Pension Agadir, 16 rue de Palmier. In a respectable part of the *medina* near the Place Aissoua. Moroccan-clean, basic rooms. Roof level advised.

A full hotel-list is available from the ONMT, 29 Boulevard Pasteur.

Where to eat

Tangier lacks good restaurants. It is as well to avoid anywhere patronised by local British expatriates, who are generally more concerned with economising than the standard of cooking. Restaurants to try are: **Nautilus Ville** and **Nautilus Plage**; **San Remo** serving Italian fare; **Le Marquis** for more up-market dining and **Guitta's** – a lingering ambience of old Tangier days with a lovely garden and good Martini cocktails. **Restaurant Valencia** near the Hotel Rif is reputed for seafood. Also **Romero's** – Spanish atmosphere. **Chez Miami** on the town beach serves summer barbecues.

Largely because package tourists demand no better, Tangier's Moroccan-style restaurants are pretty awful. Those in the *medina*, such as the **Palace Mamounia**, **Dar Tajine** (tel. 34514) and **Hammadi's** (tel. 34514), follow the *brochette* and couscous theme. Hammadi's, with red and white nylon flock wallpaper and sad-eyed musicians, is particularly vile. Fresh, simple and cheap meals are served at **Al Andaluz**, off the Petit Socco. A family-run business, it has six tables, one usually occupied by a son making brochettes: fish and grills from 30 dh. In the *Nouvelle Ville*, **Raihini's** is your average tourist-style Moroccan restaurant. In the **el Khorsan** Moorish restaurant in the El Minzah Hotel, I ate couscous listening to 'Home on the Range'. Moroccan cabaret (Tuesday–Friday). With your own transport, a trip out to **Chez Abdou** in what is known as the Diplomatic Forest, 17 km from Tangier, is worthwhile for good seafood.

Café-terraces

The *café-terrace* might have been invented in Tangier, where tables and chairs do not face each other as in Rome or Paris, but are arranged looking out at the passers-by. The best-known *café-terraces* stretch along the **Boulevard Pasteur**: the Café de Paris opposite the Semiramis; the Manila and the Metropole catching the morning sun; the Esquima and the Zagora in partial shade; Claridge's, with the longest line of tables in Africa; La Colombe and the Café Atlas. All have their regulars. Changing your *café-terrace* causes as much sensation in local circles as does a best-selling author swapping publishing houses.

The first *café-terrace* in Tangier was the **Café de Paris**, built in 1920, managed by a strict *patronne* called Madame Léontine. A popular intelligence rendezvous during the Second World War, the Café de Paris is a local landmark. It serves excellent coffee, but you are unlikely to get more than a croissant. The lively *Rogue's Guide to Tangier* mentions how Alec Waugh, a local celebrity, could be seen every morning walking towards the Café de Paris with an egg-cup in his hand. Waugh liked boiled eggs for breakfast; true to the perversity of Muslim character, the management refused to buy him an egg-cup.

Some of Morocco's most extraordinary contrasts are seen in the *café-terraces*. One afternoon in the **Metropole** I sat reading the paper between a man wearing a huge, hooded *djellabah* and a youth in a turquoise nylon tracksuit, a Walkman plugged into his ears. From the crowd countermarching along the Boulevard Pasteur, a boy dancer appeared, clicking metal castanets and swinging his red tasselled fez. Sweeping it off, he toured the tables for money. No one gave him anything, and, replacing it with a flourish, he danced on towards the Manila.

Tea places

George Greaves, the cynical Australian journalist with the foulest mouth in Tangier, used to hold court between 6 and 7 p.m. in Madame Porte's Salon du Thé. A beat-character given to wearing striped pyjamas under his clothes, he knew Tangier. 'The whole bloody place was full of spies. But not a sparrow falls and the Lord and George Greaves knows,' he told me. Like many old expatriates, George wanted to go home but never made it. He died in 1983. Sadly Madame Porte's Salon du Thé has now closed. Today's equivalent is the **Vienne Tea-House**, designed in French Empire style with fish tanks set in the bar. The most colourful local place for mint-tea is the **Petit Socco**, where *café-terraces* are ranged like a theatre in the round. Seated in the front row of the Café Tingis one evening, I was approached by vendors wanting to clean my shoes, read my palm and sell me everything from *kif* to day-excursions to Gibraltar. There was also a man selling a porcupine, a Rifian delicacy.

What to do
Entertainment

Tangier has no sophisticated entertainment. The best place for an aperitif is **Caid's Bar** in the El Minzah Hotel, a comfortable spot with quiet piano music. The painting over the bar by John Lavery depicts *caid* Sir Harry Maclean. In side-streets off the Boulevard Pasteur are several bars. **Rubi's, Scott's** and the **Regine Club** are popular with local tour guides. The colourful **Morocco Palace** is a fun place to go with friends. Most beach bars and discos charge London prices.

There is an evening *fantasia* at the Ahlen Village hotel complex, with a traditional Moroccan tent-dinner, belly-dancing and spectacle.

Shopping | Tangier sells attractive artefacts as well as souvenirs. Scores of tiny markets are hidden here and there – walking around and sussing them out is half of the fun of shopping.

The *medina* is stuffed with shops selling the bric-à-brac beloved of tourists: copper trays, hubble-bubble pipes, leather pouffes and poorly made kaftans. The Volubilis boutique sells more stylish Moroccan garments. You will pay dearly for carpets in Tangier, as in other cities for the tout needs his cut – if you do not buy anything, you may find it hard to leave the shop: more mint-tea is served, more rugs are unrolled, and, as a final gesture, an exercise book is produced with the signatures of satisfied clients. The Parfumerie Medani at 14 Rue Sebou, is popular. Mr Mohammed Medani, the present nose, has perfected over fifty copies of famous perfumes based on oils rather than alcohol. They cost a fraction of the price of original scents, but discerning souls will stick to the original. Closed 1 to 4 p.m.

In the *Nouvelle Ville* there are several expensive antique-cum-junk shops on the Rue de la Liberté, opposite the El Minzah Hotel. Below the steps, the Bazaar Tindouf sells silver jewellery, especially *fibulas*. Gold 'Hands of Fatima' are sold by the jeweller next to the El Minzah Hotel. The Librairie des Colonnes, at 54 Boulevard Pasteur, is a good bookshop. Adolfo de Velasco has one of Morocco's best antique shops at 26 Boulevard Mohammed V. Junk is sold in the flea market off the Grand Socco: everything from crystal chandeliers stripped from Spanish homes to coins. Near here is a basketware market, and a 'ladies market' near the mosque. Beneath a white wall opposite, Rif women sell flowers and country produce. They look so attractive, but do not photograph them: they will throw their eggs at you.

The old markets from the Grand Socco line the Rue de Portugal. The entrance to the **Funduq Market** – an old caravanserai – is on the right, through the arch. Weavers now work in upstairs rooms, where you can buy blankets and *djellabahs* straight off the looms. Stands downstairs sell pottery and olive-wood cooking utensils. On the other side of the road a small market expatriates call 'Hong Kong alley' will make even the proprietor of a modest shop feel like a millionaire. Arranged on bags are nuts, bolts and spent batteries, empty deodorant sprays and pill-jars, cracked sunglasses, broken sandals, buckles, electric plugs, disposable syringes. Nothing discarded by tourists is wasted – a poignant reminder of local poverty.

Sports | **Golf** Royal Country Club (4 km, 18 holes).

Tennis Emsallah Tennis Club, Rue de Belgique. Municipal Tennis Club, Rue Raymond Lulie. M'Sallah Garden Tennis Club, Avenue Hassan II.

Riding Club de L'Etrier, road to Boubana.

Yachting Tangier Yacht Club, inside the port.

Swimming Tangier's main beach has good swimming. It is surveyed by tourist police, but take nothing of value. Outlying beaches are more attractive but you need transport. All major hotels have swimming-pools.

Fishing Stay in one of the beach hotels if you like fishing. The port and breakwater near the Malabata Hotel are good spots. From a boat you can fish in the Straits but wind is a problem, as are police who watch for smuggling. They may inspect your fishing bag. Bait is sold at the bottom of the steps leading to the Rue de Portugal.

Flying Royal Aero-Club Tangier, airport.

Useful information

Royal Air Maroc, Place de France; tel. 935505.
British Consulate, Rue d'Angleterre; tel. 935895.
American Consulate, Rue el Achouak; tel. 935904.
American Express, Voyages Schwarz, 54 Boulevard Pasteur; tel. 937546.
Banks, Boulevard Pasteur and Mohammed V.
PTT, Midway down Boulevard Mohammed V.
Pharmacies, Boulevard Pasteur and Mohammed V.
Newspapers, from stalls on the Boulevard Mohammed V, *tabac* near the Café de France, Rue de la Liberté.
Bookshop, Librairie des Colonnes, 54 Boulevard Pasteur.
ONMT, 29 Boulevard Pasteur. Open Mon–Sat, 8 a.m. to 2 p.m.

Moving on

International and domestic flights leave from Tangier's **airport**, 18 km from town (fifteen minutes by *grand-taxi*). The **railway station** is outside the ferry terminal. You can buy tickets in advance from Wagons-Lits, 85 Rue de la Liberté. The **CTM bus terminal** is opposite the entrance to the ferry terminal. Other companies are on the Avenue des FAR. **Taxi ranks** are also near the port. The *petit-taxi* fare within Tangier centre is 5 dh.

If you have a car, you will find parking is more difficult than in most towns. Choose a hotel with private parking and leave nothing of value in view.

Excursions from Tangier

Cape Spartel

Route 5701 to Cape Spartel (14 km) winds over the *Vieux Montagne*, where many wealthy expatriates own villas screened by high walls. The large complex on the right belongs to King Fahd of Saudi Arabia, who also has a palace in Casablanca, and King Hassan owns 'Ravenscraig', the former residence of the British consul. The lighthouse marks the far north-west tip of Africa.

The **Café-Bar Sol** on the large bay after Cape Spartel is a nice place for a seafood lunch, although it is crowded at weekends. Licensed.

Hercules' Caves

Beyond Cape Spartel are the Grottes d'Hercules, huge, eroded caves in the cliffs where Hercules is said to have rested after slipping a disc while performing the Twelve Labours. They hold little of interest and hawkers are a nuisance.

Atlantic beaches

To the south are long surfing beaches. The Arabian Sands complex at Robinson's Plage is owned by Princess Lalla Fatima Zhora, a cousin of the king. Leased out to German tour operators, it has been allowed to become run down. The site is attractive and rooms have an Atlantic view. Tour-groups. Camel rides. Hawkers. Further south, the Oued Tahardatz has river and beach fishing. Scruffy camping-ground.

Cape Malabata

A quiet, picturesque road winds round the hills from Tangier to Ceuta. At the eastern end of Tangier Bay is the Club Méditerranée, on the site of 'Villa Harris', where Walter Harris used to live. Beyond the marina, you begin climbing to Cape Malabata: a rough track gives a splendid view back to Tangier. The road then curls around the coast where fields of *kif* wave in the Atlantic breezes. Rifian women are usually found sitting by the roadside. Baskets are good buys.

Ksar es-Seghir

Ksar es-Seghir (37 km) is a ruined Portuguese settlement, overlooking the river. Its sheltered, less-developed site is a foil to overcrowded Tangier. There are cafés but no hotels. Beyond the town, the road to Dallia is badly pot-holed. **Dallia Beach** is a gorgeous north-west-facing beach 1 km off the road. It is protected from the persistent wind and is highly recommended for swimming and a picnic. Bikinis may frighten the fishermen.

Djebel Moussa

Beyond Cape Cires lighthouse, the road climbs up to Djebel Moussa (60 km), visible on a clear day from Tangier. There are excellent views of Gibraltar and Ceuta from the headland.

Mediterranean resorts

The Route P28 from Fnideq cuts through the western Rif, or Rif Occidentale, to Ouezzane and thence to Fez. Built parallel to the coast, the initial stretch follows what will be the new 'Riviera of the Maghreb', if investors are right. The following beaches are under two hours' drive from Tangier.

Restinga-Smir has a collection of tourist hotels and a Club Méditerranée, built beside the estuary of the Oued Smir. I made a special effort to visit the Marina Smir complex, but it had run out of brochures and the assurance that information would be sent to London was one of many broken promises made to me in Morocco.

Kabila, about 2 km east, is a more attractive proposition, with a marina and villa complex built along a good beach. As well as swimming and sailing there are tennis courts and an eighteen-hole golf course is under construction. A lagoon offers good bird-watching.

Accommodation is at the excellent **Kabila Hotel** (****A); tel. 975013. On the main road, twenty minutes' drive from Tetouan. Spanish management. Ninety-two rooms serviced by forty maids; gardens tended by twenty gardeners. Rooms are small but comfortable.

M'Diq is a pleasant fishing village changing into a tourist resort, ten minutes from Kabila. A Spanish church and a mosque face each other across the P28. Local restaurants are off the road; in the small fishing harbour at the foot of the hill the bistro-style **Restaurant du Port** serves reasonable meals. Licensed.

There are guest-houses on the road to Cabo Negro and the **Golden**

Beach Hotel (****B). Clean, package-tour hotel, with plastic-flower garden in the foyer. Pool. Bar-restaurant. Parking.

On the other side of the hill from M'Diq is **Cabo Negro**, a long beach spoiled by an ugly hotel-villa complex, exposed to all weathers. The **Restaurant La Ferme** is shrewdly sited above the Club Mediterranée. Rustic ambience, French-Moroccan menu. Licensed. Avoid mid-summer. Riding facilities, and smell of horses.

An old corsair port, now a weekend resort for the residents of Tetouan, **Martil**'s holiday houses need painting and the beach is very windy – avoid during summer. In the old Spanish town a curious church and the former *Seguridad Nacional* building are worth seeing. 10 minutes' drive from Tetouan.

Tetouan

Tetouan, in Berber 'open your eyes', is greatly underestimated by travellers. Built against a bluff in the Rif, it contains some fine examples of Hispano-Mauresque architecture. Tetouanis claim to be the authentic heirs of Morocco's Andalusian heritage and the *medina* is filled with working craftsmen.

History
In 1399 Tetouan was sacked by Henry III of Castille and lay neglected until refugees from Granada settled there in the late fifteenth century. Some became corsairs based in Martil; others rebuilt the *medina*, adding arches, patios and other touches of their beloved Andalusia. Harried by Rifian tribes in 1859, it was defended and temporarily occupied by Spain (1860–62) from Ceuta. The Spanish returned in 1913 to establish the administrative headquarters of the Spanish zone. Campaigns against the Rif continued until the 1920s.

What to see
A guide is unnecessary in Tetouan, but one will insist on coming with you. Official guides are available at the ONMT. The Boulevard Mohammed V leads off the elegant Place Moulay el-Mehdi, flanked by the PTT, a Spanish cathedral and various banks. At the other end of the boulevard is the Place Hassan II, dominated by the old Khalifa's Palace (closed) and the imposing Ministry of Justice. The social centre of Tetouan, its *café-terraces* are filled with students, shoeshine men and little boys selling contraband cigarettes. The *Nouvelle Ville* has typical white houses, with green or blue shutters. Women yell at each other from wrought-iron balconies just as they do in Spain.

Medina
The Bab er-Rouah (Gate of the Wind) leads into the old town, filled with mosques, monuments and craftsmen. It is one of the best *medinas* in Morocco, without the usual crowds of hasslers. The Rue Terrafin cuts through the *souqs* to the museum exit at Bab Okla. Bab Sebta leads out to the Andalusian cemetery.

Souq el-Hots is a shaded pottery market beneath the walls of a fifteenth-century *alcazaba*, or castle. **Guersa el-Kebir** is a photogenic Rifian textile market, but photographers beware. Ask your guide to take you to the Atlas Bazaar selling memorabilia from the Spanish Protectorate. The **Place de l'Oussa** is an attractive square with an ornamental fountain and nineteenth-century almshouse. In **Souq el-Fokj**, a central commercial area selling bread, beauty products and *babouches*, various craftsmen work along the Rue el-Jazzarin leading to Bab Ceuta.

The area around Bab Okla, the north-eastern gate below the Grand Mosque, is traditionally well-off, noted for elegant houses. In the **School of Traditional Arts**, opposite Bab Okla, artists learn traditional techniques of Moorish arts – pottery, tile-making, carpentry. Open 9 a.m. to 12 noon and 2.30 to 5.30 p.m., closed Sundays. The **National Museum of Tetouan**, inside Bab Okla, houses superb costumes, embroidery, carpets, Rifian armoury and saddles. Note the exquisite *secrétaires* with 'Hand of Fatima' hinges. In the Andalusian garden my guide suddenly picked and handed me a glorious red rose, revealing the romantic nature of the unsmiling Moroccan. Open 8.30 a.m. to 12 noon and 2.30 to 5.30 p.m., closed Tuesdays and Sundays; admission 2 dh.

The **Archaeological Museum**, a short walk from the Place Hassan II, is a corner of calm, with classic mosaics from Lixus in the garden and relics of ancient 'Tamuda' (Tetouan) – oil-lamps, amphorae, funeral vases. Note the large tribal and antiquities map. The library contains 60,000 books on Islam and the Maghreb, in Spanish. Open 9 a.m. to 12 noon and 2 to 6 p.m., closed Tuesdays; admission 3 dh.

Where to stay

There are many *pensions* in Tetouan, but few are comfortable. Although attractive outside, the *pensions* surrounding the Place Hassan II are hot, rough and noisy. The town's only four-star hotel, the Safir, is perpetually booked with package tours.

Hotel Dersa (★★A), Rue de Prince Sidi Mohammed; tel. 94215. This is the old, imperial hotel in Tetouan. Fading glamour. Seventy-four large rooms. Convenient location in the *Nouvelle Ville*.

Hotel Oumaima (★★A), Avenue du 10 Mai; tel. 963473. Clean, central and dull.

Paris Hotel (★★A), 31 Rue Chakib Arsalane; tel. 966750. Central.

Hotel Regina (★A), 8 Rue Sidi Mendri; tel. 962113. Fifty-nine rooms all with bathroom. Old and clean but probably noisy. Convenient location in the *Nouvelle Ville*.

Where to eat

You have a reasonably good choice of local restaurants serving mainly Spanish-Moroccan cuisine. The **Zerhoun** is popular, as is the cheap and friendly **Restaurant Moderne** in the *Nouvelle Ville*. Walking through the *medina* you will pass the **Restaurant Marrakech de Tetouan**, which offers Moroccan food and an *orchestre folklorique* in a converted Hispano-Moorish house. Groups eat here at lunchtime. Cheap local eating places are found on the Rue Luneta. Tetouan is justly famous for its sweetmeats.

Moving on

Tangier Airport is about 1¾ hour's drive. Regular buses depart for Tangier, Rabat and Fez from a terminus near the covered Central Market. Coastal buses leave from the splendid old railway station, no longer in use. An ONCF coach service to Rabat runs twice daily. Excursions from Tetouan

Excursions from Tetouan

Oued Laou (44 km) is a poor fishing village with two basic hotels. The road from Tetouan around the headlands (Route S608) is pleasant. If you have a car, you can drive on to quiet, black-sand beaches beyond Oued Laou, but do not go further than el-Jebha – from here the *piste* crosses a lawless part of the Rif which is not recommended. From Oued Laou you can cut across to Chechaouen, following the course of the river, through the Gorges de Laou.

The western Rif

Chechaouen

According to legend the road from Tetouan to Chechaouen (Route P28, 60 km) was traced by a donkey wending its way through the Rif. The approach is dramatic: rounding a final bend, you confront Chechaouen with its back against twin peaks of the Rif. *'Choof ichaouen'*, its name in Berber, means 'look at the mountain horns'.

It is a picture-postcard town of extraordinary light and colour. Its houses are a rustic fusion of Hispano-Moorish architecture, painted white or blue, with ochre tiled roofs that contrast with the flat-roofed houses in the rest of Morocco. Many have small balconies and tiny patios planted with oranges, roses and a mulberry tree. The *moriscos* introduced silk-worm rearing, which at one time occupied every family.

History

Chechaouen was founded in 1471 by Moulay Ali Ibn Rachid, and in the late fifteenth century was settled by Muslim refugees from Granada. Fortified, with its gates locked against dissident Djeballa tribesmen, over the centuries Chechaouen grew increasingly isolated and xenophobic. When the Spanish arrived in 1920, it had only been entered by three Christians, one of whom was the intrepid Walter Harris. They found people who still spoke a form of medieval Castilian and were pining for Andalusia. Until quite recently, some of the elderly citizens offered prayers to Allah to liberate Spain from the infidels. Abd el-Karim, leader of the Rifian resistance movement in the 1920s, conquered the town in 1924, forcing the Spanish to withdraw to Tetouan. Spanish rule returned from 1926 to 1956.

What to see

The Place Mohammed V, a former Andalusian garden, is the heart of the Spanish-built New Town. Above it is the shady Place el-Makhzen, in front of the Parador. A guide is unnecessary to explore the *medina*, but local Berber boys are pleasant. Boy markets for Djeballa tribesmen were held in the *medina* as late as 1937. You will pass the **kasbah** on the way to the *medina*. Restored by Sultan Moulay Ismail, the Spanish imprisoned the resistance leader Abd el-Karim in its dungeons in 1926.

The easiest route through the medina is from Bab Ain above the bus station to Uta el-Hamman, the open square lined with multi-storey *café-terraces*. At night their upper rooms are frequented by *kif* smokers.

Shopping Long-stemmed clay pipes for *kif* smoking are sold in the shops around the Place Uta el-Hamman. Chechaouen is also one of the best crafts centres in Morocco for metalwork, wood-carving, embroidery, pottery, carpets and leather-work. A typical item is the large, red, many-pocketed *zaaboula*, or 'Berber briefcase'. Some 3,000 people, many of them women working at home, are employed in these cottage industries.

Where to stay Chechaouen lacks middle-range hotels. Cheap, basic and clean pensions are found in the *medina*; many are not adequately heated in winter.

Hotel Asmaa (***A); tel. 986265. A modern building overlooking Chechaouen, twenty minutes' steep walk. Built for package-tours, it has comfortable rooms with a stunning view. Quiet location. Recommended.

Hotel Parador (****B); tel. 986324. Central location. Used by groups. Recommended.

Hotel Magou (**B), 23 Moulay Idriss; tel. 986257. Below the *medina*. Thirty-two clean, pleasant, but possibly noisy rooms.

Hotel Rif (*B), 29 Rue Tarik Ibn Zaid; tel. 986207. Edge of the *medina*. Clean, pleasant rooms with good beds. Top rooms have a valley view.

Hotel Salam (*B), 39 Tarik Ibn Zaid; tel. 986239. Near the town centre. Back rooms have a view.

Pension Ibn Battuta Traditional house in the *medina*. Clean with shared facilities. You will need bedclothes. Cheap.

Where to eat Chechaouen is renowned for Berber cooking. *Herza*, a warming garlic and egg-yolk soup, and *khliaa*, dried meat conserved in butter, are specialities. You will see tubs of *khliaa* in the *souq*. Unfortunately the choice of restaurants is limited. The **Restaurant Tissemal** serves Spanish/Moroccan dishes and has a friendly fireside ambience. The **Granada** is a tiny *medina* restaurant serving good *brochettes*. **Al Barraka** in the *medina* serves good Berber-style food in the evening. The chef is Fassi. Avoid midday tour-groups. Licensed.

Trekking There are several attractive mountain walks from Chechaouen. It is about a four or five hour hike to ascend the left-hand peak. Take provisions and be prepared to be questioned by vigilant officers watching for drug smugglers.

Moving on Regular **buses** to Tetouan, Meknes and Fez. Book seats in advance.

Daily buses to Ceuta and Oued Laou. **Grand-taxi** rank near the market place.

Ouezzane

The twisting P28 between Chechaouen and Ouezzane (60 km) is little frequented by travellers, but you can take this route through the western heartland of the Rif and on to Fez (145 km).

Ouezzane was built by local *sherifs*, or sheikhs, in the eighteenth century and, unlike most Moroccan towns, was not troubled by dynastic quarrels. One of the rulers married an English girl whom he met riding; she insisted on a Christian marriage and local aristocrats are descended from their union.

What to see

The Place de l'Independence at the foot of the *medina*, is busiest during a Thursday *souq*. An authentic old **medina** winds uphill, a rustic maze of cobbled streets and houses with arched buttresses and tiled eaves. Weavers, tailors, cobblers and metalworkers work in the bazaar – there is no pressure to buy. An Artisanal Centre is open 8 a.m. to 7 p.m. The Ouezzani *sherifs* were also spiritual leaders and their eighteenth-century **zaouia** with its octagonal minaret is the most striking building in Ouezzane. The town is known for figs, olives and *kif*.

From Ouezzane to the P26 is a tortuous, but entirely enchanting, secondary route to Fez. I passed a trio of wandering minstrels, a man riding a mule with an open umbrella, reminiscent of northern Ethiopia – and fields and fields of *kif* in lonely mountain areas.

Kif **country**

The P39 winds across the Rif from Chechaouen to Nador. It is a good road with some spectacular views, but it passes through the main *kif*-growing area, where bandits pose considerable risk.

Cannabis sativa, the Indian hemp plant, has grown in Morocco as long as anyone can recall. Originally it was used in the manufacture of string. Its use as a drug stems from the euphoric state it induces when smoked or eaten. The leaves are dried and smoked by local farmers after a hard day's work, and *kif* cakes, made by compacting the cannabis resin with *majune*, or honey, are common; eating a small piece is usually sufficient to put you on cloud nine.

Until the 1960s, *kif*-smoking was an innocent activity; a British woman in Tangier told me of driving up to Ketama and buying *kif* for fun. But now the drug barons have moved in, kif has become big business, and in your travels through the Rif you will notice that the feathery-leafed plant is the principal crop. By cultivating a hectare or two, a local farmer can net as much as £2–3,000 a year. Conscious of the problems posed by the European demand for *kif*, Rabat is trying to find an alternative crop, but the western Rif is very barren and life would be very hard for the farmers if they substituted something with a lower return.

If you are driving from Chechaouen to al-Hoceima, make an early start: at night your fortunes cannot be guaranteed and several foreigners languish in jail through folly. Even the adventurous *Rough Guide to*

Morocco cautions against visiting Ketama. Leave Chechaouen with enough petrol so you do not have to stop until Ketama. Climbing the scrubby hills of Bab Taza (1,675 m), you will see the first aggressive *kif*-hustlers. Sighting a car, they strain to see the driver – alone, with hire-car plates from Casablanca, I felt especially vulnerable as headlights flashed urgently from black Mercedes parked in woodland clearings. If you slow down, a man will spring into action: a quick rolling mime with his fingers and a piercing whistle signifies he has *kif* to sell. Bab Berred is a sinister town; drive straight through. Between here and Ketama everyone aged nine to ninety offers *kif* as you pass.

In the pine-woods outside Ketama I passed hustlers on every bend. Down the home stretch, as it were, two old Renaults, each with five men in hooded *djellabahs*, escorted me to the Hotel Tidighine where I parked. 'Business, Madame?' they enquired, as we all got out.

Ketama

Ketama is a damp, alpine town which used to be a popular base for hunting and langlaufing during the Protectorate. The peak of Djebel Tidirhine, the highest in the Rif, remains snow-capped most of the year. Today no one visits Ketama and sightseeing is not advised. There is a petrol station and miserable little market. If you spend the night, the **Hotel Tidirhine** (★★★A) in the town centre (tel. 16), still in a pristine state from the 1930s, is clean and has a bar-restaurant. Bookings unnecessary.

From Ketama you can drive to Fez on the S302, or 'Route de l'Unité'. Hacked out of the Rif in the initial years of Independence, it succeeded in linking north and central Morocco. I have not driven it: few travellers do.

The eastern Rif

Particularly in the eastern Rif you will still see cafés and petrol stations named 'Abd el-Karim'. Abd el-Karim and his brother are Rifian folklore: their spectacular resistance to Spanish occupation in the 1920s forced the withdrawal of entire battalions and in 1925 Abd el-Karim declared an independent Republic of the Rif. However a combined Spanish and French army of 500,000 men defeated him on 25 May 1926.

Many Rifian warriors were seconded into the Spanish army, and General Franco, who fought as a major in the Moroccan campaign, invaded Andalusia with Rifian troops in 1936. Rifians played a significant role in Morocco's struggle against the French, but they were largely excluded from Parliament when it gained independence in 1956.

The main road from Ketama to al-Hoceima (Route P39) is considered one of the most exhilarating journeys in Morocco, the *kif*-

salesmen providing an extra buzz. Following the spine of the Rif, it snakes around ridges and doubles back on its tail. Guide-books speak of drops to deep valleys and of glimpses of the Mediterranean from heights where only eagles dare. Unfortunately the Rif can also be fogbound, and when I drove this section in April I could not see more than 10 m in front of the car.

Targuist

Targuist, the last refuge of Abd el-Karim, effectively marks the end of *kif* country. Five km before Targuist you can turn off on a coastal detour to al-Hoceima (approximately 90 km). I passed the odd *kif* vendor from the Beni Frah tribe of Berber farmers on the lonely, 30-km descent to the Mediterranean. **Torres de Alcalá** is a poor hamlet with shabby fishing boats pulled up on a pebble beach. A rough *piste* leads east to the site of Badis, an important trade outlet for Fez in the Middle Ages.

Cala Iris

Cala Iris lies 4 km west of Torres de Alcalá. An attractive beach enclosed by off-shore islands, it is destined to become a tourist resort one day. Excellent swimming, diving and fishing. Camping. Take all requirements.

The drive across the **Massif des Bokkoyas** to al-Hoceima takes an hour. I gave some excited schoolboys a lift to Had Rouadi. There is no bus service and they had a 15-km hike each day.

Al-Hoceima

Al-Hoceima is a pleasant resort if you do not clash with Ramadan (when it is closed) or mid-summer (the Club Mediteranée alone receives 1,400 tourists a week). A white town on a hillside above the rocky port, it was built by Spain after victory in the Rif, and still feels and looks very Spanish. Since 1673, Spain has occupied a tiny off-shore island, the Peñon de Alhucemas, more for nuisance value than anything else, as even water must be shipped from Melilla. Only one in ten families in al-Hoceima is employed. Farming is a struggle in the hard, red soil, but fishing is important and there is no pollution, so fish caught off al-Hoceima actually taste like fish. Tourism provides seasonal work. The first charters from France arrive mid-April at the airport 12 km away.

What to do

See the morning fish market when the *lamparo* boats return at 6 a.m. Tuesday town market. (In the countryside the province of al-Hoceima has four unique women-only *souqs*.) Hire a boat to visit the local beaches. The black-sand Plage Suani has a camp site. There is good skin-diving – the clear inlets are similar to the Calanques region around Marseilles. An efficient tourist office on Rue Tariq Ibn Zayed is open 8.30 a.m. to 12 noon and 2 to 6 p.m.

Where to stay

The town divides naturally around two centres: the Place du Rif and the turquoise bay. I hesitate to recommend a hotel overlooking the street, but the best middle-range establishments are in the centre of town. Cheap hotels around the Place du Rif are not recommended.

Hotel Mohammed V; tel. 2233. Quiet location near the beach, fifteen minutes' walk from town. All facilities.

Residence Caballo (****A). 600-bed complex in the town centre with pool, sauna, restaurant and snack bar. Self-contained.

Hotel Quemado (***A), Plage Quemado; tel. 982371. Ugly, but comfortable rooms with excellent beds and sea views. Superb swimming and wind-surfing, tennis court. Parking. Recommended off-season.

Hotel Maghreb el-Jadid (***A), 56 Avenue Mohammed V; tel. 982504. Clean, well-run hotel with small but pleasant rooms. Licensed restaurant. Town centre.

Hotel Nacional (**A), 23 Rue de Tetouan; tel. 982141. Very clean and comfortable. No restaurant-bar, but cheap places nearby. Town centre.

Hotel Karim (**B), 27 Avenue Hassan II; tel. 982184. Unexceptional, but clean. As with the other town hotels, it is a downhill walk to the beach.

Where to eat   There are several fish restaurants around the port. Rough, but good value, is the **Café Economique** on the Place du Rif opposite the Café-Hotel Florido, the odd building which resembles a synagogue but was the old Spanish casino. Try also the **Café-Restaurant Paris**, 21 Boulevard Mohammed V. **El Bouyadi** is a good supermarket above the crossroads near the mosque.

Moving on   The road from al-Hoceima to Nador (157 km) climbs steeply into the Rif. There is little of interest en route. Kassita, at the junction of the S312 mountain road to Taza, is as good a stop as any for petrol or snacks.

Nador   Nador, a transit stop for the Spanish town of Melilla, 15 km north (see p. 119), is of no interest but you can stay in a comfortable hotel and enjoy a seafood meal in civilized surroundings. I found it very welcome after the Rif. When Spain withdrew in 1957, Nador was just an ordinary Rifian port. Today it is the largest industrial town and port complex in Mediterranean Morocco: iron ore, a sugar refinery and commerce. The town is laid out on a grid pattern, facing a salt-water lagoon. Shops sell all requirements.

Where to stay   Nador has good, middle-range hotels.

Hotel Rif (****B), Avenue Youssef Ibn Tachfine; tel. 606535. A big, impersonal, waterfront hotel with pool, tennis, night-club and garage. Quiet location at the end of the main commercial area.

Hotel Mansour Ed-Dahabi (***A), 105 Rue de Marrakesh; tel. 606583. Town centre. Rooms with small balconies. Rather dark inside. Handy for restaurants. Licensed.

Hotel Khalid (**A), 129 Avenue des FAR; tel. 606726. Eighteen very clean rooms with hot showers. Good restaurant. Centre of town.

Hotel Mediterranée (**A), opposite Hotel Rif; tel. 606495. Small, comfortable hotel. Unlicensed restaurant with good menu.

Where to eat   Nador has good, reasonably priced restaurants with Spanish seafood menus. Opposite the Gare Routier, the **El Mahatta** restaurant specialises in fish and crustaceans, or try the **Restaurant Romero** opposite the *souq*.

Moving on

From Nador you can visit the Spanish town of Melilla or go on to Oujda, 25 km from the Algerian border. The most attractive route follows the coast via Ras el-Ma and Saidia (see p. 116); on the direct Route P27, you will be swept along by traffic and reach Oujda in about 1½ hours. The Grotte du Chameau, with a hot mineral spring, and Zegzel Gorge, 8 km from Berkane, are moderately interesting detours. Ignore hustlers wanting to change money near Oujda; they are trying to fleece Algerians of left-over dirhams.

Oujda

While traditionally conservative, Oujda is an open, easy-going town. Jeans outnumber the white *haiks*, or robes – worn by women here – and café-bars are busy. A cathedral clock chimes the hour.

History

Like all strategic towns, Oujda has experienced bloody dynastic rivalry, in particular between the Merenids and the Ziyanids based in Tlemcen, in Algeria. While Algerians and Oujdas are blood-brothers, their personalities differ: Algerians are dour and cheeky, Oujdas more *soignés* – perhaps a reflection of the different fates their countries suffered at the hands of the French.

What to see

The *Nouvelle Ville* in Oujda is extremely clean and it is easy to find your way about. A helpful tourist office is located on the Place du 16 Aout. Banks, the PTT and shops are on the Avenue Hassan II. There are no *faux-guides*.

The *medina* is enclosed by recently restored Merenid walls. The heads of criminals were displayed on the main gate, Bab Abd el-Wahab, until the practice was outlawed by the French. At dusk the area is animated with shoppers, entertainers and food stalls selling grilled *brochettes* and *chorizo*, or spicy sausage. There are many shrines. In the shady Place el-Attarine is the white *koubba* of Sidi Abd el-Wahab. The *kissaria*, or central covered market, is one of the rare places in Morocco where you can browse. Most shops sell household goods. The Rue Saboni is crowded with brides, relatives and friends choosing lavishly embroidered textiles. Opposite number 19 is a women's *hammam*. Inside I was amazed to find the bathers watching *Dynasty* on a portable television. The fashionable modern *rai* music was developed in the brothels of Oujda and in Algeria's Oran.

Where to stay

There are plenty of small hotels, but cleanliness is not next to godliness in Oujda.

Hotel Terminus (****A), Place de l'Unité Africaine; tel. 683212. Quiet old ONCF hotel 100 m from the railway station. Comfortable rooms. Popular bar. Gardens, pool, parking.

Hotel al-Massira Salam (★★★★B), Boulevard Maghreb al-Arabi; tel. 685600. No frills, but a clean hotel with excellent beds and friendly staff. Near shops and *medina*.

Grand Hotel (★★A), Rue Beni Marine; tel. 680508. Clean hotel near the Palais de Justice.

Hotel Simon (★B), Boulevard Tark Ibn Zaid; tel. 686304. Central hotel. Horrible *objets d'art*.

Hotel Lutetia (★A), 44 Boulevard Hassan Loukili; tel. 683365. Reasonable and central. Bar. Parking.

Where to eat

Oujda has many small café-restaurants and bars. The **Brasserie-Nightclub de France** is popular with well-heeled locals and visiting businessmen. A Spanish bistro-style restaurant, it has an extensive menu and a huge bar. The hole-in-the-wall **Restaurant Bab el-Garbi** (near Hotel al-Massira) has cheap home-cooked chicken, tripe, etc., from 10 dh. The main hotels all have licensed restaurants.

Moving on

The **airport** is 15 km north of Oujda; the RAM office is in the Oujda Hotel, Boulevard Mohammed V; tel. 4072. The **petit-taxi** rank is on Place du Maroc; grand-taxi rank outside Oujda railway station. The **CTM terminus** is the Oued Nachef depot. The **railway station** is at the end of the Rue es Zerktouni.

Sidi Yahia Oasis

A mysterious tradition links the shrine of Sidi Yahia, Oujda's patron saint, with John the Baptist. Effectively the Sidi Yahia Oasis (6 km) is a village of *marabout* shrines in a shady grove of trees. The *Ghar el-Houriyat* is a shadowy grotto believed to be haunted by *houris*, the sensual handmaidens awaiting Muslims in Paradise.

Saidia

Saidia (60 km) is a local holiday resort which the Portuguese plan to develop into an international resort – a 5,000-bed complex with a 200-boat marina and an 18-hole golf-course. A superb beach stretches 10 km to the Oued Moulouya; eastwards you soon reach the border. A tiny market under the gum-trees sells Algerian-manufactured products which are unobtainable in Morocco.

The present small village has a couple of hotels and a number of holiday villas geared to locals. Saidia is good for a swim, a picnic or off-season camping. **Al-Kalaa** (★★A), on a backstreet behind the beach (tel. 5123) is Saidia's biggest hotel, with a bar-restaurant and nightclub. **Hotel Hannour** (★A), Place du 20 Aout (tel. 5115) has only nine rooms. Walking distance from the beach. Nightclub, bar-restaurant. Could be noisy.

Ras el-Ma

The most delightful drive on the Mediterranean coast is a circuitous secondary road skirting the coast from Saidia to Nador via Ras el-Ma. Take a picnic. *Ras* means headland in Arabic. Ras Quebdane is a small boat-building village with grocers and bakers. Nador is 63 km from here across the alluvial plains of the Oued Moulouya rising in the Middle Atlas near Khenifra. The country is sown with cereals and vines. The Moulouya estuary teems with birdlife and is a popular camping-spot. Kariet Arkmane is a pretty fishing village spoilt by the smell of sewage. There is a straight tarmac road into Nador.

The southern Rif

Route P1 across the southern base of the Rif links Rabat and Oujda on the Algerian border. The journey from Fez to Oujda via Taza (344 km) takes five or six hours.

Taza

The town of Taza sits on a lofty peak overlooking the strategic corridor through the Rif and Middle Atlas. Historically Algeria saw the 'Taza Gap' as a route to the Atlantic until focus shifted to the Western Sahara. Every local dynasty and foreign invader has left some sort of mark on Taza. During local power struggles, it was fought over by the Almohads, Merenids and Alaouites. In 1914 it was occupied by the French, who established a large garrison here in their struggles against dissident tribes in the Rif and Middle Atlas.

History

What to see

Taza is built in tiers. At the base of the steep hill is the road and railway station. The *Nouvelle Ville* begins here and runs all the way up the hill to the *medina*, with a bus service connecting the two. The centre of the *Nouvelle Ville*, built by the French in the 1920s, is the **Place de l'Independence**. Here you will find the main hotels, café-bars and shops. Because Taza is not on the tourist 'circuit', there are no *faux-guides*. You can sit in the *café-terrace* of the Grand Hotel du Dauphine and watch Taza pass: no one hurries, the hill is much too steep.

The *medina* is still enclosed by ramparts 3 km long. A bus sets you down on the *mechouar*. From here you can follow the main *souq* street past the Grand Mosque and exit through the **Bab er-Rih** on the northern ramparts. There is a good view of the 'Taza Gap' from this point. The **Grand Mosque**, founded by Abd el-Moumen in 1135, is of great historic interest; the Andalus Mosque has a twelfth-century Almohad minaret. When I visited Taza the Merenid *medersa* was also closed to non-Muslims. Apart from a few carpets woven by the Ben Ouarine, the local Berber tribe, the *souqs* sell mainly domestic items.

Where to stay

With little choice of hotels or restaurants, Taza is best seen as a pause, rather than a nightstop. I cannot recommend anywhere to eat. The town was locked and bolted when I visited during Ramadan.

Grand Hotel du Dauphine (★★A), Place de l'Independence; tel. 3567. Fifty-eight comfortable rooms. Lingering ambience of the French Protectorate. Centre of the *Nouvelle Ville*.

Hotel Friouato-Salam (★★★A); tel. 2593. Clean, quiet but depressing. Garden, pool. Parking. Upper *Nouvelle Ville*, a long walk from the commercial area.

Moving on

Buses and *grands-taxis* leave from the **railway station**. There are two trains daily to Oujda, and two buses daily to Nador, departing

4.30 a.m. and 5 a.m. – a long drive.

From Taza you can visit the Gouffres du Friouat (23 km) in the **Djebel Tazzeka National Park**. These caves, 180 m deep, are the largest in North Africa. You need a guide and a lamp. Entrance 5 dh.

Eastwards from Taza the P1 crosses an arid plain broken by dusty market towns. **Guercif** is a major road junction for Midelt and the Deep South. Petrol, but no satisfactory accommodation. **Taourirt** has two very basic hotels. Refreshments and clean WC at the Café Mauritania. Mechanics and petrol stations. El Aioun restaurant on the Oujda exit. Wind-blown sand often covers the final stretch of road to Oujda (224 km from Taza).

Spanish outposts in Morocco

A day-trip to Melilla on the central Mediterranean coast of Morocco or to Ceuta, two hours' drive from Tangier, has novelty value. The longer you have been in Morocco, the more attractive they seem. If you are in Morocco during Ramadan, lunch at either place is irresistible. Both keep Spanish time, i.e. two hours ahead of Morocco.

Melilla

A Spanish colony since 1497, Melilla is the more picturesque of the two, especially the old quarter *Medina Sidonia*. You can see the citadel, a rocky acropolis enclosed by sixteenth-century walls, from the border at Nador (15 km). Inside is the monumental Gate of Santiago emblazoned with the royal arms of Carlos V. If you cross early to avoid the queue of Moroccan workers, women can be seen scrubbing the porches just as they do in Spain, but not in Morocco. Steps near the harbour lead up to the Plaza Maestranza, named after the celebrated bullring in Seville. There is a local *plaza de toros* and how could there not be a Plaza de España? A circular garden above the port, it divides the *medina* from the *Nouvelle Ville*. Melilla's population of 60,000 survives on the passing tourist trade and on contraband. Hotels are scarce and three times more expensive than in Morocco. The tourist office is at 20 Calle del General Aizpura. Open Mon–Fri 9 a.m. to 2 p.m., 4 to 6 p.m. and Saturday 10 a.m. to 12 noon.

Note that you may not take a hire-car into Melilla unless it is insured for driving outside Morocco. If not, you must park at the border and take a bus or taxi. There are delays at the border at ferry times.

Cueta

Ceuta was where I landed off the night ferry from Algeciras on my first visit to Morocco, more than twenty-five years ago. The sight of hooded figures at the border, where we slept on the customs' bench because the last bus to Tangier had gone, has never left me.

On my most recent visit to Ceuta I did not have international car insurance and so had to leave my car with a *gardien des voitures*. Tired of waiting for a bus, or *grand-taxi*, I hitched a lift with a Moroccan driving a bronze Mercedes. Where did he live? Maastricht, he told me reluctantly. What did he do? Live, he grunted. On noting his gold rings and a Rolex wristwatch, I decided he was a drug-smuggler. Like Melilla, Ceuta thrives on down-market duty-free shopping – perfume, alcohol and computerized gadgets are smuggled into Morocco.

History

Ceuta has known many visitors – Phoenicians, Romans, Vandals, and during the thirteenth century, in particular, it was enmeshed in shifting alliances between Portugal, Spain and the Moorish dynasty in Andalusia as well as at home. Captured by Spain in 1580, it remains a heavily fortified Spanish garrison.

What to do

Ceuta is probably quite boring for the people who live there, but it strikes the visitor from Morocco as clean, orderly and picturesque. A corniche lined with tall, healthy palm trees encircles a marina filled with expensive boats. Residents usually drive or sail out of Ceuta to swim, as the grey-sand town beach is horrible. Still, you do not go to Ceuta to swim, as you have beautiful beaches beyond Fnideq. You go to Ceuta to stock up on drink and for lunch in a European country.

Where to eat

La Torre and **La Terraza** are two good restaurants. The **Casa Silva** and **Casa Fernandez** at Benitez Beach are exclusively Spanish, with excellent seafood. More central is the **Restaurant Marina**, where I ate lunch surrounded by businessmen in suits with white linen napkins tucked under their chins. My choice of *sopa de pescados*, grilled *calamares*, salad and a San Miguel lager came to 1,450 pesetas.

Where to stay

As in Melilla, you will probably wish to see Ceuta in a day and return to Morocco where hotels are cheaper.

Hotel La Murailla (****A), Plaza de Africa; tel. (956) 514940. Clean, well-run busy hotel. Eighty-three huge bedrooms overlooking the garden. Suites are converted from ancient vaults in the ramparts. Garden. Pool. Booking essential. Double room 8,000 pesetas.

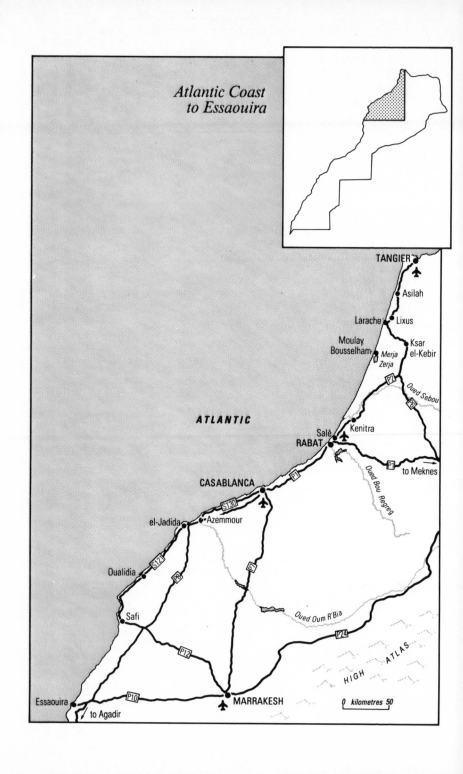

Atlantic Coast to Essaouira

TANGIER

Asilah

Larache • Lixus

Moulay Bousselham
Merja Zerja

Ksar el-Kebir

P2

Oued Sebou

P6

ATLANTIC

Salé • Kenitra
RABAT

P1

to Meknes

CASABLANCA

P1

S130

Oued Bou Regreg

el-Jadida • Azemmour

S121

P8

P7

Oualidia

Oued Oum R'Bia

Safi

P24

P12

HIGH ATLAS

Essaouira

P10

MARRAKESH

to Agadir

0 kilometres 50

The Atlantic Coast to Essaouira

Introduction

Morocco has roughly 2,000 km of glorious Atlantic coast stretching from Asilah to Mauritania, which includes the political and commercial heartland of Rabat and Casablanca and old Portuguese ports such as el-Jadida and Safi. Morocco's long, tormented relationship with Europe began when the Portuguese started chipping away at this coast in the fifteenth century.

Whether travelling north, or south, if you have a car try to stay on the coastal routes. Bus or taxi passengers will travel on busy highways linking the major cities. Do not expect de-luxe hotels and restaurants outside Rabat or Casablanca, but you will find comfortable, hopefully clean accommodation and simple restaurants, serving fresh food.

If you are into fishing or wind-surfing, take everything you need. And be careful swimming: the Atlantic off Morocco has a treacherous undertow.

Most towns in this chapter can be seen in a leisurely ten or fourteen days; allow longer for seductive spots such as Moulay Bousselham.

The northern Atlantic littoral

Asilah

Asilah is like a clean basket of laundry compared to Tangier (46 km). Its sparkling white *medina* sits behind long sea ramparts which are pounded by the Atlantic on a windy day. Asilah is busy during the brief summer, but in winter you may have it to yourself with the odd Spaniard or Tangerine who drives out for lunch. The **Asilah Arts Festival** in August draws singers and musicians as well as the élite of Morocco's contemporary painters. Traditionally each artist paints a mural in the *medina* as a gift to the town.

History

Ancient 'Zili' was an important port of call for shipping from the western Mediterranean. Beyond this point, sailors were out in the open Atlantic. It was a Roman colony and in the tenth century became a refuge of the Idrissid dynasty retreating from the Christians in

Spain. Normans, Arabs, Portuguese and Spaniards at one time or another clashed swords over the small port. Sultan Moulay Ismail finally sent the Portuguese packing in 1691. Vestiges of these transient civilizations remain, including a Phoenician cistern, a portion of Roman wall and the sixteenth-century Portuguese tower and ramparts.

What to see Asilah can be visited in forty minutes, but why rush? The best plan is to arrive mid-morning, see the town, have a swim, and enjoy a sea-food lunch. From the tower, stroll along the **ramparts**, past the *alcazaba*, an early twentieth-century palace belonging to the legendary Ahmed er-Raisuli. The most famous *caid* of Asilah, Raisuli was the well-educated son of a respectable family who became a bandit. His hostages included Sir Harry Maclean and Walter Harris, who describes him as a flamboyant, Errol Flynn-type character, charismatic but insensitive. Raisuli made captives walk a plank from the windows of his palace, known as the 'House of Tears', an 80 m drop to the rocks.

Walk along the ramparts to the white *koubba* of Sidi Mamsur and turn left into the ***medina***. Spotlessly clean, it looks more Greek than Moroccan – and the milk is delivered by donkey.

A small **street market** inside the ramparts has Rifian women traders selling panniers of goat's milk cheese, buckets of snails and sour milk in earthenware jars. The sight of a camera is likely to change the easy-going atmosphere into a slanging match. Thursday is *souq* day.

Shopping Several houses have been converted into art galleries. Old coins, Rifian belts and powder-bags are sold in shops opposite Bab Homar.

Where to stay A lunch-stop rather than a resort, Asilah is short of accommodation. Avoid the two- or three-star hotels used by groups. Self-catering apartments are available.

Hotel Asilah (*B), 79 Avenue Hassan II; tel. 97286. Central, with eleven simple but spotless rooms with shared facilities. Pleasant ambience.

Where to eat Lunch in Asilah is one of the pleasures of a visit to Morocco. Several restaurants specialize in seafood, with a Spanish bias to the menu. The Spanish-owned **Casa Garcia** on the Rue Yaccoub el-Mansour serves generous helpings of prawns, *calamares* and shellfish. The **Alcazaba** near the Portuguese tower and the pavement restaurant known as **Pepe's** are equally good. All three are licensed. You need to secure a table by noon.

Moving on Tangier is thirty-five minutes by car on the main road, or 1½–2 hours' leisurely drive around Cap Spartel (recommended). The **bus** journey takes one hour. Hourly departures outside the CTM office, Avenue Mohammed V. The ***grand-taxi*** rank is in the main square outside the *medina*. The **railway station** is 2 km north. Tangier is 1½ hours by train.

Larache

About forty minutes' drive south of Asilah is Larache, built on the southern bluff of the Loukkos estuary. An amalgam of Tetouan and Tangier, it was obviously a handsome town under the Spanish Protectorate, from 1911 to 1956. Today the blue and white paint is peeling off the buildings around the Place de la Libération, the former Plaza de España. Larachis are fishermen and boat-builders by tradition – they used to build the shallow-draught sailing vessels used by the Bou Regreg corsairs. The port that is under construction should give the town a new lease of life.

There is a beach on the north bank of the estuary with a good view of the ruined *kasbah*.

What to see

From the Place de la Libération walk through the arch into the *medina*. Wedged between the upper town and the harbour, it is attractive in a wistful way, with aged galleries and cobbled streets. A lively focus of activity is the market held in a colonnaded square built during the first Spanish occupation of Larache in the seventeenth century. The **Kasbah de la Cigogne**, on the battlements overlooking the river mouth, was built to hold Portuguese prisoners taken at the Battle of the Three Kings at Ksar el-Kebir in 1578.

The **Archaeological Museum** at the entry to Larache is a pocket-size Spanish fort bearing the royal arms of Charles V. Open daily, except Tuesday, from 9 a.m. to 12 noon and from 3 to 5 p.m. Admission free. Relics from Lixus and various ceramics. Hesitant piano music issues from the Larache Conservatorium of Music opposite.

Jean Genet, the famous French novelist and playwright, is buried in the **Spanish cemetery** to the south of Larache. It is better to have a car rather than to walk through the slums on the southern outskirts of the town.

Where to stay

Most travellers come to Larache to visit Lixus and move on.

Hotel Riad (**B), Rue Mohammed Ben Abdullah; tel. 912626. Once owned by French nobility, a quiet but depressing hotel, with hideous décor. It is hard to say it, but this is the best place to stay in Larache.

Hotel España (*A), 2 Avenue Hassan; tel. 913195. Once grand, still quaint. Fifty rooms, ten with showers and a balcony.

Pension Amal, Rue Abdullah Ben Yasin; tel. 912788. In a quiet side-street near the Place de la Libération. Fourteen rooms without showers. Clean bathrooms.

Where to eat

Restaurants on the Place de la Libération and inside Bab Khemis have Spanish-type menus with sardines and paella as well as grills; 2 km south on the Rabat road is the **Paco y Pili**, a spotlessly clean, *nouveau-riche* Spanish bistro which is open for breakfast, lunch and dinner. Licensed. You would be unlikely to stop at such a place in Spain, but you will seize the opportunity here.

Moving on

The **bus station** and ***grand-taxi*** rank is on the Rue Mohammed ben Abdullah, five minutes' stroll from the Place de la Libération. Frequent services to Rabat and Tangier, and to Fez. There are petrol stations at the Rabat roundabout and a café-restaurant with WC in the Total garage.

Lixus

You can miss Lixus, 5 km north of Larache, if you plan to visit Volubilis, but do not miss both. The town was built on the site of an early Phoenician settlement but the oldest ruins date from 600 BC. Most of what you see are Roman ruins. The town enjoyed its greatest prosperity during Roman times, exporting salt, olives, wild animals, fish and *garum*. The main sites are the garum factories by the roadside. These were sited well away from the civic and residential area of 'Upper Lixus', reached via a track 100 m up the road to Asilah. From a confusing network of ruins overgrown with grass you can make out the amphitheatre where the Romans staged gladiatorial combats. A wall 3 m high prevented the animals from leaping into the audience. In the front are the remains of cisterns and public baths. An acropolis and other temples once stood on the hill-top.

Ksar el-Kebir

The P2 Tangier–Rabat highway bypasses Ksar el-Kebir. The town does not merit a 10-km detour unless you have a car. An expanding market town, its shabby modern façade conceals several historic monuments, but its claim to fame is that it is the site of the Battle of the Three Kings.

History

Ksar el-Kebir, or 'Great Enclosure', was the Merenid defence against Portuguese incursions on the Atlantic coast in the fifteenth century. Twelve km to the north is the battlefield where a Portuguese army of 20,000 led by the young king Sebastian was crushed by superior Moroccan forces under the Saadi Sultan Abdul Malik. The sultan, the ex-sultan El Mutawakkil and the king all died in the confrontation on 5 August 1578, leaving Abdul Malik's brother Ahmed el-Mansour to continue Saadi rule.

What to see

You enter the *medina* through Bab el-Oued (River Gate), which leads into the spice market. Weavers work in a former *funduq* and an old tannery is sited on the downwind side of the *souq*. The **Grand Mosque** was built by the Almohad dynasty in the twelfth century. There is a Merenid *medrassa* nearby and other mosques, *zaouias* and shrines. Fragments of Almohad walls surround parts of the town.

South of the walls is **Sidi Ben Abbase Tower**, an eight-sided monument venerated by Christians and Jews as well as Muslims.

Shopping

A large Sunday market drawing people from the surrounding Loukkos Plains is held outside the station. Ksar el-Kebir is a thriving centre for contraband: whisky, cigarettes and assorted electronic gadgets.

Souq el Arba du Gharb

Souq el Arba du Gharb, at the junction of the P2 and the P6 to Meknes, is an important market town for the surrounding Gharb Plain. Shops, mechanics and café-grills line the roadside. One hopes you will not have to stay in the Gharb Hotel (★★A), although it has a licensed restaurant – Les Fleurs du Sud. There is a Wednesday market, 2 km from the town centre.

Moulay Bousselham

Moulay Bousselham, 44 km from Souq el Arba du Gharb, is a tiny village with a lagoon on one side and the Atlantic on the other; the site is one of the most beautiful in all Morocco. So far it is quite unspoilt, with only one avenue of shops and cafés leading down the hill to the beach. Moulay Bousselham was a tenth-century *sufi*, or *marabout*. During the summer *moussem*, animals are sacrificed at his *koubba* behind the mosque.

What to do

The edge of the **Merja Zerja** (blue lagoon) nature reserve in Moulay Bousselham is one of the most picturesque spots on the Atlantic coast. Extending inland beneath the cliff, the lagoon shelters the village fishing fleet. Until the last century, fishermen put to sea in reed-lashed boats. Barely seaworthy local skiffs are safe for sightseeing on the lagoon – the cost is refunded if you do not see flamingoes. A resident flock of 400–500 in the upper shallows of the Merja Zerja is joined by other waders during the migratory period. Best birdwatching 7 to 8 a.m. and dusk.

The **beaches** below Moulay Bousselham are excellent, but the surf is dangerous. In summer, when Moroccan families are on holiday, there are lifeguards.

The ocean and the estuary provide excellent **fishing**. There is a maximum high tide depth of 4 m on the lagoon bar. You can buy bait – worms and shrimps – from local boys. Restaurants will cook anything you may catch.

Where to stay

Moulay Bousselham is crying out for tourist investment, but the lack of package hotels adds to its charm.

Hôtel le Lagon (★★★A); tel. 902603. This small, comfortable hotel is built on the shoulder of the cliff overlooking the lagoon. Lagoon access. Licensed restaurant and disco. Commandeered by French families at weekends. Open all year.

Moulay Bousselham has an attractive **camp site** under shady trees by the lagoon. No water or electricity. This is where I found a horse in the discotheque but I never found the owner to enquire how much it cost to get in. Ideal if you are self sufficient but take mosquito repellent.

Where to eat

The **Hôtel le Lagon** or local restaurants may, or may not, have fresh fish. It depends on the weather and the refrigerator.

Kenitra

The coast road to Kenitra (44 km) from Moulay Bousselham is flat and traffic-free with several picturesque detours along irrigation canals, but you need a car, or a bicycle. Take a picnic as there are no facilities until Kenitra. Across the Oued Sebou river bridge, you join main-road traffic.

Kenitra is a wholly French-built town which they called Port Lyautey. It was meant to be the industrial capital of Morocco, but it was overtaken in no uncertain terms by Casablanca. It is of no touristic interest, but there are several comfortable hotels, restaurants and bars.

Mehdia

Mehdia (12 km) is the local beach resort. Tacky villas and several hotels overlook a broad ocean beach on the south side of the river mouth. Farther up the estuary is a fifteenth-century *kasbah* which changed hands many times. The Portuguese built it in the fifteenth century, pirates occupied it, the Spanish conquered it, Sultan Moulay Ismail recaptured it and it was finally damaged during the American landings in 1942. The gates are impressive. The **Café Belle Vue** is a simple but pleasant spot for a fresh fish lunch. On the main beach, the **Restaurant-Café Dauphine** is another possibility mid-week. Mehdia is crowded at weekends and holidays.

Rabat

The Rabat-Salé conurbation has a population of about 1 million. Coming by train, you step out of the railway station into a twentieth-century city, but the Avenue Mohammed V brings you to the seventeenth-century *medina* surrounded by twelfth-century Almohad walls. While the capital lacks Casablanca's summery style, Casablanca has none of Rabat's rich heritage, which is often overlooked by travellers concentrating on Fez or Marrakesh.

History

Rabat's rather bland personality belies a swash-buckling past. The great tenth-century *r'bat* after which it is named, was built to oust a heretic Berber tribe who occupied the old Roman site of Chellah. In the twelfth century the victorious Almohad sultan Yaccoub el-Mansour decided to expand the *r'bat* area into a new imperial city. He built the massive ramparts and gates and was constructing the great Hassan Mosque when he died in 1199. The subsequent Merenid rulers added refined touches such as fountains and gardens, but Leo Africanus, who visited Rabat in the sixteenth century, found it was still a small, relatively quiet place.

Things changed when a group of Moorish refugees from Andalusia moved into the *r'bat* in 1609 and turned to piracy as a *modus vivendi*. With no allegiance to the Saadian dynasty, they declared the independent Republic of Bou Regreg in 1627. Known as the 'Salé Rovers', the pirate fleet struck as far afield as Cork, in Ireland, and the Caribbean. Between 1620 and 1630, the corsairs captured 1,000 merchantmen, whose crews were held hostage. Some escaped. The village of Bhalil, near Sefrou, has some red-haired Moroccans whose descent is obvious.

As the rebel state thrived, its inhabitants built a Spanish-style extension to the *medina*. By the eighteenth century the lawlessness of

Rabat had become too much even for the sultans. Several clamped down, but Moulay Ismail, in need of slaves for his massive building works, encouraged the piracy. An Austrian clipper was captured as late as 1829. In 1912 the French, wary of the old imperial cities in the hinterland, chose to govern Morocco from Rabat and built a typical *Nouvelle Ville*.

What to see Rabat long ago spread beyond its ramparts but the main interest lies within them – the *kasbah*, Oudaia Gate and Andalusian Gardens, the Hassan Tower and mausoleum of Mohammed V. Outside, but also enclosed by walls, is the original settlement of Chellah. A car simplifies sightseeing; on foot you will need three days. Bargain hard with the *petit-taxi* drivers. Few meters work and they are used to fleecing business visitors.

Nouvelle Ville Built during the French Protectorate, the *Nouvelle Ville* does not seem to have enjoyed the same budget as Casablanca. The main administrative buildings such as the parliament and the PTT line the Boulevard Mohammed V, while the ministries are grouped near the great **Cathédrale de Saint Pierre**, which is worth seeing. Rabat can be rather depressing, but you can always count on someone coming up to sell you something, to offer to show you around, or to practise speaking English.

Medina Built along the lines of a Spanish town, the *medina* has none of the eastern allure of Fez, but it is easy to find your way about. The main commercial streets, the **Rue Souiqa**, and **Souq es-Sebat** are crossed by three other thoroughfares of which the **Rue des Consuls**, leading to the *kasbah*, is the most interesting. Unlike a traditional Islamic *souq* where trades and crafts are segregated, in the Rue Souiqa they are all mixed up. You will find a butcher next to a shop selling handbags, next to household goods, and so on. A tiny **spice-market**, under the arch at number 193 Rue Souiqa, is worth seeing. The **Grand Mosque** near the junction with the Rue des Consuls is nineteenth-century with Merenid foundations. Walking towards Bab Chellah, you will pass a fourteenth-century Merenid fountain. The Bab Mellah opens into the cramped Jewish quarter where Jews were settled by Sultan Moulay Sliman in the early nineteenth century. Below the *mellah* are ferries to Salé.

Before they were transferred to the *mellah*, many Jews lived in the Rue des Consuls, which has some elegant old houses and several former *funduqs*. Number 109 is worth looking for. There are some interesting shops selling leatherware and carpets at the Oudaia Gate end of the Rue des Consuls.

Kasbah des Oudaias On the southern bluff of the Bou Regreg river, the *kasbah* stands on the original site of the great *r'bat*. It is named after the Oudaia tribe as a reward for loyal service in the FAR, or armed forces, under Moulay Rachid. Its walls contain Almohad masonry, and are nearly 10 m high and 3 m thick. The **Oudaia Gate** was the ceremonial entrance to the

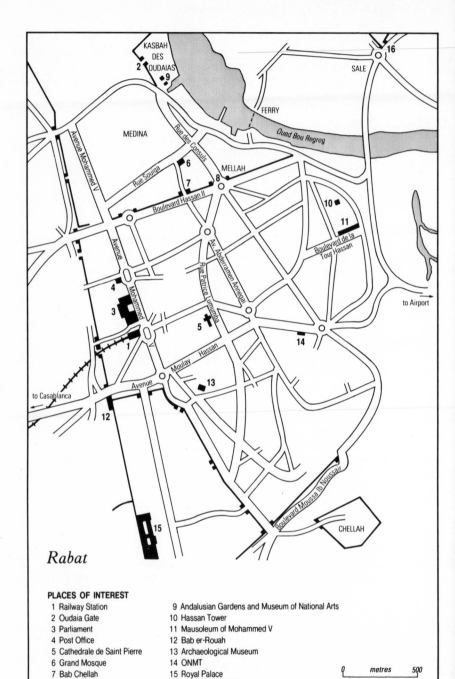

KASBAH
DES
OUDAIAS
2
9

SALE

16

FERRY

Oued Bou Regreg

MEDINA

Rue des Consuls

Rue Souiqa

6

MELLAH

7

8

10

11

Boulevard Hassan II

Boulevard de la
Tour Hassan

Avenue Mohammed V

Av. Abderramen Amegai

Avenue Mohammed

Rue Patrice Lumumba

4

3

5

to Airport

1

14

Moulay   Hassan

to Casablanca

Avenue

13

12

Boulevard Moussa Ib Noussair

CHELLAH

15

Rabat

PLACES OF INTEREST

1 Railway Station
2 Oudaia Gate
3 Parliament
4 Post Office
5 Cathedrale de Saint Pierre
6 Grand Mosque
7 Bab Chellah
8 Bab Mellah

9 Andalusian Gardens and Museum of National Arts
10 Hassan Tower
11 Mausoleum of Mohammed V
12 Bab er-Rouah
13 Archaeological Museum
14 ONMT
15 Royal Palace
16 Bab El-Mrissa

0   metres   500

kasbah, built by Yaccoub el-Mansour in the twelfth century. Overlooking the *medina*, the great gate is a masterpiece of Moorish stone-carving: 'a floating, evanescent thing . . . full of controlled passion,' extols Christopher Kininmonth in *The Traveller's Guide to Morocco*. This powerful impression is created not by mere size, but by its exuberant decoration. Note the scallop shells and the *darf w ktarf* pattern, like an interlocking *fleur de lys*, along the arch. This pattern is repeated on other Almohad monuments.

Inside the *kasbah* you find yourself in a Spanish village created by the Andalusian refugees. Walk straight down to the terrace overlooking the **Bou Regreg**, a perfect spot to reflect on the exploits of the 'Salé Rovers' – any vessel that challenged them either grounded on the shallow river entrance or was blitzed by cannon-fire. The Bou Regreg is only now being dredged for shipping. The main street passes the **Kasbah Mosque**, whose foundations date from the twelfth century. It was restored by an English renegade who joined up with the corsairs and then worked for Sultan Sidi Mohammed Ibn Abdullah (1757–90).

The **Andalusian Gardens**, in fact designed by French landscape gardeners, are part of the original grounds of a seventeenth-century palace, within the lower bastions of the *kasbah*. A small fountain has become a meeting place for women on Friday afternoons. Avoid on Sundays, when the gardens are filled with women and unruly children.

Moulay Ismail's former palace in the gardens is now a museum of arts and crafts. Built around a charming courtyard, the rooms display pottery, carpets, musical instruments and costumes including eighteenth- and nineteenth-century fashions from 'Corsair Society'. **Museum of National Arts**: open 8.30 a.m. to 12 noon and 4 to 6 p.m., closed Tuesdays. Admission 3 dh.

Hassan Tower

Like the Eiffel Tower, the stone minaret planted on the left bank of the Bou Regreg is a symbol of nationhood. Unlike the steel tower, however, it does not provide the perfect movie-set and no one has been up it to get married, to endeavour to fly, or to commit suicide. The tower stands out while you are still some way from Rabat. Once level with it, it loses much of its impact, because it is set at the end of a platform where former lofty marble columns are now mere stumps. Begun by Yaccoub el-Mansour in 1195, the mosque was no doubt just as mammoth a construction project as the Hassan II Mosque in Casablanca (see p. 135). The earthquake which devastated Lisbon in 1755 threw its masonry about like matchsticks. Pilfering for later buildings has done the rest. The solitary minaret seems to grow out of the platform like a carved trunk. Set in the centre of the mosque, rather than at the corner, it lacks balance. Apart from glorious stone-carving, it is a graceless structure of immense historic value. Walk around it. Carved with the *darf w ktarf* and other stylish Almohad patterns, each side is different.

Mausoleum of
Mohammed V

Morocco's tribute to the man who brought it independence, this twentieth-century mausoleum detracts from the regal austerity of the Almohad Hassan Tower. Non-Muslims are permitted inside to view the sarcophagus carved from a block of white onyx. Heraldic banners from all the provinces of Morocco flutter in the draught. A colossal bronze chandelier is suspended from the ornate gilded ceiling. Outside royal guards wearing red jumpsuits and white burnouses stand ill at ease. Other mounted guards flank the entrances. I tried to imagine a horseguard outside St James's Palace in London saying, *'Fous le camp!'* when I took his picture.

Walls

Still almost complete, the Almohad walls around Rabat are 5 km long. Of five gates surviving in some form, **Bab er-Rouah**, the Gate of the Winds, is worth close scrutiny. Built for defence, its shallow, floral relief is as delicate as piped icing. Within the gate you have to turn several corners; the design gave soldiers under siege time to reload their weapons. Works of art are displayed in the rooms which are open from 8.30 a.m. to 12 noon and 2.30 to 8 p.m.

The **Archaeological Museum** near Bab er-Rouah, has a small but interesting collection of pre-history remains and Roman bronzes. Look for the bronze head of Juba II, governor of the Roman province of Mauritania-Tingitana, and the guard dog, also from Volubilis. Open 8.30 to 12 noon and 2 to 6.30 p.m., closed Tuesdays. Admission 3 dh.

Chellah

The original Phoenician settlement known as Sala was probably built beside a spring which still courses out of the hill above the Bou Regreg. A flourishing Roman settlement, Chellah had been reduced to little more than a tell by the eleventh century. It was then used as a burial-ground by the Merenids. The ruins are now partly invaded by overgrown gardens. Of great historical significance, they have little architectural merit except for the huge gate, beautifully worked in gingerbread stone with the Almohad shells and an elegant *kufic* inscription above the Islamic horseshoe arch. The Gothic-type bastions are disturbing, but they later became a feature of Merenid architecture. You will need a guide to point out the tomb of Sultan Abou Hassan who died in 1351. He is surrounded by his favourite wives and slaves.

Where to
stay

Rabat is short of all grades of hotels, and reservations are essential. Visitors tend to be politicians and businessmen rather than tourists, but some people fly thousands of miles to swing a club on the town's celebrated Dar es Salaam golfcourse.

Hyatt Regency (*****A), Place Sidi Makhlouf; tel. 771234. A member of the exclusive five-star club in Morocco. The foyer is filled with valuable kitsch. Quiet location. Inconvenient without a car, but *petit-taxi* service available.

La Tour Hassan (*****A), 26 Avenue Abderraman Annegai; tel.

721401. Convenient and calm, but does not deserve its rating.

Hotel Moussafir (***A); tel. 774326. Old ONCF hotel next to the railway station. Sixty rooms, traditional Moroccan design. Modernised and pleasant.

Hotel Balima (***A), Avenue Mohammed V; tel. 707755. Old 1930s hotel, full of bureaucratic ghosts. Waning elegance. Over-rated, but convenient.

Hotel Bou Regreg (**A), 1 Rue Nador; tel. 724110. On the corner of the busy Boulevard Hassan II, it might be noisy. Large, clean rooms. Garage. Near the *medina*.

Hotel Majestic (*A), 121 Avenue Hassan II; tel. 722997. A fairly comfortable hotel with fifty beds.

Where to eat Mercifully Rabat has more restaurants than Tangier, but nothing like the range in Casablanca. In the Hyatt Regency, **Justine's** has an excellent French menu. Other tables of repute are the **Relais Pierre Louis**, seafood; **Les Martinets**, European; and **La Mama**, Italian. The best and cheapest Moroccan food in Rabat is sold in and around the *medina*. Try the **Saadi** and the **CTM Café** (licensed). With a car, **Le Provençal** , 16 km from Rabat on the road to Temara (the P1), is very good. Dishes cooked to order.

Coffee-houses The **Comédie**, **Capucines** and **Balima** *café-terraces* on the Boulevard Mohammed V are recommended. **Jour et Nuit**, near the bus station, is more Western. The best spot for mint-tea with a view is the **Café Maure** behind the Andalusian Gardens.

What to do Rabat is as dead as a dodo after 8 p.m. Entertainment is mainly in
Nightlife hotel discos.

Shopping Rabat is not the place to shop unless you want to buy a locally made carpet, and even then I would suggest you first see other carpet centres such as Meknes, Midelt and Rissani. A carpet market is held at the Oudaia Gate end of the Rue des Consuls on Thursdays. Shop number 18 sells rugs and other bric-à-brac. Buy handicrafts in Fez, Marrakesh or Taroudannt.

Sports The 45-hole Royal Dar es Salaam golfcourse, 15 km from Rabat, is among the top fifty in the world. The Hyatt Regency has the best sports facilities: swimming-pool, tennis, mini golf, fitness centre and a jogging track within the grounds. Mohammedia Beach, thirty minutes' drive south, has sailing, water-skiing and riding – more for the local élite than independent travellers.

Useful **Royal Air Maroc**, 281 Avenue Mohammed V, tel. 767066.
information **British Embassy**, 17 Boulevard de la Tour Hassan, tel. 720905/6.
Canadian Embassy, 13 bis Rue Jaafar Assadik, tel. 771376.
American Embassy, Avenue de Marrakesh, tel. 762265.
Banks, Avenues General Kittani and Hassan II.
PTT, midway down the Avenue Mohammed V.

ONMT, 22 Avenue d'Alger, tel. 721252.
SCIT, Rue Patrice Lumumba, tel. 723272.
Police, tel. 19.
Ambulance, tel. 15.

Moving on   Six buses a day leave from outside Hotel Terminus (Avenue Mohammed V) for Casablanca **Airport**; 45 dh. Excellent, frequent **train service** to Casablanca, Fez, Tangier and Oujda. Café and lockers at the station. Local **buses** leave from the Boulevard Hassan II, CTM buses from the main bus station, Place Zerktouni. *Grand-taxi* ranks are on the Avenue Hassan II and on Place Zerktouni for Casablanca.

Salé   The classic white town of Salé stares at the *kasbah* across the Bou Regreg. It is 2 km over the bridge or you can catch a boat beneath the *mellah*; they leave as soon as they are full. On the other side just follow other passengers walking up to the *medina*.

History   In the tenth century Salé was the headquarters of an independent Berber tribe who incited Almohad wrath at the same time as the Berbers lodged in Chellah. The town was attacked by Spanish forces in the thirteenth century but under Merenid rule it became a prosperous port trading with Europe. The Merenid sultans built mosques and *medressa*. Unwilling to throw in their lot with the 'Salé Rovers', many Moriscos settled in Salé. When Rabat gained prominence, development ceased and Salé has not changed in the past 200 years.

What to see   **Bab el-Mrisa**, the Sea Gate, is the most curious of the six gates in the remaining walls. It was built in the thirteenth century to control shipping entering the town from a small canal off the Bou Regreg. The old *mellah* was inside.

The most interesting part of Salé is the concentration of elegant old houses and *zaouias* around the **Grand Mosque**. The mosque, built in the thirteenth century, is entered by a flight of steps beside the *medrassa*. The richly worked arched entrance to the *medrassa* gives on to a small but lavishly decorated courtyard. Columns covered with bright tiles carry the eye upwards to swirling bands of calligraphy and stucco-work. The students lived in small cells around the gallery, each room separated by a cedar screen carved with elaborate floral and geometric motifs. There is a view of Salé from a flat roof-terrace.

Behind the mosque is the *zaouia* **of Sidi Abdallah Ibn Hassoun**. A greatly respected *sufi*, he became Salé's patron saint following his death in 1604, and like Saint Christopher, his shrine is visited by travellers. Each year, on the eve of *Mouloud*, the Prophet's birthday, fishermen wearing pirate costumes and descendants of the corsairs carrying decorated candles make a procession through the town to the mausoleum. A large, wind-swept cemetery extends beyond the shrine. There are several *koubba*, but locals do not like Christians walking about the graves.

Souqs

Both the Bab Bou Haja and Bab Fez lead into the markets. You cannot get lost so you do not need a guide. Most shops sell domestic items. There are stone-masons and carpenters in the Rue Kechachine. I also saw a man carving flutes. Souq el-Ghezel is the wool market and Souq el-Merzouk is the textile market, where tailors run up dazzling gowns on ancient sewing machines. Souq el-Kebir is a busy second-hand clothes market. The absence of touts makes browsing pleasant; crowded on Thursdays and Fridays.

Where to stay

Most people stay in Rabat, but there is a camp site by the river. Excellent café-grills and hole-in-the-wall restaurants are found inside both main gates. The **Café Marhaba** near the SGMB bank sells tasty cooked fish, *brochettes* and chicken.

Jardins Exotiques

The Jardins Exotiques, about 20 minutes' drive north of Rabat, are the work of a French horticulturist in the 1950s. The gardens are a pleasing confusion of many different species of native and exotic flora. Open 9 a.m. to 6.30 p.m.

Plage des Nations

The Plage des Nations, about 15 km north of Rabat, takes its name from Rabat's diplomatic circle who descend at weekends. Western women will feel more relaxed here than in the male-dominated areas of Rabat and Salé. It is quiet during the week. If you take bus 28 from Salé, alight at the turning. The beach is 2 km walk.

Where to stay

Hôtel Firdaous (*****A), Plage des Nations-Sidi Bouknadel. Large, clean hotel with friendly staff. Bar-restaurant. Parking. Huge pool open to non-residents for a small fee. Busy at weekends.

Mohammedia

70 km south of Rabat (and 30 km before you reach Casablanca) is a long coastal strip known as Mohammedia. On the Casablanca side it is an untidy industrial sprawl – oil, port and industrial zone. On the Rabat side, or East Mohammedia, are good beaches backed by villas, hotels and sports facilities. More a local playground, it has no lasting interest – an urban railway will link it to Casablanca by the year 2000. A subway is also planned for the large coastal metropolis.

Casablanca

Many people still like to imagine Casablanca as the city depicted in the steamy film starring Bogart and Bergman. Unfortunately this not only presents an archaic image of the robust Atlantic port, but not a single scene was shot in Casablanca. It is just as untrue to describe Casablanca as a city of *bidonvilles*. Its expanding population of more than 4 million includes many poor rural workers drawn to its bright lights in the hope of earning a better living. Every metropolis in the developing world has slums; Casablanca is no exception, but it is also the most handsome city in the Maghreb. Thanks to the French it is a model of urban planning and very easy to find your way about. There are no historic monuments, unless you count the statue to General Lyautey, but its 1930s architecture is unique. The discerning traveller will find Casablanca has a certain elusive style which is not encountered elsewhere in Morocco. It is not at all apparent when you fly into Mohammed V Airport direct from overseas, but returning to Casablanca after several weeks out in the *bled* is like splashdown from the moon. It is time to jazz up the tune, Sam.

History

The remains of a primitive human being, dubbed 'Casablanca man', were discovered on the road to Sidi Abderraman in 1955. Ancient Casablanca, known to the Portuguese as 'Anfa' (a possible reference to aniseed) was built around a large coastal swamp. You can dig a hole anywhere in downtown Casablanca and it still fills with water and you will see many flooded building sites. When the Merenid dynasty weakened, fifteenth-century Anfa became a popular base for pirates, a forerunner, perhaps, of the Bou Regreg Republic. Sultan Sidi Mohammed Ibn Abdullah reclaimed the town in 1770 and built the old white *medina*, Dar el-Beida, along the seafront. By 1857 it had 8,000 inhabitants and 20,000 by 1900. Trade with Europe flourished thanks to a direct French shipping service and work began on extensions to the port. In 1907 nine French dock-workers trespassing on sacred ground were murdered, providing France with a pretext for landing troops in Casablanca and also Oujda, on the Algerian border. The French Protectorate was formalized in 1912.

What to see

Nouvelle Ville

Casablanca's metamorphosis began when the first resident general Louis Hubert Lyautey (1912–25) instructed the celebrated French architect d'Henri Prost to design a *Nouvelle Ville*. Within five years, Dar el-Beida was surrounded by a new town based on a simple grid of long, elegant avenues linked by roundabouts. Today 'Greater Casablanca', divided into six *arrondissements*, or boroughs, covers more than 50 sq km and is ringed by a motorway. The *Nouvelle Ville* is the centre of administrative, corporate and social activity. Hidden behind the Hyatt Regency Hotel, the old town is almost forgotten; parts are to be levelled for an approach to the Hassan II Mosque.

Casablanca's 1930s architecture is just as much a part of Morocco's heritage as Almohad monuments. Overlooked by handsome administrative buildings such as the Palais de Justice and the Préfecture, the centre of Casablanca, the **Place des Nations Unies**, is full of vitality. The local architecture is an eclectic marriage of Moorish, rococo and colonial French design. The clocktower on the Préfecture is unmistakably colonial – a monument also erected in Delhi, Malacca and Noumea – wherever Europeans have tried to teach the meaning of time.

Downtown Casablanca is rather scruffy but some of the most interesting architecture is on the long **Boulevard Mohammed V**. Number 3 is a beautiful building from *la belle époque*, while numbers

12 and 97 are examples of the bizarre Islamic-rococo style. Balconies decorated with elaborate friezes and heads of Pan are characteristic. The PTT and Chamber of Commerce are French-Islamic, while number 125 is colonial overlaid with Arab motifs, as is the Bessoneau building, facing the Central Market. The imposing Hôtel de Paix and the Hôtel Transatlantique, built by the ONCF in 1926 are gems of Atlantic-coast style, in contrast to the modern Sheraton.

Dar el-Beida

The architecture of the old white town of Dar el-Beida is less interesting. You can see some fine old homes on the Place Sidi Bou Hamra and along the Rue de la Marine. A 2-km walk around the *medina* walls takes you around the battery lined with Portuguese cannons and up the Boulevard Mohammed el-Hansali to the Hyatt Regency hotel. Dating from the eighteenth century, the *medina souqs* are clean and orderly, but filled with cheap clothing and leatherware.

Habbous

Built by the French, the *Quartier Habbous*, or new *medina* has aged well and today looks quite folksy. Visitors are welcome to watch proceedings in its law courts (9 a.m. to 12 noon). Moroccan law is based on the Napoleonic code and *Sharia*, or Islamic law, although not the off-with-the-hand variety of Saudi Arabia.

Hassan II Mosque

A jewel of Islamic architecture, the great Hassan II Mosque on the seafront in Casablanca was designed by Frenchman Michel Pinseau. A building of truly Pharoanic proportions, it was begun in 1980 and officially inaugurated by King Hassan II in 1993. Why Casablanca? According to the king, the mosque is to compensate the citizens of Casablanca for having promised them the Mohammed V mausoleum and then chosen Rabat instead.

25,000 labourers were employed on the construction of the mosque, including 10,000 of Morocco's master craftsmen. As well as a prayer hall, the building comprises an ablutions room, *hammams*, a vast library, a museum and a *medrassa* or religious school. There is room for 25,000 believers inside the mosque and a further 80,000 on the esplanade. The central part of the prayer hall can be electronically transformed into a vast patio, whose mobile ceiling opens to the sky. Part of the mosque extends out over the sea, illustrating the Koranic verse 'And his throne was over the Waters'. The mosque façades and those of the minaret are covered with sculpted marble; embedded in the axis of the southern façade, the minaret soars upwards 200 m. The top, or *jamour*, weighing 3 tons, is fitted with a laser beaming device. With a range of 5 km, it is focused in the direction of Mecca.

300,000 cu m of concrete, 40,000 tons of steel, and quarried marble the equivalent of 65,000 tons went into the mosque. Everyone in Morocco also contributed to the cost – including expatriates although, as non-Muslims, they are not permitted inside.

Going to Casablanca today and not seeing the Hassan II Mosque equates with visiting Cairo and missing the pyramids. If not indeed the

'Eighth Wonder of the World', it is an inspirational image of modern Morocco. It is unfortunate that tourists must view it from afar.

Sidi Beliout shrine

Sidi Beliout, the patron saint of Casablanca, was a humble man who preferred animals to humans. Legend says a lion took care of him when he became blind and on his death carried him to the cemetery. The saint's shrine, in the Boulevard Felix Houphet-Boigny, draws love-sick Moroccan teenagers, who go there to seek consolation. 'Sidi Beliout gives us hope that we will not die of love,' a tear-stained secretary told me.

Sidi Abderraman shrine

In the bay beyond Ain Diab a white sanctuary encrusts a rocky outcrop. It is five minutes' walk at low tide, or ten minutes' breast-stroke when the tide is up. Sidi Abderraman, a Muslim ascetic who was born in Baghdad, found this bay near Casablanca ideal for meditation. His disciples buried the *sufi* among the rocks and his shrine became a pilgrimage for the mentally ill. Lodgings accommodate relatives and a *guardian* sells talismans and flags which are tied to the cells where the mad must remain exposed to the waves for seven nights. Non-Muslims, no matter how deranged (and I certainly qualified after weeks of driving in Morocco) may not visit the shrine. People returning speak of Dantesque scenes of the insane, hair whipping in the wind, gripping the bars and staring into the crashing waves. To exorcise all the devils, the hapless creatures are also fumigated, and, according to the family's means, a goat or a chicken is sacrificed and shared with the *guardian* and various camp-followers.

Where to stay

Casablanca has the best up-market hotels in Morocco. Cheap hotels are hard to find.

Sheraton Casablanca (*****A), 100 Avenue des FAR; tel. 317878. Built in 1989, 306 de-luxe rooms with large beds. All amenities plus health club. French, Oriental and Morocco's first Japanese restaurant. Downtown.

Casablanca Hyatt Regency (*****A), Place Mohammed V; tel. 261234. A familiar landmark near the *medina*. Well-run, friendly hotel in the business centre.

Royal Mansour (*****A), 27 Avenue des FAR; tel. 313011. Trust House Forte management. California-style atrium with British bar on one side and Moroccan and French restaurant on the other. Complimentary mint-tea or almond milk on arrival. Downtown.

Riad-Salam-Meridien (*****A), Boulevard de la Corniche, Ain-Diab; tel. 392244. On the lido – twelve minutes' drive from central Casablanca. Africa's first *thalassothérapie* (salt-water treatment) centre. Attracts glitzy European, mainly French, clientele. Resident doctor and dietician. Treatments modestly priced.

Hôtel Moussafir (***A), Place de la Gare; tel. 364110. Convenient and good value.

Hôtel Transatlantique (****B), 79 Rue Colbert; tel. 260763.

Pleasant, old, male-chauvinist hotel. 1930s 'Fantasia Bar' with leather chairs. Tufted carpet, pseudo-Moorish fountain and frightful paintings. Large, clean rooms, soft beds. Midtown.

Hôtel Excelsior (**A), 2 Rue Nolly; tel. 200048. Built 1930. Marble staircase, eclectic Oriental décor. No atmosphere. Soft beds. Downtown.

Hôtel Majestique (*A), 57 Boulevard Lalla Yacout; tel. 310951. Rococo façade. Oriental foyer. Rooms facing the street are noisy. Central.

Hôtel Louvre (*B), 36 Rue Nationale; tel. 273747. Large, fairly comfortable rooms. Popular with young tourists. Near the pedestrian mall.

Grand Hôtel de Paris (***B), 2 Rue Branley; tel. 273871. Less grand than the Louvre but clean, small and convenient for shops and restaurants. Off the mall.

Where to eat Casablanca has some of Morocco's best restaurants, especially for French cuisine and seafood. Several of the best restaurants are fifteen minutes' drive. **A Ma Bretagne** (tel. 362112), beyond the Sidi Abderraman shrine, is the only restaurant in Africa with a Michelin star and owner-chef André Halbert is a member of the 'Maîtres Cuisiniers de France'. *Spécialités poissons*. An extensive wine list includes rare Moroccan reds. Every table has a view of the Atlantic.

The group of restaurants around the lighthouse has a loyal following of local gourmets: **Le Cabestan** (tel. 363265) – sea view and excellent seafood; the Swiss-managed **La Mer** (tel. 363315); and, facing the Hassan II Mosque, **Le Petit Roche** (tel. 361195). None is cheap.

Good restaurants in town are the **Restaurant du Port**, the **Taverne du Dauphin** and **La Paix**, located behind the Central Market with a *Relais des Routier* type menu. **Al-Mounia** is a long-established Moroccan restaurant; the **Douira** in the Royal Mansour Hotel enjoys a reputation for good local cuisine. So too does the **Andalus Restaurant** in the Sheraton Hotel. All top hotels offer lunchtime buffets. Cheap eating places are found along the Avenue Prince Moulay Abdullah.

What to do Entertainment centres on hotel bars, nightclubs and a few seedy
Nightlife strip-joints. **La Fontaine** on the Boulevard Mohammed el-Hansali has belly-dancing; drinks for bar staff are *de rigueur*. Bar-clubs on the corniche are packed at weekends. Searching for Rick's Bar as in the film, American tourists end up in a nostalgic mock-up in the Hyatt Regency. A pianist plays 'As Time Goes By' and there are black and white photos of the Bogart–Bergman team. The **Black House** disco is one of Casablanca's trendy spots, as is **Caesar's** in the Sheraton.

Swimming The surf off Casablanca is notorious. Play safe and swim in one of the sea-water pools on the lido at Ain-Diab. Standards and prices vary, from 20 dh. Recommended are **Miami** and **Tahiti Plage**. Lined with beach-clubs and café-snacks, the lido – 3 km from the centre of Casablanca – is reminiscent of south Beirut. French residents used to take Sunday tea on the terrace of the old Hôtel Belle Rive.

Shopping Except for silver samovars, teapots and *couscoussiers*, Casablanca is not known for locally made handicrafts. Shops at the top end of the Boulevard Mohammed el-Hansali sell souvenirs. Occasionally you can buy a good pair of blue jeans, but locally manufactured garments are usually decades out of date. In up-town Casablanca, the modern Riad Complex sells smarter goods. Alpha 55, a depressing department store in mid-town Casablanca, sells anything you may have lost or forgotten to bring on holiday. In the *Habbous* you will find a good variety of handicrafts around the mosque. Number 12 bis Joutia, in the carpet market, sells jewellery, rifles and 'Hand of Fatima' doorknockers. Most are new items made to look old, but your friends will never know.

The Central Market on the Boulevard Mohammed V has excellent displays of fruit, vegetables, fish, cheeses and spices and is worth a visit.

The garden Surrounded by lush gardens, the suburbs of **Anfa** and **Ain-Diab**
suburbs are comparable to Sydney's North Shore or Beverly Hills. Villas start at £150,000; many Arabs own mansions. **Anfa Golfcourse** has nine holes and is laid out around the racetrack, which constitutes one of the hazards. Visitors are welcome at the **Churchill Club**, Rue Pessac, Ain-Diab (tel. 261441), the usual, rather tacky home-from-home patronized by English expats and Anglophile Moroccans. Only English may be spoken.

Useful **Royal Air Maroc**, 44 Avenue des FAR, tel. 2311122.
information **Olive Branch Tours**, 35 Rue de Foucauld.
InterRent-Europcar, Tour des Habbous, tel. 2313737; 144 Avenue des FAR, tel. 2314069.
British Consulate, 60 Boulevard d'Anfa.
British Chamber of Commerce, 291 Boulevard Mohammed V.
US Consulate, 8 Boulevard Moulay Youssef.
Protestant Church, 33 Rue d'Azilal.
Catholic Churches, Rond-Point Europe; 2 Rue de l'Eglise; 44 Boulevard Ab del-Moumen; Rue d'Hendaye.
American Express, Voyages Schwarz, 112 Avenue Moulay Abdullah.
PTT, central office Place des Nations Unies; sub-office Boulevard Mohammed V.
SCIT, 98 Boulevard Mohammed V.
ONMT, 55 Rue Omar Slaoui.
All-night pharmacy, Place des Nations Unies.

Newspapers, French and British newspapers are sold from stalls in the Boulevard Mohammed V and in hotel bookshops.

Banks, SGMB, 84 Boulevard Mohammed V; Credit du Maroc, 48–58 Boulevard Mohammed V; Banque de Maroc and Citibank, near PTT; others near the Hassan II roundabout.

Moving on

The Mohammed V **Airport** is about 30 km south of Casablanca on Route P7 to Marrakesh. There is a regular bus-service from the CTM terminus. Airline offices are mainly on the Avenue des FAR. Casablanca Port is the **railway station** within walking distance of the town centre and main hotels. There are excellent, regular services to Rabat and elsewhere. ONCF: tel. 271837. The CTM **bus-terminus** is on the Rue Vidal, behind the Safir hotel, in downtown Casablanca. There are **petit-taxi** ranks outside the Hyatt Regency and on the Avenue des FAR. The inner-city fare should not exceed 15 dh.

The central Atlantic littoral

Azemmour

Azemmour, on the S130, 1¼ hours' drive from Casablanca, is rarely visited by tourists. There is a stunning view of its old white *medina* strung along the Oum R'bia from the bridge. Rising in the Middle Atlas, the river brings down billions of tonnes of sediment, which make the estuary unnavigable. A Moroccan bed-time tale relates how a *djinn* offered to clear the entrance. Locals thought his payment – the lives of forty men – was exorbitant, but they hid and watched him roll away a giant boulder blocking the estuary, and were engulfed by the rush of water. It is said the same number of boatmen are drowned every year around Azemmour.

History

Walking around the ramparts is an instant history lesson. Azemmour's official guide chants dates like a litany, but ask him to show you the interesting sights: the subterranean canals where the Portuguese manoeuvred small boats inside the safety of the fort and the brackets where their flag fluttered over the battlements. The town was occupied by the Duke of Braganza in 1513. It was evacuated in 1541.

What to see

The *medina* cannot have much changed since the sixteenth century. It is picturesque but filthy, and children are a nuisance. Persevere, however. The narrow, unpaved streets are flanked by white-washed houses famous for their heavy wooden doors. Many are painted blue, and have 'Hand of Fatima' knockers. Intricate locks are opened with heavy, moulded keys. Hole-in-the-wall shops sell simple foodstuffs and the famous Azemmour bread. Everyone sells bread, and children seem to spend their day trailing back and forth carrying a tray of dough to the public oven.

Azemmour had a large Jewish community. From the northern

ramparts you can look down into the *mellah*. Its once-elegant houses are shedding their masonry like rotting fruit – most remain empty following the Jewish exodus from Morocco. A riverside synagogue is still used by visitors.

A market leads from the *Nouvelle Ville* up-hill to the shrine of **Moulay Bou Cho'aib**, the patron saint of Azemmour. The herbalists selling dried lizards and seeds are a contrast to the modern pharmacy. Outside the sanctuary stalls sell candles, flags and other jingle-jangles. A *zaouia* to the saint was established in the twelfth century. Every male in Azemmour is named Bou Cho'aib and the population of 30,000 is greatly augmented by pilgrims during the annual *moussem* on 15 August.

Beaches

Swimming in the Oum R'bia river is dangerous. The bank is also strewn with rubbish – there is no refuse collection, so residents throw everything out of their windows. A country road off the Place du Souq leads to Hazouzia beach (3 km) and to the local railway station. The Atlantic here is treacherous and soccer-games spoil sunbathing. A better beach lies north of Azemmour.

Where to stay

People do not normally stay in Azemmour. The **Hôtel la Victoire**, 308 Boulevard Mohammed V, is clean but basic. Various café-grills face the Portuguese ramparts draped in purple bougainvillea. The tourist office is at 141 Avenue Mohammed V.

El-Jadida

Old differences between Morocco and Portugal were buried when el-Jadida, 16 km south of Azemmour, was twinned with Cintra. 'Mazagan', as the town was known until Independence, is the most popular local holiday resort on the central Atlantic coast. It has a population of 100,000, mainly employed at the Jorf Lasfar phosphate terminus. Local prosperity is evident in the new housing and commercial development; prostitutes in Azemmour are also benefiting.

El-Jadida is a striking, European-looking town built at the end of a sweeping bay. A long avenue lined with palms leads in to the town centre. Like Estoril on a summer evening, the corniche is packed with promenaders. Locals love el-Jadida, but it lacks charm for an independent traveller – particularly for a woman on her own. There is nowhere pleasant to sit, as the *café-terraces* are noisy and packed with men.

History

El-Jadida's history lies in the *Cité Portugaise* founded in 1513. Locked inside colossal ramparts, it resisted all attacks until 1769. The town then remained uninhabited until it was transformed into a *mellah* in 1815. As trade flourished, Europeans joined the wealthy Jewish community.

What to see

If you do nothing else in el-Jadida, you must walk around the **walls**. The bastion of Saint Ange overlooks the harbour and walls lined with cannon. The bastion of Saint Sebastian was the former prison and tribunal of the Inquisition. It was converted into a synagogue – note the star of David cut in the wall. A complete tour takes about one hour. Women on their own may be bothered.

Entering the main gate, you pass the Church of the Assumption, now closed. Walk down the Rua de Carreiro lined with shops selling souvenirs. Once graceful shades of pink and grey, restoration has coated everything a uniform dung-colour. Happily the **Portuguese cistern**, halfway down on the left, was spared. Built as an arsenal in the sixteenth century, it was converted into a tank. The mysterious subterranean chamber is a magical sight at midday, its vaulted roof lit by the sun mirrored in a sheet of water. Orson Welles used it as the backdrop for a scene in *Othello*. Open 8 a.m. to 12 noon and 2 to 6 p.m.; admission 3 dh. A guide is compulsory.

The ***Porta do Mar***, or Sea Gate, at the end of the Rua de Carreiro is where the last Portuguese governor slipped out by sea. A bakery within the ramparts exudes a bewitching aroma of fresh bread. The Rua Nazareth, on the right, is worth a picture. Early morning is the best time for photography in el-Jadida.

Where to stay   El-Jadida has a good choice of middle-range hotels; booking is essential from June to early September.

Hôtel Palais de Andalous (****A), Avenue de la Nouie; tel. 033906. Converted palace with comfortable rooms with high, large beds. Tiled courtyard. The bar is the best spot for an aperitif in el-Jadida.

Hotel-Club Doukkala Salam (****B), Avenue el Jamiaa Arabia; tel. 343737. Ugly exterior but well-maintained. Small rooms with huge bathrooms. Sea views. Good tennis. Pleasant ambience despite package-tours.

Hôtel Royal (*A), 108 Avenue Mohammed V; tel. 341100. Old hotel in ugly commercial street. Tiled entrance and attractive courtyard. Eighteen large, airy rooms, some with showers. Bar.

Hôtel Suisse (*A), 145 Rue Zerktouni; tel. 342816. If the Royal is full; twenty quiet rooms around a patio.

Hôtel de Provence (**B), 42 Avenue Fkih Rafii; tel. 342347. This is a home-from-home, under genial British management. Clean, quiet rooms. Pleasant dining-room. Central location. Courtesy bus to the railway station. Recommended.

Where to eat   The **Restaurant du Port** beneath the Portuguese citadel serves fresh seafood and Moroccan cuisine, licensed. **Chez Chiquito**, near the port, serves cheap fish in basic surroundings. **Restaurant La Marquise** is a popular local restaurant. The dining-room of the Hôtel de Provence serves a cheap three-course menu. Good restaurants outside el-Jadida are **Le Requin Bleu** at Sidi Bouzid – excellent for a seafood lunch – and **Auberge Beauséjour** on the road to Jorf Lasfar.

Moving on   Travelling south from el-Jadida, you can take the P8 to Safi or the S121, a good coastal road crossing the Doukkala Plain. The S121 is more interesting and has several charming roadside restaurants. If you leave el-Jadida around noon, you can eat lunch en route and break the journey in Oualidia (73 km). To find your way out of el-Jadida follow the lighthouse road to Sidi Bouzid.

Moulay Abdullah

Moulay Abdullah (11 km) is a rustic fishing village built on the ruins of the Carthaginian settlement known as Titus. On the left are the remains of a twelfth-century *r'bat*, known as Tit. Crumbling walls enclose a prominent white-washed *zaouia* built in Almohad times, when Moulay Abdullah was an important base for Islamic orthodoxy opposing heretic Berber tribes. In August one of Morocco's most important *moussems* is held at the *zaouia* and Moulay Abdullah becomes a sea of tents and foodstalls.

The Doukkala Plain

Skirting Cap Blanc, the S121 ascends the rocky hills overlooking the new Jorf Lasfar phosphate terminus. The Doukkala Plain is one of the most intensively farmed regions in Morocco. The sight of a camel-drawn plough silhouetted against a modern plastic cloche symbolizes the rapid changes Morocco is undergoing. Tomatoes are the main crop. Excellent coastal road with plenty of petrol stations.

Le Rélais bar-restaurant, 26 km from el-Jadida, is a rustic, French-colonial-style establishment, with six rooms, open from May to August. It has a splendid seafood lunch menu. Allow time for a swim. **La Brise** is about 4 km down the road on the left. It also serves an excellent lunch, including local Oualidia oysters. Eleven spotless rooms overlook the lagoon.

Oualidia

The road to Oualidia crosses a marshy coastal plain dotted with salt pans, oyster beds and market gardens. An unspoilt holiday village, Oualidia is built around a huge inlet which an eighteenth-century traveller estimated was large enough 'to contain 500 sail of the line'. Shipping cannot enter through the cleft in the rock wall where the Atlantic pours in and out with great ferocity. Swimming, fishing and wind-surfing are excellent. Boats may be hired. There is a Saturday *souq*.

Where to stay

There are a few simple hotels and a camp site.

L'Hippocampe; tel. 346499. Clean, cheap, basic rooms. Holiday atmosphere. You can potter about in your costume offending no one. *Fruits de mer* are a speciality. A melancholy sea-horse, or *hippocampe*, swims in a tank on the bar. Licensed.

Auberge de la Lagune (*A); tel. 346477. Village centre. Lacks the charm of L'Hippocampe, but has better food in the Restaurant d'Or. Seafood and oysters are specialities. Excellent *tartes au maison*. Small rooms.

Motel de l'Araignée Gourmande. A small motel on the lagoon which also serves seafood meals.

The coast between Oualidia and Cap Beddouza resembles the rugged west coast of Ireland. In winter it is often shrouded in sea mist; during April and May the clifftops are covered in wild flowers. Safe side-tracks lead down to glorious sandy beaches which are worth a detour. The fishing looks good. A modest roadside restaurant at Cap Beddouza serves plain fish dishes. The WC is filthy, but there is no alternative for miles. There are more stunning beaches between here and Safi (23 km). Camping is free. Fishermen will appear with the odd long-legged spider crab, but take with you everything else you may require, including water.

Safi

Safi and its white *medina* framed against the Atlantic – the exact shade of ultramarine – looks like an early Hockney. Most days, however, the view is obscured by haze, a mixture of sea-air and industrial pollution. Safi's population of 314,000 works mainly in the fertilizer complex and there are more than 100 sardine canneries. Local sardines are exported internationally. The ceramics industry is as old as Safi itself. A visit to the potteries followed by lunch at Le Refuge in Sidi Bouzid are the reasons to stop.

History

Safi's defences date from Portuguese occupation in 1508 (Lisbon had a consul there as early as 1450). When the Portuguese were obliged to withdraw from Agadir in 1541, they also pulled out of Safi. The last Portuguese garrison blew up the fort.

What to see

The most impressive sight is the sixteenth-century **Dar el-Bahr**, or *Château de la Mer*, which overlooks the port – the governor's residence during years of Portuguese occupation. Good views from the south-west bastion. Open Monday to Friday, 8 a.m. to 12 noon and 2 to 4 p.m.

The walled *medina* extending uphill from the waterfront encloses the *souqs* and *kechla*, or citadel, on the summit. Its huge crenellated towers are emblazoned with the royal Portuguese coat-of-arms. Near the Grand Mosque is a small chapel, once the choir-hall of a cathedral. The stone boss is engraved with the arms of the Holy See and the Bishopric of Safi; an episcopal mitre and the keys of St Peter can be discerned.

The **Place de l'Independence** is the social heart of Safi. The busy, crowded streets of the *Nouvelle Ville* hold no interest for tourists.

Potteries

Potters' kilns smoke among dozens of white shrines on the hillside outside Bab Chaabah. (In the Middle Ages, Safi was quite fanatical and before Jews could enter this or any other gate, they had to remove their shoes. If riding, they had to dismount and walk.) A centuries-old guild, Safi's potters work in rabbit-warren workshops by a stream that washes down the red clay. Much of their work has mass-market appeal, but the Safi salt glaze, blue on a white backdrop with yellow *entrelacs*, is attractive. The typical green-glazed Moroccan roof-tiles are made here. Ask a young apprentice to show you Ahmed Serghini's workshops above the pottery *souq*.

Where to stay

Safi is more of a lunch-stop between Essaouira and Casablanca, but there are several comfortable hotels.

Hotel Safir (★★★★A), Avenue Kerkouni; tel. 464299. A modern hotel in a quiet location, twenty minutes' walk downtown. All amenities.

Hôtel Atlantique (★★★★A), Rue Chaouki; tel. 462160. Questionable rating when compared to the Safir. Older-style with clean, basic rooms. Above the old town.

Hotel Assif (★★A), Avenue de la Liberté; tel. 462311. Fifty-two beds, spacious rooms.

Where to eat

One of Morocco's biggest fishing ports, Safi is renowned for its seafood. If you have a car, drive out to **Le Refuge** (tel. 464354) on the cliffs at Sidi Bouzid. Its menu features crab, lobster, prawns . . . Open for lunch. Recommended for the view of Safi. In town the **Restaurant Calypso** off the Place de l'Independence has a cheap three-course menu. All classified hotels have licensed restaurants. Cheap café-grills around the Rue du Socco.

Moving on

From Safi the P8 direct to Essaouira is an uninspiring journey of about three hours. There is a Saturday *souq* at Sept des Gzoula, 40 km south of Safi. There are several very important shrines to the Regrada saints, a tribe of Berber Christians who lived in the vicinity of Djebel Habid, accessible only by rough track. Glowering on the western horizon, Djebel Habid is an indication of the southern landscape: dark red soil, silvery-leaved olives, *thuya*, or gum sanderac, and the native *argan*, which only grows in the Souss region of Morocco. At Ounara, where you take the P10 to Essaouira, there is a beautiful avenue of gum-trees.

Essaouira

Essaouira is a splendid break between Casablanca and Agadir. If you are in Marrakesh, come up for the day – the 175-km road-journey is uninteresting, but Essaouira is worth it. Its dramatic coastal battlements and thriving wood-crafts industry are two reasons to visit. It also has some of the best seafood in Morocco. Occasionally you may find it crowded with tourist coaches from Marrakesh, but Essaouira wears its holiday hat with a rakish indifference. On a grey January morning its mood can be grim, as the Atlantic lashes its *sqala*, or battery, lined with Spanish cannons. Were it human, Essaouira might be a Scorpio: dramatic, romantic and seductive. It will not leave you unmoved.

History

Essaouira was named Mogador in ancient times after the off-shore islands still known as Mogador, from the Berber words *moga* or bull, and *or* or gold. They were visited by Phoenician sailors who may have called them 'Migdol'. Juba II founded a settlement here in order to extract the reddish-purple dye from a local mollusc – 'Tyrian purple' was a popular colour among the Roman élite. In the fifteenth century the Portuguese commanded a Merenid fortress but it fell to the Saadians before the demise of Agadir. The town you see today was planned by a French architect, Théodore Cornut, who was held captive by Sultan Sidi Mohammed

Ibn Abdullah in the mid-eighteenth century. The port prospered when Moulay Ismail moved the Jews from Agadir to develop trade with Europe.

Well-run and free of customs duties, Essaouira was handling half Morocco's exports by the nineteenth century. Among items listed from the 'Barbary port of Mogador, January–July 1806' were almonds, beeswax, skins, raisins, olive oil and gum sanderac; 5,536 lb of elephant teeth, 556 lb of ostrich feathers and 2,860 lb of wild thyme were shipped to European ports. Imports included 1,000 dozen razors, ninety-three silk handkerchiefs, 9,000 tapestry needles, 18,696 looking-glasses, 242 copper kettles and four cases of the Torah.

Isaac Disraeli, the father of the British prime minister Benjamin, was born in Essaouira. The town had four synagogues until the Jewish exodus in the 1950s. Today fishing and wood-carving are the most important occupations. A few tourists stay, but beachside holidays are spoilt by blustery Atlantic breezes. The average August temperature is 22°C (72°F).

Social

Although Essaouira women are without exception in purdah, the local attitude to tourists is friendly and relaxed. Women can wear shorts.

What to see

Begin sightseeing in the small but animated **port**, where gulls swoop over fishermen cleaning their catch. Its bastions date from 1769. The 'Marine Gate' leads into the **Place Moulay Hassan**, the social centre of Essaouira, lined with elegant old blue and white shuttered houses, and *café-terraces*. A grocer stocks every need. There is also a bookshop with day-old international newspapers. Any street to the left takes you to the *sqala*, or marine battlements; the seaward battery holds a line of Dutch cannon, throats rusting in the salty air. On the north bastion sniff the good sea air and descend the steps to the **wood-carvers' souq**, heralded by the sound of saws. Beneath the ramparts carpenters and young apprentices work blocks of *thuya*, and its rich, resinous smell fills the air. Artefacts can be bought direct from the craftsmen, who make anything from dice-sets to dining-tables. They also excel at marquetry, inlaying strips of silver, bone and mother-of-pearl. Essaouira-made objects are among the best buys in Morocco.

You will need a morning to explore the old *medina*. The central area surrounds the Rue Sidi Mohammed Ibn Abdullah. Some of the streets are actually tunnelled through the houses. Dark and not a little thrilling, they are perfectly safe.

The **Sidi Mohammed Ibn Abdullah Museum** is in a nineteenth-century palace used as a Town Hall during the French Protectorate. If you have seen the crafts museum in Tetouan or Rabat, you can miss it. Marquetry, costumes, jewellery and musical instruments. Open 8.30 a.m. to 12 noon and 2.30 to 6 p.m., closed Tuesdays; admission 3 dh.

Essaouira has several comfortable hotels.

Hôtel des Iles (★★★★A), Boulevard Mohammed V; tel. 472329. ONCF hotel convenient for the *medina*. Excellent beds. Pool, tennis, parking.

Hotel Tafouk (★★★A), Boulevard Mohammed V; tel. 472504/5. Forty pleasant rooms, pleasant staff. Bar-restaurant. Fair hike to town.

Villa Maroc (★★★B), 10 Rue Abdullah Ben Yaeine; tel. 473147. Moroccan houses converted to make a pleasant hotel. Twenty-two rooms.

Several clean, cheap hotels are located inside the *medina*. **The Hôtel des Remparts** is built into the walls overlooking the ocean. Ask for an outside room, which will have fresh, salty air flowing in the window. Interior ones are musty and claustrophobic. The **Smara** also overlooks the ocean above the wood-carvers' *souq*. Clean, simple rooms with rather soft beds. Popular with better-heeled backpackers is the **Hotel Sahara** (opposite the *medina*); clean rooms with bath. The **Auberge Tangaro**, P.O. Box 8, 8 km south of Essaouira, 500 m beyond Diabat, has clean, pleasant rooms. French-run, Saturday-night dances used to be held here for the French officers posted to Essaouira. Weekends may be crowded. Booking advised. Meals available but take all requirements. Beach, forty minutes' walk, has good surfing.

Seafood is the speciality in Essaouira. This is the place to try *couscous aux poissons*. **Chez Sam**, a delightful port restaurant, serves some of Morocco's best fish dishes (licensed, about 90 dh per head). Open lunch and dinner (tel. 473513). Stalls at the port end of the Place Moulay Hassan grill sardines which you eat sitting on the beaches. Beware of 'tourist traps' in the *medina*. The **Café l'Horloge** inside the clock-tower gate offers the chance to eat in a former synagogue. It is unlicensed, but the *patron*, Monsieur Kanane, will send a waiter out for wine. It may take a long while to arrive, but the décor is much more interesting than the food. Upstairs is the gallery where women used to pray. More expensive is the bar-restaurant **Chalet de la Plage**, on the waterfront, opposite the Hôtel des Iles. Or dine at the hotel itself if you are too tired to go out.

The Cape Sim sand dunes lie 14 km south of Essaouira, accessible only by *piste*, due to a broken bridge over the Oued Ksab. There is no road sign. Bear right beyond the village of Diabat and travel roughly 7 km. The track ends at a lookout. Take a picnic.

The coastline between Essaouira and Agadir is ruggedly beautiful, with mountains dropping to the sea. Tracks require four-wheel drive and there are no facilities. The P8 to Agadir skirts the western edge of the High Atlas. It is a twisting road, a four- or five-hour drive through colourless scenery. Simmou sells petrol and refreshments. Tamanar is a novel lunch-stop, with roadside cafés selling simmering *tajines*.

Choose a café with a fly-proof fridge. The Hôtel Etoile du Sud has rooms in an emergency. After Tamri (33 km), the P8 widens into a motorway following the coast to Agadir.

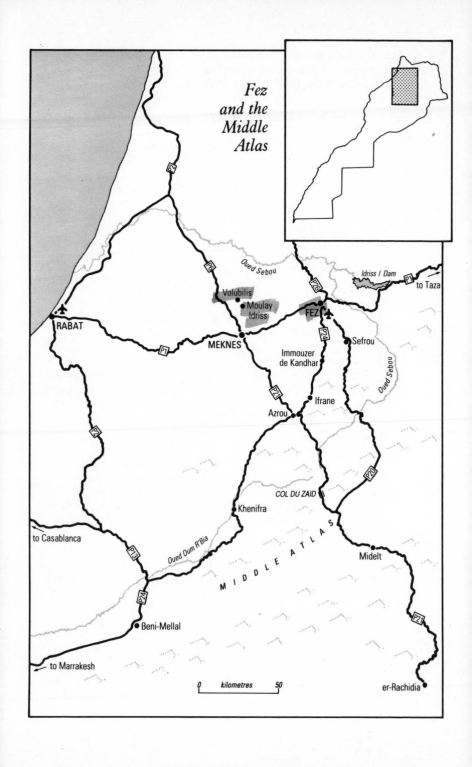

Fez
and the
Middle
Atlas

Fez and the Middle Atlas

Introduction

The heartland of Morocco is the Middle Atlas surrounding the imperial city of Fez. Arterial highways crossing at Azrou link the moist, green north with the parched brown south. The Tizi N'Talghemt, or Pass of the She-Camel, north of er-Rachidia, marks the dramatic transitional zone. It is a fresh, pastoral region of forests and lakes, where you can enjoy nature in peace, yet if you start a tour of the Middle Atlas in Fez or Volubilis, there are centuries of history to digest.

Package tours generally pass quickly through the Middle Atlas, which lacks large de-luxe hotels but has pleasant middle-range establishments for independent travellers. The region was popular during the French Protectorate: the chalets of Ifrane are copied from the Alps. Ifrane, Azrou and Mischliffen are popular winter-sports resorts. Snow occasionally closes roads from January to March. Secondary roads are generally good.

The two main approaches to the Middle Atlas are the P6 from the north and the P1 from Rabat. The P28 from Ouezzane (see p. 111) is a direct route for buses and *grands-taxis*. The journey to Fez from Rabat (136 km) on the P1 is of no interest. Khemisset is a partly industrialized town with a Tuesday carpet *souq*. The **Hotel Diouri** (**A) on the Meknes exit has clean lavatories and a restaurant with Vietnamese as well as French-Moroccan food. M'Haya, halfway between Meknes and Fez, consists of a long arcade of mechanics, café-grills, butchers and photocopier shops, typical of Moroccan roadside towns.

Meknes

In the centre of one of the richest farming areas in Morocco, the town of Meknes spreads over gentle hills, with the Oued Boufekrane running through the valleys. It was an important wine producing area during the French Protectorate and the tree-lined streets and café-bars of the *Nouvelle Ville* retain a Gallic feel. Meknes, however, is associated with a single man, Sultan Moulay Ismail (1672–1727), who ruled Morocco from the great city he built next to the *medina*.

Only 60 km west of Fez, Meknes is inevitably overshadowed by the older, more famous imperial capital, but it is an interesting town in its own right. When Fez is bursting at the seams with tourists, you can frequently find accommodation here. The town is a good base to explore Roman Volubilis and the holy village of Moulay Idriss, both less than an hour's drive by car. Allow two or three days for sightseeing. A guide is recommended to explain the lay-out of imperial Meknes.

History

The old Meknes, known as Mequinas, was settled by the Meknassa Berbers in the tenth century. A hill-top *kasbah* was repeatedly fought over by the various dynasties but the town did not become significant until Moulay Ismail, the second Alaouite sultan, elected to rule Morocco from here.

Moulay Ismail

Writers commonly dwell on Moulay Ismail's cruelty and megalomania, but his long period of rule should be judged in the context of the world at that time. Australia was yet to be discovered when the sultan, a compulsive builder, was laying roads, bridges and irrigation works throughout Morocco. He was a despot, but he was also the first sultan to contain the dissident *caids*. Backed by a loyal army, shrewdly balanced with Berber and Arab troops and his crack Abid regiment, he maintained absolute control. His success in routing Christian forces from Moroccan soil won further respect from potential enemies in their mountain *kasbahs*. His siege of Tangier in 1674 forced the British to withdraw and he liberated Asilah from the Spanish in 1691. The hard-working sultan also found time to father a vast progeny – some sources say 800 sons – but his failure to prepare a suitable successor exposed Morocco to renewed anarchy.

What to see

Today Meknes consists of three towns: Moulay Ismail's Imperial City, the old *medina* and the *Nouvelle Ville* built by the French. From Route P1 you are confronted by an apparently endless *enceinte* – not the dramatic red ramparts of Essaouira, but an intimidating, buff-coloured wall which seems to imprison the town. The Place Hedim, outside Bab el-Mansour, the ceremonial entrance to the Imperial City, is the best spot to get your bearings. Once a square for itinerant entertainers, it is now remodelled with bazaar-type shops.

Bab el-Mansour

Almohad in the concept of its design, this ponderous ceremonial gateway was designed by a Christian convert to Islam, Aleuj el-Mansour. When Moulay Ismail enquired whether the architect thought he could design a better gate, he was summarily executed for replying in the affirmative. No longer covered by lustrous *zellij* tilework, the Bab el-Mansour today seems rather large for the amount of decoration. But big was beautiful to Moulay Ismail. Everything in his Imperial City is built larger than life: gates, walls, store-houses, barracks, and stables for 12,000 horses. The bastions flanking Bab el-Mansour sit on marble columns which were dragged over the hills from Volubilis by a vast slave-army, including many hostages captured at sea by the Bou Regreg corsairs.

Imperial City   Inside is a parade ground, where the sultan used to inspect his famous Abid regiment, a force of 140,000 negro bodyguards. The angular building of the **Koubat al-Khayattine**, with a glazed green tile roof, is seen at the far end of a second square laid to grass. Here foreign ambassadors presented their credentials to the Alaouite court; in the audience-hall Moulay Ismail received them seated on a throne. Beside the Koubat al-Khayattine is an entrance to a series of vaulted, subterranean storerooms, which guides misleadingly call the Christian slave-prison. It is unlikely that it was a jail; the shafts you can see in the lawn were probably chutes for tipping grain into the silos. The vaults may be visited for a small sum. The *guardian*, apparently asleep under a rose-bush, has a loud voice, should you go down without paying.

Moulay Ismail's **mausoleum** is on the left, beyond the double gate. Restored in 1959, it is open to non-Muslims whom the guards consider to be correctly dressed – it is not unusual to see a scantily clad little figure waiting outside for 'the group'. In the tiled inner sanctum an eighteenth-century sundial still tells the time as accurately as a Swiss watch. The sultan's tomb is flanked by two clocks presented by Louis XIV. Touching the sarcophagus is believed to bring the *baraka*, or blessing, a Berber word that has been assimilated into colloquial French. It is barred to tourists.

Inspired by tales of the French court at Versailles, Moulay Ismail built a Moroccan equivalent: the **Dar el-Kebira** consists of twenty-four palaces and pavilions interlaced with gardens and streams. Completed in 1677, it so appealed to the sultan's ego that he sent a message to Louis XIV inviting him to send one of his daughters to join his harem. An eighteenth-century European traveller, having obtained permission to view the Dar el-Kebira, wrote that the 'horem' (sic) had two large apartments surrounded by galleries, 'the largest of which are appropriated to the women (the smaller rooms being for the eunuchs and female attendants) . . . built on a causeway which divides the gardens. Here the females look through the iron latticed windows, and take the air, which, in the summer, is perfumed with the smell of violets, jasmines, roses, wild thyme, and other delectable odours.' He speaks of other long and lofty rooms with ceilings 6 m high, of walls inlaid with coloured tiles, and courtyards paved in black and white marble. Today, the Dar el-Kebira is a confusing network of ruins.

The **'Strangee'** is a walled corridor, some 3 km long, connecting the mausoleum and the Aguedal Gardens, which reflects a penchant for privacy verging on paranoia. Now tarred and paved, in Moulay Ismail's time it was shaded by trees and he used to ride along it in a chariot pulled by eunuchs. He even considered building an extension to Marrakesh (700 km), saying, in an unusually humane moment, that it would help the blind find their way. The great walled corridor is probably the *'strangee'* referred to by visitors to eighteenth-century Mequinas. It should be auctioned at Sotheby's, or exhibited at the World Fair.

The long walk between the walls brings you to the **Heri es-Suani**, a massive store-house standing on the edge of the Aguedal Basin. Four hectares long and four metres deep, the Aguedal Basin doubled as a reservoir for the sultan's gardens and a boating-lake for his court, which included 500 concubines. From the 'hanging gardens' you can see the **Dar el-Makhzen**, an eighteenth-century palace built by Moulay Ismail, now the royal residence in Meknes.

Adjacent is the battlemented quarter of **Heri el-Mansour**, with the ruins of the *rouah*, or royal stables. Covering 6 km, the complex once stabled 12,000 horses used on the great *harkas*, or marches. Horses which made the pilgrimage to Mecca and back were accorded special privileges and buried wrapped in shrouds.

Medina

The *medina* follows the traditional pattern of monuments and markets built around the **Grand Mosque**, which dates from the tenth century.

Opposite the Grand Mosque, the **Bou Inania *Medrassa***, built in the 1350s, is a smaller, less elaborate version of the celebrated college in Fez. A lofty courtyard paved in black and white marble surrounds an ablutions tank. Decorative materials include bands of stucco-work, *zellij* tiles and carved cedar-wood. The wooden screens between the students' cells are beautifully carved. One can imagine them walking around the gallery memorizing passages from the Qur'an; the classic Arabic of Mecca must have been difficult for Berbers to learn. The *Medrassa* gives a roof-top view of the *medina*.

A nineteenth-century Moorish-style palace with Andalusian garden, the **Dar Jamai** was built by the Jamai brothers, who owned the Palais Jamai in Fez. It is now a museum exhibiting ceramics, weapons, Berber crafts and carpets. Open daily 9 a.m. to 12 noon and 3 to 6 p.m., closed Tuesdays. The entrance is off the Place el-Hedim.

A street behind the museum leads to the *kissaria*, or covered market of seven different *souqs*. *Souq es-Sebat* is an up-market place for clothes and shoes. The *babouches* are replaced by thousands of gym-shoes slowly spinning on their laces. Wanting to buy a pair when my own shoes got wet, I found I needed a sense of humour. One salesman, unable to find a matching pair of size 39, insisted that size 42 was the same. Another lad valiantly tried to sell me two left feet rather than lose a sale. Feeling like Alice on a shopping expedition with the Red Queen, I finally bought some in Fez. *Souq Nejjarine* is lined with carpenters and metal-workers; Rue des Serairia is the blacksmiths' *souq*, with key-cutters and knife-grinders; saddlers and weavers work in *Souq Bezzarin*, while the dyers' street is behind the Sebbarine Mosque. A stroll round the *souqs* takes an hour or two – more if you are buying gym-shoes.

The *mellah* is downhill from the Place el-Hedim. A large Jewish community lived in Meknes under Moulay Ismail, whose own financier was a Jewish accountant. Tailors and textile shops line the Avenue du Mellah.

The shrine of **Sidi Mohammed Ibn Aissa**, one of Morocco's truly fanatic *sufis*, is in the large cemetery near Bab el-Jedid. His doctrines were as darkly mysterious as the saint himself, who used to eat prickly pears and scorpions, possibly to illustrate his indifference towards material pleasures. Sidi Mohammed Ibn Aissa died in the 1520s, but membership of the Aissa brotherhood continues to grow. Members meet at the tomb on Friday afternoons. Some work themselves into a trance through dance; others scrabble among the headstones for scorpions. It is emphasized that such cults, similar to customs practised by Hindu fakirs, have no place in Islam. You should visit the cemetery with some caution.

Nouvelle Ville

The *Nouvelle Ville* is on the eastern bank of the Oued Boufekrane. It is an animated place with tree-lined streets and café-restaurants where young men and women openly congregate.

Where to stay

Meknes has a good choice of middle-range hotels, almost all in the *Nouvelle Ville*.

Transatlantique (*****A), Rue el-Meriniyine; tel. 525050. Fine old ONCF hotel with 240 beds. Quiet location, but inconvenient without a car (15 minutes by taxi to the medina). Pleasant gardens. Large swimming-pool. Recommended.

Zaki (****A), Boulevard el-Massira; tel. 520990. Modern, tourist-style hotel geared to groups, with 163 rooms overlooking the swimming-pool. Outside the walls near the Aviation School. Quiet. Parking.

Rif (****A), Zankat Accra; tel. 522591. Modern Moorish-style décor and 120 comfortable rooms. Centre of the *Nouvelle Ville*. Groups.

Hotel Bab Mansour (***A), 38 Rue Emir Abdelkadir; tel. 525239. Next to the Regent Cinema in the *Nouvelle Ville*.

Hotel Palace (**A), 11 Kenkat Ghana; tel. 525777. Sixty beds. Pleasant reception. Clean rooms, but soft beds. Popular bar. Centre of the *Nouvelle Ville*.

Hotel Majestic (**A), 19 Avenue Mohammed V; tel. 522035. Pleasant old-style hotel in the centre of the *Nouvelle Ville*. Clean rooms, with central-heating. Most with shower. Recommended.

Hotel Continental (**B), 92 Avenue des FAR; tel. 525471. Once grand, with forty-nine beds. Hot water. Near centre of the *Nouvelle Ville* and CTM bus station.

Hotel Excelsior (*A), 57 Avenue des FAR; tel. 521900. Thirty-nine beds. Pleasant reception. Large, clean rooms. Hot water in the morning. Horrible paintings. Centre of the *Nouvelle Ville*.

Where to eat

Local cooking resembles Fassi cuisine. Some Meknassi dishes are *tajine t'faya*, made with meat, eggs and hazelnuts, and *djaja taret* – chicken with chick peas and raisins. *Couscous au lait* is popular. The aromatic mint-tea is considered the best in Morocco. There is a good choice of restaurants in the *Nouvelle Ville*.

Transatlantique Hotel. French and Moroccan cuisine in civilised surroundings. Cocktail-bar.

Le Dauphin. Moroccan and seafood. Licensed. Excellent reputation.

Café-Restaurant Camprinos. French, Spanish and Moroccan menu. Licensed. Lunch-time groups.

Brasserie Métropole. Cheap three-course menu. Licensed. Pleasant ambience.

La Cupole. Bistro-style with an international menu. Licensed.

Restaurant Zitouna. Near Bab Tizimi, the north gate of the *medina*. Moroccan cuisine in a refurbished palace.

Café-grills are found around Bab Berrima and Bab el-Jedid. These are cheap but insalubrious cafés outside the Bab el-Mansour.

What to do

Meknes has an unusual number of bars. The **Roi de la Bière**, **Du Trésor** and **Jour et Nuit** are on the Boulevard Mohammed V. The **Bar American** and the **Bar Vox Brasserie** are on the Avenue Hassan II. **La Caravelle** at 6 Rue de Marseilles is a nice spot. Of the hotels, the **Transatlantique** is the most elegant place for an aperitif. The bar in the Hotel de Nice is popular. **The Bahia Nightclub** in the Rif Hotel has a cabaret at 8 p.m. **Cabaret Oriental** is a local-style nightclub on the Avenue des FAR, with live bands until 3 a.m. Make the most of Meknes by night: you will not find such variety elsewhere in the Middle Atlas.

Useful information

Royal Air Maroc, Avenue Mohammed V, tel. 20963.

Wagon-Lits, 1 Rue du Ghana, tel. 21995.

Banks, Avenue Mohammed V and Avenue des FAR.

PTT, Place de France.

ONMT, Place Administrative, tel. 21286.

All-night pharmacy, next to the Hotel de Ville (Place Administrative).

Moving on

The bus and taxi **station** is near Bab el-Khemmis. The main railway station is on the Avenue de la Basse, about 1 km outside the *Nouvelle Ville*. Frequent trains in all directions. The CTM **bus station** is at 47 Avenue Mohammed V. Shuttle buses 5, 7 and 9 between the *Nouvelle Ville* and the *medina*. There is a **taxi** rank below the Place el-Hedim.

Two interesting sites are within easy reach of Meknes.

Moulay Idriss

The holy city of Moulay Idriss (24 km) is worth a visit if combined with Volubilis. Christians and Jews were forbidden entry to the city until 1912, and entry to the mausoleum of Moulay Idriss is still rigorously forbidden.

History   A *shorfa*, or descendant of the Prophet, Moulay Idriss came to Morocco in AD 786 to escape the religious schisms in Iraq. Accompanied by his servant Rachid, he settled in Volubilis, but perhaps finding the site too exposed, moved to Moulay Idriss. The Berbers welcomed him as their *imam*, or leader. When news of his achievements filtered back to Baghdad in 791 he was poisoned on orders of the Caliph Harun al-Rachid, but one of his Berber concubines gave birth posthumously to Moulay Idriss II (791–828), the founder of Fez.

What to see   Moulay Idriss jumps into view round the final bend from Meknes. Built in a cradle in the Zerhoun mountains, its houses cluster around the white mosque and mausoleum with their distinctive shiny green-tile roofs. A curious mixture of nougat, reed plates, flags and religious trinkets is sold in a long dark hallway leading into the sanctuary. It is reminiscent of religious markets in Pakistan, or the Philippines. A wooden rail at the end of the hall prevents non-Muslims from proceeding any further. There is a good view of the secret sanctuary from the hillside terrace of Sidi Abdellah el-Hajjim, left, about 140 steps' climb.

Where to eat   Western travellers do not normally stay in Moulay Idriss, which has only rough lodgings for pilgrims (the *moussem* is in September). Cafés sell *brochettes*, doughnuts, dates and figs, but I was left with an overwhelming impression of huge blocks of sticky nougat. I ate almond and strawberry nougat, pistachio and banana nougat, until my jaw ached. If you require sustenance, half-way up the hill the **Restaurant el-Baraka**, 22 Ain Smen-Khiber, is a modern house converted into a clean restaurant. Tasty main course dishes cost from 50 dh. Unlicensed.

Volubilis   Volubilis is 5 km from Moulay Idriss, off the road to Ouezzane. Less dramatic, perhaps, than Roman cities in the Middle East, it is a picturesque site of classic Roman houses peopled by civilized ghosts.

History   Built on a plateau in the Zerhoun massif, Volubilis was the old Berber capital of Mauritania-Tingitana. Brought under direct Roman rule in AD 45, it became a base-camp for punitive expeditions against dissident tribes. At its peak, the walled city topped with forty bastions enclosed a population of 20,000. When the Romans withdrew at the end of the third century, they left an eloquent testimony of their lifestyle. Volubilis flickered into life again with the arrival of Moulay Idriss c. AD 788, but its light went out permanently after he moved.

What to see   Volubilis is open daily, 8 a.m. until dusk. The complex has a café and clean WCs. A museum displays statues and Roman fragments. Guides are available.

Begin the tour by crossing the stream on the left and climbing the hill. Note the ruins of ancient olive-oil presses.

House of Orpheus. The large mansion in the southern quarter of Volubilis is named, like most houses, after its main mosaic. Note the central-heating system and the niches in the kitchen for oil-lamps. The mosaic in the central atrium shows Amphitrite, the wife of Poseidon, in a chariot pulled by a sea-horse. The large mosaic in the dining-room depicts Orpheus plucking a harp watched by a number of docile creatures.

Baths of Gallienus. Remains of a large *hammam* restored in the third century by the Emperor Gallienus.

Forum. The path now heads towards the former forum, the capitol and basilica.

Capitol. The temple is dedicated to a trinity of gods – Jupiter, Juno and Minerva. The inscription is to the Emperor Macrinus, AD 217.

Basilica. The Roman court-house has various inscriptions to magistrates on the front plinth.

House of the Athlete. This contains a mosaic depicting an athlete with a cup. The bronze dog in the Rabat Archaeological Museum was discovered near here. Roughly opposite is the remains of a public fountain and aqueduct.

Triumphal Arch. The ceremonial gateway to the great Decumanus Maximus. It is dedicated to the Emperor Caracalla and his mother Julia, whose defaced medallion is vaguely discernible. In AD 217 the arch was topped by a chariot pulled by six bronze horses.

Decumanus Maximus. The 'Champs-Elysées' of Volubilis. Once flanked by great Corinthian columns, this runs as straight as a Roman javelin to the Tangier Gate. It used to be lined with the smartest shops and houses.

House of the Ephebos. With the posh address of 1 Decumanus Maximus, this is a classic Roman house. A mosaic shows Bacchus in a chariot pulled by panthers which were plentiful in the Zerhoun forests during Roman times.

House of the Labours of Hercules. This is named after the series of mosaic panels depicting the twelve labours assigned to the popular god of Greek mythology. Most of the finest mosaics in Volubilis date from AD 193 to 235.

House of the Bathing Nymphs. This contains a mosaic showing the three maidens disporting themselves by the Hippocrene spring.

House of the Venus Cortège. Number 3 on the south side of the Decumanus Maximus has some wonderfully fluid mosaics, including Diana, Goddess of the Hunt, surprised by Acteon in her bath, and the acclaimed mosaic of a naked Hylos being carried off by the water nymphs.

If you can identify these buildings you will have done well. Allow about two hours. The mosaics are undoubtedly the main attraction of Volubilis, but I couldn't help wondering whether they wouldn't be better off in a museum. At present they are exposed to water, fungus and the occasional tourist's shoe. There is a good panorama from the hillside. Go early.

Fez

To visit Morocco without seeing Fez is like playing cricket without stumps. Built in a bowl of hills, it is the gem of the Middle Atlas; some might say the jewel in the imperial crown of Morocco. Of the imperial cities, Marrakesh is better known abroad, but Fez has made no concessions to tourism. Apart from electricity, it is a pristine medieval town, whose *medina*, known as Fez el-Bali, is a World Heritage Site. If you have to choose between the two cities, see Fez. Marrakesh is for the hedonistic traveller who likes to see a monument and lie by the swimming-pool. Fez makes you work. Its treasures are concealed in an enigmatic maze filled with haunting images of a past civilization, and exploring can be intimidating for anyone unfamiliar with a Moroccan *medina*. You are assailed by hucksters, insulted by *faux-guides*, and the single utterance, 'Allah,' spoken over and over by the blind, rings in your ears long after you have unscrambled the way out. Fez el-Bali is a full-scale assault on your senses – the smell of the tanneries will never leave your nose – but it is your last ticket on a journey to the 'thousand and one nights'.

Fassi character   Observant travellers will notice the difference between Fassis and other Moroccans. Fez has been a melting-pot for generations of Berbers mingled with Arabs, Moors born in Andalusia, and Islamized Jews. There are hundreds of old Fassi families who are descended from Jewish converts to Islam. Your prototype Fassi has paler skin than the average Moroccan Arab, and his hands are finely tapered. A thoughtful conversationalist, he is an equally good listener and meticulously well-mannered. Socially he is imbued with an appreciation of Hispano-Moorish culture, finding the desert lifestyle as alien as any foreigner. Upper-class Fassis, mainly of Andalusian ancestry, are very houseproud and there are hundreds of superb old Moorish mansions hidden in the *medina*. Adventurous in commerce, the Fassi's success in business is matched by a desire to educate the children well and to dress his wife smartly so she mirrors his generosity. While beautiful and intelligent, the average Fassia still knows her place, although Moroccan-style liberalism has crept in in some quarters – I did meet one young couple who were 'living in sin'.

Main areas   Fez is effectively three towns within a city of more than half a million inhabitants. **Fez el-Bali**, the original Idrissid settlement, dates from the end of the eighth century. It covers the bottom of the basin bisected by the Oued Fez, with the Andalus Quarter on one bank and the Kairouan Quarter on the other. Counting the town's oldest mosques and houses, Fez el-Bali is at the heart of UNESCO's preservation order. It contains the major crafts area and *souqs*. **Fez el-Jdid** is the royal town constructed around the rim of the bowl in the thirteenth century. The ***Nouvelle Ville*** is the French-built new town, set back on a hill-top, about two minutes' drive west of Fez el-Jdid and a further ten minutes from Fez el-Bali.

Guides

The best way to get your bearings is from the hill overlooking Fez el-Bali. Bordj Nord, the Saadian fort, is a good vantage point. There is an even better view higher up, from the Merenid tombs, where child-gangs prey on visitors. The lads apparently studying under the trees, or sitting casually with an open book on the wall, are not students, but *faux-guides*. You will need a companion in Fez, not just to show you around, but to protect you from the unemployed – all of whom want to be your guide. There are 214 official guides working for the Tourist Office, so you do not have to use one of these young men, but many official guides bore with their bland resumés of the city's history. Official or not, everyone will lead you a merry dance through the shops, where handsome commissions are made, so take as much care in choosing your guide as you would a fine Berber carpet. Have mint-tea with him, determine his command of French, or English, win his confidence. You can endeavour to ferret out Fez's secrets with a guide-book, but without a guide you are lost. And even with an apparently willing guide, you will still be left with the impression he could have shown you that much more.

History

Fez was founded at roughly the same time that Scheherazade was spinning her tales of 'a thousand and one nights' to the Abbassid caliphs in Baghdad, but it is Fez, not the Iraqi capital, that remains the perfect example of that exotic era.

At the beginning of the ninth century, when the young Idriss II became king he moved his court to a site by the Oued Fez where his father had planned to establish a new capital. As building started on the city, there was an influx of Moorish refugees escaping from the turbulent politics of Spain. They were welcomed by the sultan and settled into what became known as 'Adwat al-Andalus' (the Andalusian Quarter), on the east bank of the river. Their impact on local society is still evident: the haunting *ala* lament has its origins in Andalusia; crafts such as metalwork, leatherware and wood-carving are also traditionally Spanish. In 925 another group of refugees arrived – fleeing from religious persecution in the holy city of Kairouan, in present-day Tunisia. They settled on the opposite bank of the Oued Fez; the Kairouine Mosque was financed by a wealthy Arab woman from Tunisia. The knowledge and talents of these two Muslim communities in their separate walled towns made Fez a thriving city.

Successive Berber dynasties, the Almoravids and the Almohads moved the seat of government to Marrakesh and Fez did not regain its former importance until the Merenids began to rule from there in 1248. Abou Yussef Yaccoub (1258–86), the second Merenid sultan, began the construction of an entirely new town, 'Fez el-Jdid', enclosed by double walls, outside the old *medina*. Fez el-Jdid became a self-sufficient community within Fez, with its palace, three mosques, a mint, barracks, markets and moated gardens. The wealthy Jewish community that controlled local commerce was resettled in the *mellah*, within the protection of the royal enclosure. But Fez el-Bali was not forgotten; the Merenids enlarged the Kairouine Mosque, and in a fervour of religious building constructed other smaller mosques and the magnificent *medersa*, or religious colleges, for the thousands of students coming to study in Fez. At the height of its Golden Age (from the tenth to the fifteenth centuries), Fez was the most advanced centre of learning for mathematics, philosophy and science in the medieval world. There were hospitals, hotels or *funduqs*, more than eighty fountains, ninety-three *hammams*, and the trades and crafts were well organized into 150 corporations. Each syndicate had a patron saint. It is tenth-century Fez, enfeebled by age, and also, it must be said, by neglect, which is the attraction for the modern visitor.

Fez lost its international status when the Saadi dynasty moved the capital back to Marrakesh. Apart from building the shrine to Moulay Idriss, they made few contributions to the celebrated city. In 1672 Moulay Ismail imposed high taxes to finance his building projects in Meknes. The Great Plague which ravaged Morocco in 1799 claimed between 1,200 and 1,500 lives in Fez, where it is thought to have started.

The decline of Fez was not checked until the reign of the Alaouite Sultan Moulay Hassan (1873–94), but local power was again eroded when Moulay Hafid was forced to sign the Treaty of Fez – *carte blanche* for the French Protectorate – on 30 March 1912.

Under French occupation, Fez enjoyed relative prosperity from crafts and commerce, but it lost its political importance with the decision to govern Morocco from Rabat and its economic significance with the exodus of wealthy Fassi Jews at Independence.

Today Fez waits for an elixir. No amount of aid can save the *medina* unless restoration speeds up. But what has priority in a town where eleventh-century bridges span speedily flowing canals filled with twentieth-century refuse? What can one do with inhabitants, many of whom can trace connections back to Andalusia, whose families have occupied the same house for generations? Which house do you choose when every one is a museum piece?

What to see

Fez el-Bali

An early description of Fez el-Bali comes from a nineteenth-century travelogue written by James Grey Jackson: *Empire of Morocco*, published by the Philadelphia Press in 1810:

'The houses have flat roofs ingeniously worked in wood, and covered with terrace, on which the inhabitants spread carpets in summer, to recline upon, and enjoy the cool breezes of evening. A small turret . . . is erected upon the roofs, for the use of the females of the family, who resort thither for amusement and pastime. In the centre of each house is an open quadrangle surrounded by a gallery, which communicates with the staircase, and into which the doors of the different apartments

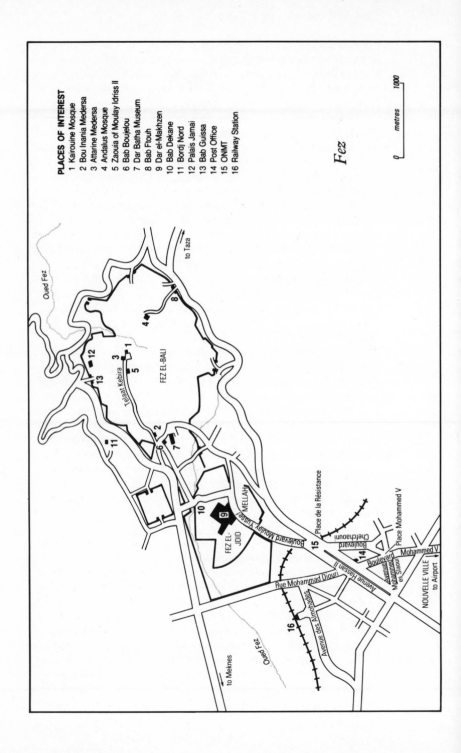

PLACES OF INTEREST

1 Kairouine Mosque
2 Bou Inania Medersa
3 Attarine Medersa
4 Andalus Mosque
5 Zaouia of Moulay Idriss II
6 Bab Boujelou
7 Dar Batha Museum
8 Bab Ftouh
9 Dar el-Makhzen
10 Bab Dekane
11 Bordj Nord
12 Palais Jamai
13 Bab Guissa
14 Post Office
15 ONMT
16 Railway Station

Fez

0   metres   1000

open. These doors are both wide and lofty, and are made of curiously carved wood painted in various colours. The beams of the roofs of the different apartments are whimsically painted with gay colours in the arabesque style . . . The principal houses have cisterns under them containing water used in the baths, which are built of marble or stone.'

The scene has little changed. Old houses and *funduqs*, or former hotels, still line the Telaat Kebira, which becomes more congested as you penetrate the *medina*. *'Balek!'* ('Watch out!') cry porters of the hereditary Guia Valley Porters' Guild. Many of their animals carry crippling loads of planks and port-a-gas cylinders. The delivery vans of Fez, they are born in the harness and will die in the harness, as donkeys and mules in Fez have done for the past 1,500 years. The streets in Fez el-Bali were measured by the width of a loaded donkey.

The best way to tackle Fez el-Bali is to tell your guide what you wish to see from the following brief. Wear comfortable shoes and pack a bandaid and an aspirin – Fez is strenuous sightseeing. To fully understand it, you need to be Fassi.

The heart of Fassi and indeed Moroccan culture is the great **Kairouine Mosque**, entirely surrounded by *souqs*. Built in AD 859 as a gift to the city from a pious but wealthy Tunisian woman refugee, Fatma bint Mohammed Ibn Feheri, it was further embellished in the tenth century and extensions by the Almoravids in the twelfth century brought it to its present size. Based on a T-plan, the Kairouine has sixteen aisles and fourteen doors; within the vast open courtyard 20,000 can worship simultaneously. It is sad one cannot enter, but it is better to keep it for worship rather than allow its worshippers to become a tourist attraction. You have a glimpse of its interior through huge bronze doors. Treasures include an ivory-inlaid cedar-wood *minbar*, or pulpit, from Cordoba. Much of the stucco-work in the central court is in mint condition, having been uncovered during recent restoration work. There is a view of the mosque from the roof-top of the nearby Attarine Medrassa. Another, even better, is had from the top of the Tetouani Funduq.

At the south-east corner of the mosque is the Place Seffarine, shaded by an ancient fig-tree. A simple door in the wall leads into the celebrated **Kairouine Library**, which has one of the greatest collections of Islamic and scholarly books in the world. Its 30,000 volumes, including a ninth-century Qur'an, were brought to Fez by Arab refugees from Kairouan. The university, one of the four oldest in the world (with Zabid in North Yemen, Damascus, and al-Ahzar in Cairo), evolved in a similar way to Christian universities and cathedral schools. Learned men like Ibn Khaldoun and the well-travelled Leo Africanus and Ibn Battuta studied there. The Kairouine remained the principal source of higher education in Morocco until the mid-1960s, when degree courses were transferred to a new university in Fez and elsewhere. Students still attend courses in *sharia*, or Islamic law, at

Kairouine University, which is for men only.

The great **Bou Inania** *Medrassa* in Fez is considered the best expression of Hispano-Mauresque architecture in Morocco. Built by Sultan Abou Inan (1351–8), it outshines all others in the sheer exuberance of decoration. A domed, stucco-work chamber leads into a spacious central courtyard paved in marble. You have a glimpse of the prayer-hall beyond a charming moated section of the Oued Fez. Do not miss going upstairs to the students' cells, separated by exquisitely carved cedar screens. The *kufic* inscriptions contain verses from the Qur'an, and also lists the properties in Fez that donated money to the great college – rather like the brass acknowledgement plaques on the walls of a church. Questioned by fourteenth-century scribes about the inordinate cost of constructing the *medrassa*, Sultan Abou Inan is reported to have said: 'What is beautiful cannot be too expensive at any price: what is enthralling is never too costly.'

Some restorations have been made to the woodwork, but otherwise the *medrassa* is in perfect condition. Open 8 a.m. to 6 p.m., closed Fridays and Tuesday morning; admission 3 dh.

The **Attarine** *Medrassa*, in the heart of the *souqs*, is notable among half a dozen other colleges built by the Merenids. Dating from 1322–5, it is not grand like the Bou Inania, but its craftsmanship is no less exquisite. The design is classic: a central ablutions area, a prayer-hall and an upstairs residential quarter for about sixty students. The ceiling in the prayer-hall from which hangs a huge bronze chandelier is considered a masterpiece of wood-carving. Note the monumental brass doors carved with the interlacing rosettes and geometric motifs typical of Islam.

The **es-Seffarine** *Medrassa* is the oldest in Morocco. It was built in 1280 by Sultan Abou Yussef Yaccoub, the founder of Fez el-Jidid. It is designed like a Fassi house where the professors lectured students when they could not get into the mosque. It has been greatly restored, but retains its historic character.

The **es-Sehrij** *Medrassa*, near the Andalus Mosque, was built by Sultan Abou Hassan, who also commissioned the colleges in Taza, Meknes and Salé. It is noted for its wealth of richly carved cedar-wood. A marble ablutions basin reflects the surrounding galleries and pillars.

These three *medersa* are open to the public between 8 a.m. to 6 p.m., except on Fridays, prayer-day; admission 3 dh.

Surrounded by a network of lanes near Souq Attarine is the *horm*, or sanctuary precinct around the *zaouia*, or **shrine of Moulay Idriss II**. When the Merinids opened his coffin in 1308 his corpse was found to be intact and a cult was launched, the devotees being mainly women. Non-Muslims may not enter the shrine, but you can glimpse the velvet-draped sarcophagus through the women's entrance. It is a mystical sight, heightened by flickering candles and the pungent aroma of burning incense. The rows of clocks are a surprise. Sundials were used to record the prayer-times, but European clocks were prestigious acquisitions among wealthy Fassi merchant families. The *zaouia* was rebuilt in the eighteenth century. A lane to the left of the women's entrance – the Bab Moulay Ismail – is lined with stalls selling votive offerings, more Catholic than Muslim.

An interesting walk that will give you a feel of Fez begins at **Bab Boujeloud**. Built only in 1913, Bab Boujeloud is an attractive, triple-arched structure with blue and gold *entrelac* patterns on its exterior façade. The minaret of the Sidi Lezzaz Mosque framed by the central arch is one of the most popular photographs in Morocco. Photography is difficult in alternate patches of light and shade in the *medina*. Inside the road forks. Either way will eventuaiiy bring you to the Kairouine Mosque, but **Talaat Kebira** is the more interesting route.

A forerunner of modern walkways, the overhead bridge dates from the twelfth century. High up on the left wall is a curious fourteenth-century **water-clock** where water used to drop out of thirteen windows into brass bowls. Seven are original but the clock is beyond repair. My guide attributed its dilapidated state to a Jewess who once passed below. Opposite the clock is a complex of ancient latrines with an ornate stucco ceiling. I caused a sensation by going in to look – public latrines being exclusively male.

On the left, before the Talaat Kebira changes to the Rue Cherabliyyin, is one of the oldest **hammams** in Fez. In the sixteenth century Leo Africanus noted that there were 100 in the city. Other public baths are scattered throughout the *medina*. The bathing times were segregated in the past, as now. When it was the women's turn, a rope was suspended from the first-floor balcony as a signal to proceed no further.

On the left as you walk down the Talaat Kebira you will see a big *funduq*, now a wholesale butter and honey market. *Funduqs*, or hostels, were built around a courtyard where travellers could hobble their horses. Some of the large *funduqs* had three storeys with as many as 100 rooms. Most of the 200 or so old *funduqs* in sixteenth-century Fez now serve as shops and warehouses. One is occupied by drum-makers and another, on the left, is the *Funduq* **el-Laine**, where mules bring loads of fresh sheepskins for stripping before going to the tanneries – if you cannot stand the smell here, strike the tanneries off your list of sights. Few of the *funduqs* have any lasting architectural interest, but the eighteenth-century *Funduq* **en-Nejjarine**, an elabo-rately decorated, tall building with a splendid entrance on the Place Nejjarine, is an exception. Ask your guide to point it out, as the eye is usually drawn to the mosaic-tiled drinking fountain.

Souqs

The Cherabliyyin Mosque, or 'Slipper-Maker' Mosque, marks the beginning of the *Souq* **Ain Allou**, dominated by leatherworkers. As well as shops selling *babouches*, there are second-hand shoe-stalls where the poor come to haggle over footwear. A sign on an arch reads

Souq **el-Attarine** (spice-market), where the scent of coriander makes you sneeze. A right turn before the arch brings you into *Souq* **el-Henna**. In a shaded square, the stalls sell sacks of henna leaves, pots of henna paste and other beauty products: tiny glass phials of anti-mony; herb and olive-oil mixtures for making facial masks; *souak*, or bark, toothbrushes; *jaoui*, a resin-like substance burned to perfume the house against the *djinn*; and creamy blocks of musk from the glands of the male deer. Aphrodisiacs are also sold. The square is overlooked by a Merenid lunatic asylum. Originally it was the Sidi Freq Sanctuary, where sick storks were looked after and a decent interment arranged for these holy birds.

The **Kissaria** on the arterial crossroads in the *medina* is rather characterless, having been rebuilt after a fire. Most of its shops stock textiles – an entire block is devoted to nothing but thread. Other places sell religious *objets d'art*: mirrors painted with verses from the Qur'an, tapestries embroidered with the sacred *ka'aba*, worry-beads, silver necklaces with miniature copies of the holy book and gold-embossed book binders. You will never see a picture of the Prophet, as his representation is strictly forbidden, whereas portraits of King Hassan are displayed everywhere.

Prowling around the Kairouine Mosque you will pass most of the other *souqs* – selling gold and silver jewellery, ornamental metalware, furniture, woven goods. In Merenid times, the artisans in Fez el-Bali were highly organized: there were 20,000 registered weavers, while strippers, scourers, dyers, harness-makers, saddlers and so on be-longed to a leatherware syndicate.

Each trade, or craft, has its quarter, allotted to it centuries ago by a *mutasib*, or prefect. There are wax chandlers, knife-grinders, station-ers and scribes, cabinet-makers and perfume-blenders. Foodstalls are also segregated: fruits here, vegetables there, a part for stalls which fry meat, another where people make a type of light dough known as *sfinge*, fried in oil and eaten with honey. Friendly shop-keepers invite you to dip your fingers in honey, to try bits of cheese and *smen*, or rancid butter, to taste a glass of yoghurt, chew a bit of nougat, smell a little orange-blossom water, suck a quarter of tangerine, to sit down and share a glass of mint-tea – all with no obligation to buy. You may get tired, but Fez el-Bali will never bore you.

Souq **Sabbighin**, the dyers' *souq*, is on the river bank near the es-Seffarine *Medersa*. A short street paved with eleventh-century cobbles, it is lined with dark alcoves containing vats of bubbling dye. Super-vised by grave-faced master-dyers, apprentices stir the heavy skeins in the vats. The swatches of dripping, steaming wool are then draped across the street which runs raspberry, chocolate, mustard and indigo. Like the tanneries, the dyeing process is photogenic, but medieval: ask your guide to show you the riverside mill where the Oued Fez crushes the seeds for the vegetable dyes to powder.

The stench of the **tanneries**, not far from the dyers' *souq*, is not disguised by the sprig of mint you are handed at the gate. Many tourists take one photo, clap a hand to their mouth and rush out. A honeycomb of wells filled with vivid vegetable dyes are surrounded by terraced houses. Between the wells are yellow vats of liquid in which the skins are softened. My guide said it was cows' urine, leaving me to speculate on how it got there. Did cows come and urinate in the vats? I subsequently learned it is made of water and pigeon shit, sold in a special pigeon-shit *souq*. Apparently oblivious of the tourists, wet-skinned tanners bob up and down in the water. Slapping down a dripping skin punishes anyone snatching a picture. The scene is medieval and the tanneries are run on a feudal basis: jobs are handed down from father to son.

Andalus Quarter

Most tourists give up after the tanneries and your guide will be pleased not to have to trudge down to the Andalus Mosque, but the Andalus Quarter, a quiet residential area, is at the root of Hispano-Mauresque culture in Morocco. A bridge over the Oued Fez separates the Andalus and the Kairouan Quarters. The former was renowned for beautiful, dark-eyed women, the latter for money.

The **Andalus Mosque** was founded in the ninth century by the equally pious sister of the Tunisian woman who financed the Kairouine Mosque. Surrounded on all sides by houses and shops, all you can see are the great doors. The Merenids added a fountain and other embellishments and established the es-Sehrij *medrassa*, but the mosque was not developed as a centre of learning like the Kairouine.

Dar Batha Museum, a converted nineteenth-century palace outside Bab Boujeloud, has a superb collection of Moroccan arts and crafts. Highlights are a fourteenth-century door from the Attarine *Medrassa*, various Qur'ans from the sixteenth to eighteenth centuries, and an edict from the City of Fez, written on parchment and dated 1710. It is unjust to single out particular objects as they are all quite magnificent, especially the ceramics, costumes, carpets and ironwork. The heart of the museum is an enchanting Andalusian garden filled with swathes of bamboo and palms, jasmine, lemon and roses. Open 9 a.m. to 12 noon and 3 to 6 p.m., closed Tuesdays; admission 3 dh.

To exit from Fez el-Bali, walk down the Rue Sidi Ali Boughaleb towards Bab Ftouh. The road passes the large **cemetery** with a shrine to the twelfth-century ascetic Sidi Harazem, who is buried in Marra-kesh. A lecturer of great repute at the Kairouine University, he became the patron saint of students and of the mentally ill. The insane who gather at the white *koubba* on a Tuesday evening and wait for Sidi Harazem to appear might be better off standing in the waves at Sidi Abderraman. The spring *moussem* is usually an emotionally charged event.

Outside the gate you can catch a *petit-taxi* or Bus 18 to the *Nouvelle Ville*.

Fez el-Jdid

Enclosed by its own walls, the Merenid town of Fez el-Jdid was built by Sultan Abou Yussef Yaccoub in 1273 as his seat of government. It was paid for by profits from olive oil produced in Meknes and by exorbitant taxes levied on the Jewish community.

You need a morning to see Fez el-Jdid; a guide is not necessary, but still advisable. It is a quiet place, with bird song replacing the coughing and hammering of Fez el-Bali and lush gardens watered by an ingenious thirteenth-century water system.

The **Dar el-Makhzen**, where King Hassan stays when in Fez, is almost a town within Fez el-Jdid. Its 80 hectares of palaces, pavilions and other retreats have been the historic privilege of royalty since Merenid times.

On the east side of the Dar el-Makhzen is the *mellah*, or ancient Jewish quarter, whose shop-houses display distinctive wrought-iron balconies. The Arabic word *mellah*, meaning salt, came to describe Jewish quarters throughout Morocco, but it originated in Fez – Fassi Jews were given the task of salting the severed heads of the sultan's prisoners and displaying them on spikes on the gate. Only one or two Jewish families still live in the *mellah*, but the wrought iron balconies and jewellers' shops are a legacy of the past.

Bab Semmarine used to separate the Jewish and Muslim quarters at the end of the Grande Rue du Mellah. At the top of the Grande Rue de Fez el-Jdid is **Bab Dekane**, until recently the ceremonial entrance into Fez el-Jdid. In 1437 the Portuguese prince Dom Ferdinand was hung up on Bab Dekane by his heels for four days when his brothers refused to negotiate a ransom deal with the sultan. Cut down, his body was stuffed and displayed in Fez for twenty-nine years. The square in front of Bab Dekane attracts storytellers, jugglers and other itinerant entertainers.

Ramparts

You can make a tour of the 15 km of ramparts. On the hill overlooking Fez el-Bali is **Bordj Nord**, a seventeenth-century Saadian fort, now a Museum of Arms (open 8.30 a.m. to 12 noon and 2.30 to 6 p.m.; admission 3 dh). If children make life unpleasant, escape into the Palais Jamai. Sipping an aperitif on the terrace as pigeons swoop over the old city and the *muezzins* make the call to prayer is one of the most satisfying moments in Fez.

A de-luxe hotel, the **Palais Jamai** was built by two brothers, one the Grand Vizier and the other the Minister of War. Completed in 1879, it incorporates fine elements of Hispano-Mauresque architecture and décor. The 'Grand Vizier's Room', built within the ramparts around Fez el-Bali, is sumptuously decorated, with carved ceilings illuminated in gold. The Jamai brothers met an unfortunate end when they fell out with the sultan and were jailed in Tetouan. The older brother died and the younger was left chained to his rotting corpse for eleven days in the height of summer. On his release in 1908, he found his family had vanished and his beautiful properties in Fez and Meknes had been confiscated by the government. The hotel was acquired by ONCF in 1933. The nearby gate into the *medina* is Bab Guissa, an Almohad structure from the thirteenth century.

Nouvelle Ville

On the hill overlooking Fez el-Jdid the *Nouvelle Ville*, built in the 1920s, feels strange after the twisting, turning *medina*. Sweeping through the town, the palm-lined Avenue Hassan II is typical of fastidious French urban planning in the Maghreb, while the Boulevard Mohammed V exudes a style rarely encountered in Morocco. In the **L'Epie d'Or** coffee-lounge, you might be in Paris or Vienna – and if you say that you do not want Morocco to feel like Europe, I say wait until you have had a week of the *café-terraces*.

Where to stay

Fez remains short of all grades of hotels. Most four-star hotels in the *Nouvelle Ville* are continually booked with tour groups.

Palais Jamai (*****A), Bab Guissa; tel. 634331/2/3/5. 245 beds and twenty suites. De-luxe with stunning views, this is arguably one of the world's great hotels, somewhat mediocre service.

Hotel Jnan Palace (*****A), Avenue Ahmed Chaouki; tel. 653965. Luxury 193-room hotel built in parkland in the heart of the new town. Shopping complex, sauna, tennis, heated pool.

Merenides (*****A), Bordj Nord; tel. 645225. Large modern hotel with the same view as the Palais Jamai. Parking available.

Hotel Zalagh (****B), Rue Mohammad Diouri; tel. 622810. 128 beds. Good view. *Hammam* and large pool. *Nouvelle Ville*.

Grand Hotel (***A), Boulevard Chefchaouni; tel. 625511/22. 145 beds, twenty rooms with bathrooms. A pleasant, older-style hotel in the *Nouvelle Ville*.

Hôtel de la Paix (***A), 44 Avenue Hassan II; tel. 625072. Fifty-four beds. Clean, comfortable hotel in the centre of the *Nouvelle Ville*. Bar and restaurant.

Splendid Hotel (***B), 9 Rue Abd el-Karim el-Khattabi; tel. 622148. Seventy spotlessly clean rooms. Swiss-management. Garden. Pool. Good bar. *Nouvelle Ville*. Recommended.

Hôtel du Commerce, Place des Alaouites; tel. 622231. Run by Madame Amar Bida and family for thirty-one years. Thirty clean, basic rooms, some with showers. Friendly atmosphere. Ideal for young travellers and spirited older ones. Between Fez el-Bali and Fez el-Jdid.

Hotel Kaskades, inside Bab Boujeloud; tel. 633086. Popular with young travellers. Old **hammam** on second floor. View from terrace. Might be noisy.

Where to eat

The bonus of the *Nouvelle Ville* is wine, or beer, with your meal. Pleasant French-Moroccan food is served at **Chamonix** and **Chez Claude**. The restaurant in the **Hotel Olympic** has a three-course lunch for 61 dh. The popular old **La Tour d'Argent** is no longer licensed, but meals remain good. The *Nouvelle Ville* has several bars – the **Bar Olympic** is behind the Central Market. The **Epicérie de Fez**, opposite, sells alcohol. The French and Moroccan restaurants in the **Palais Jamai** are excellent. Among several good Moroccan restaurants in former palaces in the *medina* are the **Palais de Fez**, the **Dar Tajine**, the **Dar Saada** and the **Palais M'Nebhi**. Near Bab Guissa the restaurant **Firdaous** offers a floor show.

What to do

Nightlife

Several hotel bars are quite lively watering-holes in the early evening; try the **Splendid Hotel**. Nightclubs in the **Sofia** and **Zalagh** are popular with young Fassis.

Shopping

Before shopping, visit the excellent **Artisanal Complex** on the Boulevard Allal Ben Abdellah (near the Volubilis Hotel). The standard is superior to other crafts centres. Ceramics and hand-embroidery are particularly fine.

Fez not only has the largest number of craftsmen, but it produces the *crème de la crème* of handicrafts. The local artisans – potters, weavers, carpenters, coppersmiths, book-binders – are often father and sons working in the same tiny space their family has owned for generations. There are men who only make delicate cow-horn combs, or *babouches*, others who embroider belts, or paint pottery. Many are youngsters so absorbed in their work that they do not look up from weaving, polishing, tapping or embossing; some have become master-craftsmen by their teens.

Fassis are born artists and pride in their work does not permit the bargaining necessary elsewhere, although if you are shopping with a guide, slash the asking price by half.

Fassi pottery and **ceramics** are one of the most beautiful traditions of Hispano-Mauresque art. Artefacts are either enamelled or varnished. Swirling floral or geometric designs in blue and green on a white background are typical. **Jewellery** designs are mainly inherited from the Jewish community who were active in Fez el-Jdid until about twenty years ago. Decorative **wood-carving** is one of the most famous Fassi crafts and Fassi **leatherwork** is known internationally under the broad term 'Moroccan leather'. Introduced by refugees from Andalusia, Fez overtook Spain in this field long ago. Briefcases and office-type items are good buys.

Embroidery, brought from Andalusia, now also surpasses that produced in Spain. You can find richly embroidered textiles, table sets and tasselled belts. Local craftsmen are masters at working both **copper** and **brass**. Ask for the Place Seffarine in Fez el-Bali.

Useful information

Royal Air Maroc, 54 Avenue Hassan II.

Wagon Lits, 41 Avenue Mohammed es Sleoui.

InterRent-Europcar, 41 Avenue Hassan II.

Banks are mainly on the Boulevard Mohammed V.

PTT. The central post office is at the junction of the Boulevard Mohammed V and the Avenue Hassan II.

ONMT, Place de la Résistance, *Nouvelle Ville*.

All-night pharmacy, Boulevard Moulay Yussef, near the Place de la Résistance.

Newspapers are sold in hotel bookshops and stalls around Boulevard Mohammed V.

English bookshop, 68 Avenue Hassan II.

Moving on

The main **train station** is on Avenue des Almohades, five minutes from the *Nouvelle Ville* by *petit-taxi*. Frequent services to Rabat and Casablanca, Tangier, Taza and Oujda. The main CTM **bus stations** are on Boulevard Mohammed V and at Bab Boujeloud. Frequent services in all directions. *Petit-taxi* ranks include the Place Mohammed V, the central post office and the railway station. Most *petits-taxis* use the meter. Fares increase by half after sunset. The inner-city bus fare is 1.20 dh. Useful numbers are: 18, Place de la Résistance to Bab Ftouh; 19, railway station to Place des Alaouites outside Fez el-Jdid; 10, Bab Guissa to Place des Alaouites.

Sidi Harazem

Sidi Harazem, the source of Morocco's famous mineral water, does not justify the 30-km round-trip from Fez. It is crowded with hucksters selling hideous stuffed toys to holidaymakers, many from Algeria. You are besieged by children begging you to buy a mug of mineral water which issues free from the spring. Seeking a cure in a thermal pool, the ill risk catching something else. A hotel with piped muzak looks like the KGB headquarters in Leningrad. Avoid at all costs the April *moussem* venerating Sidi Harazem.

Sefrou

Sefrou (28 km) is an enchanting Berber market town, built on the banks of the Oued Aggai beneath a limestone plateau. You might consider staying the night. It will also appeal to walkers.

History

Until the Arab–Israeli War in 1967, Sefrou had one of the biggest Jewish communities in Morocco, dating from the first millennium. Moulay Idriss lived in a nearby *ksar* while planning the development of Fez.

What to see

Passing through the **Nouvelle Ville**, the P20 becomes the Boulevard Mohammed V. Shops, a bank and the PTT are here. The trees lining the street are laden with tangerines in March. There is an annual Cherry Festival (23–5 June).

The **medina**, enclosed by eighteenth-century walls of ochre *pisé*, spreads below the public park on either river bank. Of the nine gates the most convenient for the *Nouvelle Ville* is Bab Merba, where a weekly *souq* is held on Thursdays. Inside Bab Merba, the Rue du Marché winds down to the Grand Mosque. There are no *faux-guides* so take time to explore the network of lanes and craft shops.

A bridge in front of the Grand Mosque crosses over to the **mellah** with its distinctive tall houses and balconies. Some of the streets are dark and tunnel-like. Rubbish lies everywhere.

The white **koubba** of Sidi Bou Ali Serghin, built on a spectacular limestone ridge above Sefrou, is a thirty-minute climb. Below the shrine is the **Source Lalla Rekia**; Berber folklore requires an annual sacrifice of a white hen, black cock and a black billy-goat here to appease the spirits of the spring.

Where to stay **Hotel Sidi Lahcen Lyoussi** (**A), tel. 660497. Follow the 'Cascades' sign behind the PTT, five minutes' walk. Seventeen clean, airy rooms overlooking a garden. Pleasant staff, but the hotel needs maintenance. Bar-restaurant. Parking. Recommended.

Where to eat Try the **Hotel Sidi Lahcen Lyoussi**, or the **Restaurant Marbaa** inside Bab Merba, which serves cheap barbecued chicken, *tajine*, etc. Excellent foodstalls sell *brochettes* of liver and other offal.

The Middle Atlas

There are many sightseeing possibilities in the Middle Atlas, which stretch across the midriff of Morocco. Rarely frequented by travellers hell-bent on reaching Marrakesh, it is a quiet region with none of the heady Hispano-Moorish culture of the north, nor the striking architecture of the south – basically a refreshing sorbet between courses, which may draw you back for a holiday once you have completed the obligatory 'grand tour' of Morocco. The best time to visit the Middle Atlas is from April to May and from September to December. Avoid June to August, when any Moroccan who can afford it hits the hills.

Two main roads cut through the Middle Atlas: the P21 from Meknes to Midelt and the southern oases, and the P24 from Fez to Marrakesh.

Immouzer de Kandhar A town of two faces, Immouzer lies within one hour's drive of Fez on the P24. In summer, the square buzzes with activity. The three-day Apple Festival in July is celebrated with eating, drinking, singing and dancing – often all at once. During winter, people withdraw to their pine-log fires. At 1,345 m, Immouzer is frequently under snow from January to March. Red-tiled European-type houses outnumber Berber dwellings. There is a Monday *souq*.

Where to stay There are three or four hotels; those on the main road are used by group tours.

Hôtel des Truites (**A), tel. 663002. A small, clean family-run hotel in a quiet location, ten minutes' walk from the town centre. French-style bar-restaurant. Parking.

Where to eat **La Chaumière** is a cosy restaurant owned by a French-Moroccan couple, on the Ifrane exit in Immouzer.

Circuit des Lacs
Dait Aoua The 'Circuit des Lacs' is about a 60-km round-trip, signposted on the left, 8 km south of Immouzer. 0.5 km off the road, Dait Aoua is a shallow, reed-lined lake with delightful picnic spots. You can also camp beside the lake, one of my favourite places in Morocco.

The only place to stay is the charming **Chalet du Lac** with eighteen comfortable rooms. An ambience of colonial France pervades the *auberge*, which is renowned for its bar. A restaurant serves good French food – generous portions. Very popular with diplomats from Rabat and crowded at weekends, when bookings are essential; tel. 0 via Azrou. On no account interrupt Madame's poker game, either to check in, or out. Highly recommended.

Dait Ifrah, 29 km from Dait Aoua is a picturesque lake; legend says the mountain here is named after a holy woman hermit, Lalla Mimouna, who was raped and killed by forest *djinns*. **Dait Hachlaf** has trout fishing.

If you do not want to do the whole circuit, you can head south on the P20 from Annonceur, a small village at the end of the road from Dait Aoua. In the winter check that the Tizi Abekhnanes pass (1,769 m) is open; the snow stays until April. **Boulemane** is an old French garrison town built above a dramatic gorge. From here the road crosses a barren plateau before joining the P21 at Boulojoul (70 km). Petrol.

Ifrane

Ifrane, 17 km south of Immouzer on the P24, is a civilized but sterile assemblage of chalets built as a summer hill station by the French. It is now a fashionable resort for wealthy Moroccans. The Alaouite Court takes up residence here from June to September, when security is strict and hotels are fully booked. A mosque and *souq* on a modern *medina*-estate is the only indication this is Morocco.

Where to stay

Accommodation is available off-season at several bland hotels.

Hotel Mischliffen (*****A); tel. 566614. De-luxe hotel used by groups. A good WC stop. Parking.

Grand Hotel (***A), Rue de la Poste; tel. 56407. Mock-alpine-style hotel. Bar-restaurant.

Meals are available at both hotels.

Activities and sports

Mischliffen is a major winter-sports centre near Ifrane. It is of no interest unless you ski. Short runs. Equipment may be hired at the **Chamonix** café-restaurant in Ifrane. Serious skiers should come equipped.

Azrou

Azrou is named after a glowering peak where Moulay Ismail built a *kasbah* to monitor the caravan routes, which are now the P21 and P24 highways. Azrou is a one-street town with a population of 45,000, a Berber market and a Tuesday *souq*.

What to see

Azrou has little of lasting interest, but it is a pleasant place to stay. There is an excellent Artisan Complex open Monday to Saturday from 8.30 a.m. to 12 noon and from 2.30 to 6 p.m. It sells carpets and handicrafts made by the local Beni M'Guid Berbers.

Where to stay

Azrou is short of hotels and booking is advisable during the summer.

Hotel Panorama (**A), tel. 562010. Clean, well-run family hotel with thirty-six comfortable rooms. The manager is a keen fisherman. Bar-restaurant. Recommended.

Hôtel des Cèdres (*A), Place Mohammed V; tel. 52326. Nine clean rooms. Friendly management. Town centre.

Auberge d'Amros. Comfortable farm-house chalet. Good meals.

8 km out of Azrou on the Meknes road.

Where to eat

The most civilised place to eat in Azrou is the Hotel Panorama. There is a limited menu at the **Hôtel des Cèdres**. Next door, the **Relais Forestière** is clean and popular. There are exceptionally good food stalls in the market. The **Laiterie Atlas** is a nice spot for coffee in the morning sun.

Moving on

Buses depart for Meknes (67 km) and Fez (77 km) throughout the day. The through service to Marrakesh is often full, so book in advance. A daily bus goes to Midelt and er-Rachidia.

The P21 passes through a dense cedar forest outside Azrou. A 5-km detour goes to the **Cedar Gouraud** – a huge tree it takes a minute to run around, named after General Lyautey's second in command, who succeeded him as resident general in 1917. Running briskly round the cedar deters local hustlers, who think you are tuppence off the shilling, or the Berber equivalent.

Sidi Ali

The 125-km drive from Azrou to Midelt is uninspiring, but a short detour to Sidi Ali, 52 km south of Azrou, is worthwhile. A slate-blue crater lake, 1 km off the P21, it lies in a tumbled pumice-stone landscape. The fishing is reputed to be good and it is a pleasant, if bleak, camping-spot. No facilities.

Col du Zaid

Back on the main road you climb the Col du Zaid (2,178 m) and slowly descend to Zaid, a rough market town. Petrol. South of here is the junction with the little-used P33 to Khenifra, winding 4 hours, 110 km to K. Tadla.

Midelt

Midelt is the main roadside town between Azrou and er-Rachidia. Stop here for petrol, snacks and the WC. Every tourist coach calls at the Hotel Ayachi between 11.30 a.m. and 2 p.m. To the west of Midelt the dark hood of Djebel Ayachi rises to 3,737 m – the ultimate view in the Middle Atlas.

What to see

The old quarter of Midelt has an excellent carpet market. Carpets are draped in the sun to allow the vivid vegetable dyes to bleach naturally. Patterns are the typical geometric styles of the Middle Atlas. You are unlikely to find anything old. The **Atelier de Tissage** is a weaving school run by Franciscan nuns.

Where to stay

There is only one good hotel:

Hotel Ayachi (★★★A), Rue d'Agadir; tel. 582161. A clean, comfortable old hotel with forty-nine beds and pleasant management. Bar-restaurant. Up to 500 lunch-covers. Quiet at night.

Where to eat

Eat at the **Hotel Ayachi** or the popular **Restaurant de Fes** run by Fatima Tazi.

Moving on

Thirty km south of Midelt you cross the Tizi N'Talghemt pass, which marks the transition from the alpine forests to the scrub-land of the sub-Sahara, where the dry air already carries particles of sand. At Ait Messaoud there is a 'Beau Geste' fort – an expression beloved of travel writers on Morocco – soon afterwards you reach the first *ksour*, or fortified mud-villages, which become commonplace in the south.

Fez to Marrakesh

The P24 from Fez heads south-west from Azrou to Marrakesh. From Tiouririne, 17 km south of Azrou, there is an enchanting detour through alpine meadows and forests of cedars and pines – the tribal lands of the Beni M'Guid – to the source of the Oum er-R'bia.

Ain Leuh

Ain Leuh is a typical Berber village of flat-roofed houses stacked in tiers above the valley. At some stage everything goes on the roofs, precisely what being dependent on the season. I have seen wind-dried beef, corn and chicken-coops, water-jars, the family bedding and one instance of Berber bourgeois living: an entire family seated on the roof watching television. In winter the roof is stacked with logs for fuel. People eat on the roof and sleep on the roof. They also die on the roof when an edge gives way. Ain Leuh has a daily market and a *souq* on Mondays and Thursdays.

Source of Oum er-R'bia

Lake Ouiouane is a pleasant picnic-spot 20 km south of Ain Leuh. The sign 'Aguelmane Azigza–Khenifra' indicates the source of the Oum er-R'bia, the river which flows into the sea at Azemmour. In the spring and summer it spews out of the limestone cliff, slowing to a trickle in November. When I was there a barber was shaving a man about to make the *haj*. Squatting by the river, he dipped his cut-throat in a pool and dragged it across his client's skull, raising flecks of bright red cranial blood. He was no Leonard of London, Manhattan and Dubai, but he had already done several farmers, the *gardien des voitures* and a strange hopping person wanting to be my guide. The pilgrim did not look as though he could afford a bus-ticket to Ain Leuh, let alone an air-fare to Mecca.

Above the bridge about forty waterfalls spill off Djebel Aang into a natural basin in the rocks.

Aguelmane Azigza

Aguelmane Azigza, 18 km further south, is a spectacular crater lake surrounded by grassy meadows and cedar forests. It is a superb camping spot with excellent bass-fishing. Swimming is safe, although the water is freezing. There are no facilities.

Khenifra

A beautiful drive across the Khenifra Valley brings you to Khenifra itself (38 km), a striking town of ox-blood-red houses with pea-green shutters and doors. It has a population of 130,000 and is an important market town for the Middle Atlas.

History

In the nineteenth century Khenifra was ruled by a powerful *caid*, Moha ou Hammou, who dominated the Middle Atlas as far as Meknes. The French suffered one of their biggest defeats here in 1914: 600 men were killed when they attempted to storm the town. Moha ou Hammou continued his resistance to the Protectorate until his death in 1921.

What to see

The mosque, a *zaouia* and *kasbah* in the *medina* were built by Moha ou Hammou. The bridge over the Oum er-R'bia was built by Moulay Ismail. There are attractive parks and riverside walks.

Where to stay

Hotel Hamou (****B), Azzayani Salam; tel. 586020 and 586532. A modern tourist hotel used by groups. All facilities.

Hôtel-Restaurant France; tel. 6114. Simple but correct. Single room 60 dh.

The **Hamou** offers a tourist menu. The restaurants of the **France** or **Voyageurs** hotels serve local food.

El Ksiba

The picturesque village of El Ksiba, surrounded by orchards, lies just off the P24, 77 km south of Khenifra. The **Hostellerie Henri IV** is a clean, basic hotel with a bar-restaurant. To travel on to the Plâteau des Lacs, with the saline lakes of Tislit and Isli, and the small village of Imilchil in the High Atlas, a four-wheel drive is recommended.

Beni-Mellal

The last major town on the P24 to Marrakesh, Beni-Mellal has become prosperous on irrigation projects from the Bin el Ouidane dam. It is surrounded by extensive orchards of figs, citrus fruits and water melons. A Friday *souq* sells rugs and carpets. A 'Tourist Walk' leads to springs and an ornamental park.

Where to stay

The four-star hotels are used by groups; cheap hotels in the *medina* are unappealing.

Auberge du Vieux Moulin (*A), Route du Kasbah Tadla; tel. 482788. Well-run, well-worn old French-style inn with ten rooms.

Hotel Gharnata, Avenue Mohammed V; tel. 483482. Small, modern, comfortable hotel in the centre of the *Nouvelle Ville*.

Where to eat

You can eat reasonably well in several places in Beni-Mellal. The **Auberge du Vieux Moulin** is renowned for its French cuisine. The **Gharnata** serves good portions of French-Moroccan food. **Al Bassatine** has a tourist menu and waiters in uniform (lunchtime groups).

Marrakesh, the High Atlas and the Oases

Introduction

Nowhere are the sudden, dramatic changes in the landscape that make travelling in Morocco so exciting as apparent as on the journey from Marrakesh across the High Atlas to the southern oases. Beyond the Atlas is what brochures call '*kasbah* country', where the flat-roofed, white-washed houses of Mediterranean Morocco are replaced by castellated, ox-blood-red *ksour*. Only a few hundred kilometres separate northern and southern Morocco, but they could be worlds apart. A date-grower from Erfoud will feel just as much a stranger in Tetouan as you, the real stranger, will feel in one of the oases in the Tafilalet.

Marrakesh, the ancient Saadian capital, is the heart of tourism in southern Morocco. That the fabled city is sold as a package resort is rather sad, but if you have never visited Marrakesh, you are unlikely to be disappointed, and the town makes a splendid base for sightseeing in the Atlas valleys. The foothills of the High Atlas are only 50 km from the centre of Marrakesh, but they are so high you can still see their snow-line from the Sahara. The Tizi N'Test and the Tizi N'Tishka passes cut through the mountains to the Deep South. Either pass is a good test of driving skills – the 'Test' is steeper, but the 'Tishka' is more exhilarating motoring.

Over the crest of the Atlas, good roads lead to the Anti-Atlas, up and over again to emerald oases in the desert. One of the most enchanting journeys in Morocco is to follow the palm-lined river Draa from Ouarzazate to Zagora, where a faded sign indicates the way to Timbuktu by camel. Further east, the road to Erfoud follows the old trade route descending into the Sahara. Wealth came on camels from the rich Saharan sub-kingdoms in pre-colonial times; several Moroccan dynasties, including the ruling Alaouites, also came from the Tafilalet and the Draa. When Morocco's economic fortunes moved north to around Khouribga and Casablanca, these flourishing oases shrank to little more than tourist attractions – but what attractions!

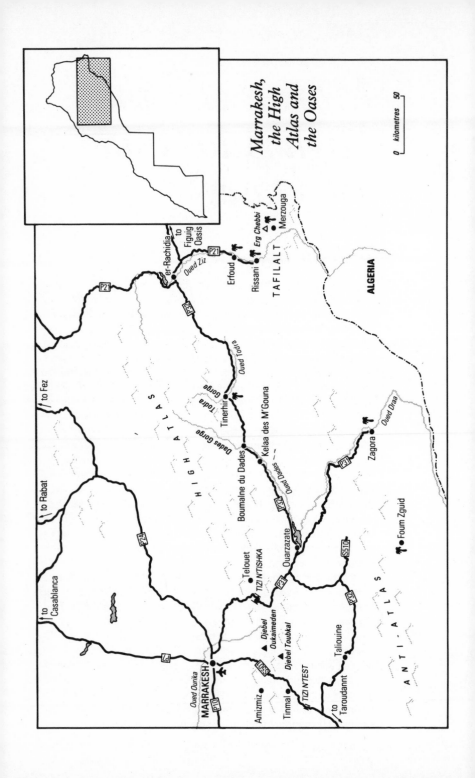

Marrakesh, the High Atlas and the Oases

Marrakesh

Marrakesh is like a huge sun-baked sandwich with an exotic filling of palaces, *souqs* and colourful peoples. Once a magic name, like Samarkand or Timbuktu, tourism has made it familiar in every household. Although the *Nouvelle Ville* has grown considerably, with scores of buildings under construction, the old *medina* remains a timeless world – shops take credit cards, but there are few other changes. Marrakesh is an Arab city with its feet dancing to an African tam-tam. Built on the flat, red Haouz Plains, it is ideal to explore by bicycle or local horse-carriage. With transport you can escape into forested valleys of the High Atlas. With excellent hotels and restaurants, Marrakesh has become Morocco's premier resort, the problem for an independent traveller being that it is hard to avoid the tourists.

With a population of more than 500,000, Marrakesh is the fourth largest town in Morocco. Crafts and commerce are traditional activities being overtaken by light industry and tourism. A 5,000-seat Congress Centre was completed in 1990.

History

Marrakesh has always been a logical stop for travellers crossing the High Atlas from central Morocco, or for people from the southern oases heading north. The first permanent settlement was founded by the Almoravids, who built the original ramparts in the eleventh century. The Sultan Youssef Ibn Tachfine added mosques, palaces and gardens. Of Almoravid Marrakesh, however, little remains.

Following the Almohad conquest in 1147, building began in earnest. Sultan Abd el-Moumen erected the Koutoubia Mosque on the site of the original Almoravid settlement. Using skilled Andalusian craftsmen, Sultan Yaccoub el-Mansour constructed gardens, irrigation works and palaces. When schisms developed between the more liberal Almohads and others entrenched in puritan philosophy, Marrakesh was allowed to decline. Almohad rule lasted only 100 years.

Merenid sultans contributed several *medressa* to the city in the thirteenth century, but they lavished most attention on Fez, Marrakesh's rival throughout the history of Morocco.

Advancing over the Tizi N'Test from Taroudannt in 1541, the Saadians found Marrakesh in ruins, but wealth from the prosperous Saharan caravan trade restored it to a glittering city. The Saadians built new mosques, fountains and *funduqs*, as well as restoring the Merenid *medressa*. Their lavishly embellished tombs assured their own immortality.

When the Saadian dynasty fell out of favour in the seventeenth century, Marrakesh was seized by local *marabouts*. In 1688 it was conquered by Moulay Rachid, the second Alaouite sultan, but when his brother, the infamous Moulay Ismail, decided to rule from Meknes, the most beautiful buildings, including the incomparable el-Badi

Palace, were stripped. Later Alaouite sultans saved the city from further destruction by alternating rule between Marrakesh and Fez. From 1893 to 1912 Thami el-Glaoui ruled the High Atlas as Pasha of Marrakesh.

Nouvelle Ville

When the French arrived in Marrakesh in 1912, they found a town still reliant largely on pack animals. A new town built to the west of the old *medina* has expanded in two directions since Independence in 1956. In the north is the wealthy, well-planned residential suburb, the Cité Mohammedia, while in the south is Sidi Youssef Ben Ali, a slum area where many rural poor live in haphazardly built houses. Expansion eastwards is hampered by the old Almoravid Palmery.

What to see

Allow at least four or five days for sightseeing in Marrakesh and its environs. The town is very hot from June to August, but the warm days and crisp nights at other times are ideal. The peak season coincides with the European winter, when hotels are at a premium.

Ramparts

When you are back home, what will you best remember about Morocco? The ever-changing landscape, certainly, and probably the walls: the great walls enclosing Rabat, Fez and Essaouira, Moulay Ismail's mad walls around Meknes, and the wonderful ramparts surrounding Marrakesh – hot, red walls which are a startling contrast to the cold, snow-capped Atlas. Built of *tabia*, a mixture of water and red mud from the Haouz Plains, the original walls, 16 km long, were raised by the Almoravids and were fortified on many occasions. One of the most delightful things to do in Marrakesh is to make a tour of the ramparts by calèche at dusk, ending in the Aguedal or the Menara Gardens, closed at sunset.

Gates

Of the twenty original gates which entered the *medina*, the following are the most significant: **Bab Aguenou**, a smaller, though no less assertive cousin of the great Oudaia Gate in Rabat, noted for a bold semi-circular frieze; the **Bab Doukkala**, from Almoravid Marrakesh with solid, but unequal towers, guards the exit to the Doukkala Plain; **Bab el-Khemis**, also originally Almoravid, is the location of a daily domestic market; **Bab el-Debbagh**, Almoravid although rebuilt, with the classic, twisting passage, leads into the tanneries quarter; **Bab er-Rob**, part of a twelfth-century Almohad extension to the *medina*, near an untidy market area; and **Bab el-Makhzen**, an Almoravid gate, greatly rebuilt, but historically the royal entry to the *kasbah*.

Imperial monuments

The imperial heritage of Marrakesh lies within the *medina*; where you begin sightseeing is merely a matter of convenience. You might like to start at the Koutoubia Mosque and work through the Djemaa el Fna to the *souqs* or you can start at Bab Aguenou, the gateway to Saadian Marrakesh. To see all the monuments will take at least two days. Marrakesh is haunted by touts and you are advised to take an official guide from the Tourist Office or a local travel agency. Knowing that *faux-guides* are not early risers is perhaps useful for independent sightseeing. Female *faux-guides* are common in Marrakesh.

You can see the minaret of the **Koutoubia Mosque** like a giant obelisk on the skyline while you are still several kilometres outside Marrakesh. Completed during the reign of Yaccoub el-Mansour (1184–99), it is the second mosque to be built on the site – the first was demolished when the *mihrab* was found to be aligned in the wrong direction. (Some writers attribute the name 'Djemaa el Fna' to mean 'mosque of destruction', *jemaa* being the Arabic for mosque.) The minaret is built on the classic 1:5 ratio tapering to 70 m. Each side features classic Almohad decorative stone-work – the *darf w ktarf* and cut-out merlons – and what remains of the band of ceramic tiles indicates what the minaret might have looked like in full dress.

On the top are three golden orbs, which legend says are the melted-down jewellery of one of Yaccoub el-Mansour's wives, who ate three grapes during the fast and was obliged to surrender her jewellery as a penance. The Koutoubia holds up to 20,000 worshippers on the occasion of *eid* prayers held at the end of Ramadan. You may not enter the mosque, but even from the outside it exerts a powerful, spiritual influence. The bare area around it is said to have been the centre of Almoravid Marrakesh.

It is difficult to obtain any perspective of the **El Mouassin Mosque**, which stands in the centre of the *medina* near the dyers' *souq*. It was built between 1563 and 1573 by the Saadi sultan Moulay Abdullah on the site of a fourteenth-century Jewish cemetery, which was considered an evil omen. Stigma still surrounds the mosque, one of the largest in Marrakesh, with a *medrassa* and fountain (see p. 183). Its minaret is stumpy, but the interior, glimpsed through the door, looks magnificent.

The **Ali Ben Youssef Mosque** is a somewhat austere building which dates from the twelfth century. It was restored by the Saadis and is held in great affection by the Marrakshis.

The **Ben Youssef *Medersa*** is a contemporary of the *medrassa* built by the Merenids in Fez, Salé and Meknes. Restored by the Saadi sultans, it features the flamboyant decorative work also seen on their mausoleums: elaborate cedar-work, *zellij* and stucco. The beautiful marble ablutions tank in the prayer-hall was made in tenth-century Cordoba. Its figurines and floral motifs are unusual, as Islam forbids representational art. Open 9 a.m. to 12 noon and 2.30 to 6 p.m., closed Fridays; admission 3 dh.

The apparently insignificant structure in the outer courtyard of the Ali Ben Youssef Mosque is the **Koubba el-Baroudiyn**, the only wholly original Almoravid structure in Marrakesh. The cupola covering a shallow washing area features the merlons and scalloped arches of many later buildings. A *kufic* frieze inside the dome attributes the *koubba* to Sultan Ali Ben Youssef.

The minaret of the **Kasbah Mosque** looks over the walls near Bab

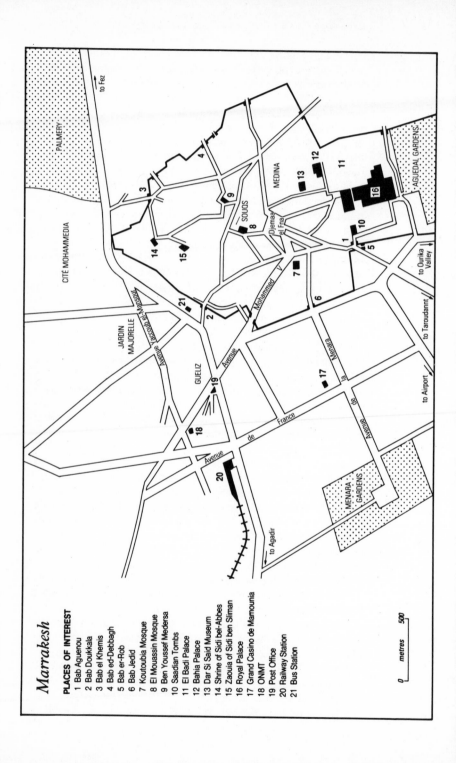

Marrakesh

PLACES OF INTEREST

1 Bab Aguenou
2 Bab Doukkala
3 Bab el Khemis
4 Bab ed-Debbagh
5 Bab er-Rob
6 Bab Jedid
7 Koutoubia Mosque
8 El Mouassin Mosque
9 Ben Youssef Medersa
10 Saadian Tombs
11 El Badi Palace
12 Bahia Palace
13 Dar Si Said Museum
14 Shrine of Sidi bel-Abbes
15 Zaouia of Sidi ben Sliman
16 Royal Palace
17 Grand Casino de Mamounia
18 ONMT
19 Post Office
20 Railway Station
21 Bus Station

0   metres   500

Aguenou. The original mosque, built in 1190 by Yaccoub el-Mansour, has been restored many times. A door beside the *mihrab*, or prayer-niche, leads into the sixteenth-century necropolis known as the **'Saadian tombs'**. When Moulay Ismail stripped the el-Badi Palace, he also sealed up the tombs. They were forgotten until the French discovered them in 1917, and a passage was cut through the surrounding wall to provide access for non-Muslims: every tour-group in Marrakesh visits the necropolis in single file, along this narrow, jasmine-draped corridor.

Surrounded by high, clipped rosemary hedges, the cemetery was the burial ground of the *shorfa*, or descendants of the Prophet. The major pavilions are occupied by the Saadi sultans, their wives, children and, according to my guide, their most faithful servants. There are two main mausoleums. The first is a large, open pavilion rather like a prayer-hall, with a beautiful *mihrab*. Shafts of light filtering through its arches add to the sepulchral atmosphere. Some sixty-six Saadi are buried in this shelter and the next with more than a hundred others dotted around the garden. The second pavilion contains the mausoleum of Ahmed el-Mansour, who died in 1603. It is supported by twelve marble columns whose upper sections are carved as delicately as hand-embroidered lace. The necropolis is one of those pools of tranquillity you suddenly encounter in a *medina* in Morocco; its almost ethereal atmosphere is reminiscent of the Alhambra Gardens in Granada. Open 8 a.m. to 12 noon and 2 to 6 p.m.; admission 10 dh.

The once-celebrated **el-Badi Palace**, whose name means the 'incomparable', was built with profits from the Battle of the Three Kings, but was systematically demolished by Sultan Moulay Ismail. Of the gold-encrusted ceilings, crystal pavilions and scented Moorish gardens, nothing remains. What you see are traces of the reception hall and entrance hall, which is illuminated for the 'Festival of Folklore'. Entry via Bab Berrima. Open 9 a.m. to 12 noon and 2.30 to 5.30 p.m.

The **Bahia Palace** was begun by the grand vizier Si' Mousa in the late nineteenth century and extended by his son. Christopher Kininmonth, an expert on Islamic architecture in Morocco, says it is 'shoddily built, tastelessly designed . . . and hideously decorated'. The vast marble-paved courtyard surrounded by galleried rooms is the most attractive aspect of the palace, which covers about 8 hectares. The interior rooms and corridors are covered with vivid, uninspiring designs, the grand vizier's personal quarters being particularly garish. He was hated by his staff, who stripped the palace when he died. Open 8 a.m. to 12 noon and 2.30 to 6 p.m. Admission is free but if you are not with a group, a guide is compulsory.

A smaller version of the Bahia Palace, the **Dar Si Said** was built for Si' Mousa's half-wit brother. It has been converted into a Museum of Moroccan Arts and has especially good displays of carpets, Berber jewellery and eighteenth- and nineteenth-century cedar-wood carving from the Glaoui kasbahs. Open 9 a.m. to 12 noon and 2.30 to 6 p.m. in winter; 9 a.m. to 12 noon and 4 to 7 p.m. in summer; closed on Tuesdays.

Medina

The **Shrine of Sidi bel-Abbes** is in the northern *medina*, which is mainly residential but has several other shrines and some Saadi *funduqs*. Sidi bel-Abbes is the most revered of seven popular *sufi* mystics in Marrakesh. Born in Ceuta in 1145, he moved to Marrakesh and retreated into a *zaouia*. His teachings attracted many disciples and Sultan Yaccoub el-Mansour encouraged his good works among the poor and the blind. His ghost is said to haunt the Koutoubia every night until every blind person in Marrakesh is fed. Entry to the shrine is forbidden.

Zaouia of Sidi Ben Sliman el-Jazuli. Another of the 'Seven Mystics of Marrakesh', the fourteenth-century *sufi* el-Jazuli is considered one of the greatest *sufis* in Morocco. His embalmed remains were brought to Marrakesh by the Saadis in the hope that some of his glory might rub off on them. Six Saadi princes who were assassinated in a palace *coup* are buried beside him. The *marabout* cult of el-Jazuli remains active. Non-Muslims are not permitted near the el-Jazuli *zaouia*, but its green tiled roof can be seen above the surrounding houses.

Djemaa el Fna

The large, open square known as the Djemaa el Fna is an antechamber to the *souqs*, a carnival of colourful charlatans buying, selling and performing for the crowds. Ironically it used to be the execution site in Marrakesh.

A good vantage spot to watch the activity on the Djemaa el Fna is the roof-terrace of a local café, where you can sip mint-tea and observe the crowds gathered around story-tellers and quacks, fortune-tellers and clowns, child-boxers, snake-charmers and magicians. The tight circles break briefly to allow someone out, then close ranks like a shoal of fish. Elbows strapped ingeniously in cut-down tyres, a cripple drags himself around the edge of one circle, tugging at trouserlegs to be let in.

A microcosm of everything you are likely to see in Morocco, the Djemaa el Fna also has its own brand of entertainers: acrobats making triple somersaults and black *Gnaoua* musicians rattling iron castanets and beating camel-skin drums with long, curved canes. Amid all this frenzied activity, a dentist painfully plucks out poor people's molars with a pair of pliers; a boxful on display shows how popular he is. Asked the cost of an extraction, he gave me a toothless smile. *'Pour vous, madame, je vous ferais un prix spécial de 20 dirham.'* People such as the dentist, the water-seller and the snake-charmer live off money made from posing for photographs.

Today on the Djemaa el Fna, as well as dried chameleons and *djellabahs* you will find fake watches and port-a-gas stoves, the gas jets turned on to explain how they function. The orange-juice vendors are fully automated, using electric juice extractors powered by small

Japanese generators.

Are you still sitting in the *café-terrace*? Go down and mingle on the Djemaa el Fna: safe as well as colourful, it is an indelible memory of Marrakesh.

Souqs There have been credible attempts to map the *medina*, which extends north from the Place Djemaa el Fna and is enclosed on all sides by walls. It is bigger than Fez, but it is easier to explore. The *souqs* branch off the Rue Souq Smarine, which you can use for orientation. If you have already visited some of the imperial monuments, many *souqs* will be familiar, but do not try to combine shopping and sightseeing as both demand your full attention.

The best time to visit the *souqs* is in the late afternoon, around 3.30 p.m. If you go early to avoid the crowds, you may find the *medina* deserted and the *souqs* with their shutters down. Take a guide as shopkeepers will drive you crazy; they will still drive you crazy, but you will not be lost. Finding an object you fancy, dip into the *souq* next day about 10 a.m. Avoid the *kissaria*, or central shopping area, on Thursday afternoons and Fridays, when the streets are packed like a subway station at rush-hour.

A map of the *souqs* is effectively useless, as you will be unable to read it in the crowded street. When I asked for directions in a shop I was asked to buy the dining-room suite the man was carving! The main archway leading into the **Rue Souq Smarine** is almost hidden by bazaars. From the Djemaa el Fna you can cut through to the Rue Souq Smarine via the small pottery market. The street is wide and well-paved by comparison with some of the alleys in the *kissaria*. A palm-matting roof filters the sunlight, making shadowy patterns. Beyond the cloth merchants on your right is the **Rahba Kedima**, or old corn market. The **Souq aux Bijoutiers** has some eye-catching shops selling chunky silver and amber Berber jewellery. Beware of buying fake amber.

Off the Rahba Kedima is the **Criée Berbère**, or Berber auction-site, where slave auctions used to be held just before sunset every Wednesday, Thursday and Friday, until outlawed by the French in 1912. Today there are carpet auctions here, the buyers feeling for knots, just as the merchants acting for the Glaoui used to scrutinize the eyes, teeth and nails of the unfortunate slaves. Slaves were also used as barter, the approximate rate in the late nineteenth century being two slaves for a camel. As well as being festooned with carpets, the Criée Berbère is piled with second-hand clothes, olive-wood walking canes, sacks of henna, dishes of cochineal, heaps of vegetables and grim remedies sold by *pseudo-guérisseurs* preying on the poor and ignorant.

The ancient **kissaria** is the traditional heart of the *medina*, framed by the **Souq des Babouches**, selling slippers, and the **Souq Charratine**, selling leather, wood and metal goods. At the end, towards the Mouassin Mosque, is the **Souq des Teinturiers**, or dyers' *souq*, featured on many postcards. Ask your guide to show you the **Mouassin Fountain**, built by the Saadis in the sixteenth century. If walking has made you hot, you can wash here in the central basin – the outer trough is for animals.

Walking north of the *kissaria*, you will pass the carpenters', copper-smiths' and metal-workers' souqs on the way to the Ben Youssef Mosque, plunged in the middle of fourteenth-century Marrakesh. Outside, shaking their tins, the blind add to other sounds which must be deafening if you cannot see: carpenters sawing, shoe-makers tapping, coppersmiths hammering, radios blaring, hustlers whistling, touts cajoling, tourists calling, shoppers bargaining, bicycle bells ringing and the muleteers yelling *'Balek! Balek!'* (get out of the way!), the *chanson* of the *souqs*.

Nouvelle Ville

Monsieur Prost, the architect of Casablanca's *Nouvelle Ville*, was also responsible for the pleasant new town in Marrakesh. The main commercial area, known as **Gueliz**, was lined with beautiful trees until they were hacked down by the local council recently. Many streets are planted with olives; the harvest in December is the property of the municipality.

The social heart of Gueliz is where the four famous *café-terraces* meet on the Avenue Mohammed V: the Renaissance, Atlas, Café les Negociants and the Glacier Adra. It is as wise to find a table in the middle of a *café-terrace*. On the outside of the Renaissance one morning, I was pestered by a tout selling lurex Y-fronts. *'Pour votre mari, votre fils, madame,'* he implored, until I finally told him that my husband and my son were dead, and that I personally had no use for such things. After a respectful pause, he shook a Rolex out of his *djellabah*.

Cycling is the best way to explore the *Nouvelle Ville* which is fifteen minutes by bike from the Djemaa el Fna.

Gardens

Marrakesh has several lovely gardens planted by the green-fingered Almohad sultans, the Palmery attributed to Almoravid gardeners, and the beautiful formal gardens such as those of the Mamounia Hotel.

The **Menara Gardens** are reached by walking down the Avenue de la Menara from Bab el-Jedid. The irrigated olive groves surrounding a large water-tank were laid out in the twelfth century. There is a good photograph of the pavilion against the Atlas snowline at dusk. The gates close at sunset. Ideal for cyclists.

The larger **Aguedal Gardens** extend south from the Royal Palace. They, too, were laid out in the twelfth century, and were restored by the Alaouites. Sultan Moulay Hassan, who built the pavilions, used the Dar el-Beida pavilion as his harem-quarters. I have a photo of me in 1964 standing on the edge of the water-tank, wearing a sundress and holding the custodian's hand. Wiser now, I wear trousers and long sleeve shirts – and the custodian charges 5 dh a picture.

You can make a circuit of the **Palmery** by *calèche*; it takes about 1½ hours from the Djemaa el Fna and costs 120–50 dh. The palms are too far north to bear dates and are grown mainly for wood. Covering more than 13,000 hectares, the Palmery is slowly being sold off for villas and time-share developments.

In the *Nouvelle Ville* off the Avenue Yaccoub el-Mansour, the **Jardin Majorelle** is a small, lush garden laid out by the French artist Louis Majorelle, who lived in Marrakesh until 1926. It was acquired by Yves Saint-Laurent, who added a touch of *haute-couture* to the pavilions and plant pots by painting them designer blue. Cacti are a feature among some fifty different plants. Open 8 a.m. to 12 noon and 2 to 5 p.m. in winter and 3 to 7 p.m. during summer; admission 7 dh.

Where to stay

Marrakesh has the best range of accommodation in Morocco. The most impressive is the Mamounia, where Winston Churchill used to paint from 1930 to 1950. Middle-range hotels include de-luxe package-tour hotels such as the Meridien, es-Saadi and the Atlas Asni. All have excellent sports facilities and you may wish to spend more for the use of a swimming-pool. There are also plenty of cheap, pension-style establishments, but they are often full.

Hotel Mamounia (*****A), Avenue Bab el-Jedid; tel. 448981. Former ONCF hotel, listed among the grand hotels of the world. It was supremely elegant until revamped, but the gardens are still superb. Quiet and convenient for the Djemaa el Fna. Excellent pool, tennis, casino.

Hotel Tichka (****A), Route de Casablanca, Semlalia; tel. 448710. If you stay in just one up-market hotel in Morocco, choose the Tichka. A jewel of a hotel with stunning interiors by American designer Bill Willis, resident of Marrakesh. Elegant, peaceful, with 138 rooms and a superb pool. In the *Nouvelle Ville*, a long walk from the shops and *medina*, so a car is useful.

Hotel Tafilalet (****A), Route de Casablanca; tel. 434518. A comfortable, relaxed, 1950s-style hotel. French-owned. Ask for a room overlooking the garden. Like the Tichka, it is a long hike from attractions, but similarly recommended.

Hotel Oudaya (***A), 147 Rue Mohammed el Beqal; tel. 448751. A new, modern hotel with ninety-two, rather small gallery-style rooms overlooking a small, sheltered pool. Excellent beds. Very convenient for the *Nouvelle Ville*. Recommended.

Grand Hotel Imilchil (***A), Avenue Echouhada; tel. 447653. Well-kept modern hotel in the *Nouvelle Ville* near the ramparts. Small pool, restaurant.

Hotel Chems (****B), Avenue Hoummen el Fetouaki; tel. 444813. Motel-type hotel with 274 beds. Car park. Pool. Garden. Two bars. Well-positioned, opposite the Mamounia.

Grand Hotel Tazi (**A), corner of Avenue el Mouahidine and Rue Bab Aguenou; tel. 442152. Eighty rooms. Like a hospital upstairs, but pleasant rear rooms. Beds variable. Clean bathrooms two steps up with good-size bath and bidet. Terrace. View of the Koutoubia.

Hôtel-Restaurant de Foucauld (★★B), Avenue el Mouahidine; tel. 445499. Forty rooms, Moroccan-clean, all with several beds. Front rooms very noisy. Traditional painted headboards and mirrors. Constant hot water. Minutes from Djemaa el Fna, this must have been a lovely hotel in its day.

Hotel Gallia (★★B), 30 Rue de la Recette; tel. 445913. Quiet, attractive hotel close to, but not disturbed by, the Djemaa el Fna. Twenty clean rooms overlooking a central courtyard. Recommended. (There are several other cheap hotels in this street; try **Hotel Souria** at number 17.)

Hotel CTM, Place Djemaa el Fna; tel. 442355. Rooms surround a small patio; those overlooking the square are very noisy, but what animation! Avoid in summer. Very popular so you are unlikely to get a room anyway.

Cheap, unclassified hotels for younger travellers include the **Hôtel du Café de France** and the **Oukaimadin**. Others are found on the Rue Zitoun el Kedim. There is a dusty camp site on the Avenue de France.

Where to eat

Local food is similar to Fassi cooking. Specialities include *m'rouzia* (mutton, prune and almond in a sweet sauce) and various other exotic *tajines*. Pigeon couscous, *kefta*, or minced meat, and *brochettes* are popular. A great choice of sweetmeats usually ends a meal: *m'hencha* (coiled pastry filled with almond paste), 'gazelle horns' and *briouats* made with honey and almonds. You can eat well in Marrakesh, but you will also pay dearly for the experience. Spoiled by patronage from the international set, many of the top restaurants are also fussy about who they let in.

La Maison Arabe (tel. 422604) is the oldest and most celebrated restaurant. Around 400 dh.

Yacout (tel. 441903), designed in spectacular fashion by American Bill Willis, is hard to find in the heart of the *medina*, but rewarding if you do. There are twelve types of *hors d'œuvre*. Good *bstilla au lait*. Roof-top salons, stunning WCs.

Restaurant le Marrakchi (tel. 443377). Attractive terrace restaurant overlooking the Djemaa el Fna, with tables around a fountain and uncomfortable Moroccan chairs. Very good food, especially *poulet au citron*. Licensed.

Restaurant Relais al Baraka (tel. 442341), on the Djemaa el Fna beside the *Commissariat de Police*. Up-market dining in a fountain court.

Many palatial nineteenth-century houses have been converted into 'Moorish restaurants'. All are doubtless exotic, but most cater to tour groups, and dinner with belly-dancing and German tourists is my idea of hell. Most menus feature *brochettes* and couscous. **Dar Marjana** (tel. 445773), **Dar el Barad** (tel. 445077) and **Dar Fez** (tel. 441793) are among the best.

Cheaper restaurants

Marrakesh has many cheap restaurants, mainly around the Djemaa el Fna and along Rue Bab Aguenou. **Chez Chegrouni** (next to the Café Montreal) enjoys an excellent reputation for cheap nourishing meals – yoghurt, *brochettes* and mutton *tajine*. Go early to get a table. The street beside the Banque du Maroque has half a dozen restaurants where you can eat a three-course meal for 50–60 dh in admittedly rather rough surroundings. **Hôtel de Foucauld** with a pseudo-Moorish dining-room adopts the common habit of slipping chicken, instead of pigeon, in the *bstilla*. At night Djemaa el Fna becomes a vast open-air restaurant, with food-stalls cooking *brochettes* over charcoal grills.

Gueliz restaurants

In Marrakesh you can eat a variety of good European, mainly French, food in civilized surroundings in the Gueliz. A number of restaurants are ideal for a quiet meal with a bottle of wine.

La Jacaranda (tel. 430069) is a good, but expensive, French restaurant with an open fireplace.

Bagatelle (tel. 430274) has a mainly French menu and al-fresco dining most of the year in pleasant atmosphere.

Le Petit Poucet (tel. 430069) is an old-bistro-style restaurant dating from the French Protectorate. Nice for lunch and reasonably priced.

La Taverne (tel. 431035). Mainly French, with a bar at one end and a fountain courtyard. Quiet dining from 50 dh for a generous four-course meal.

Villa Rossa (tel. 430832). Italian, specializes in seafood.

Rôtisserie au Café de la Paix (tel. 433118) specializes in char-grills.

What to do

Marrakesh enjoys itself at night. Apart from the traditional spectacle of the Djemaa el Fna, it has a number of worthwhile tourist attractions.

Bars

The only places to drink in the *medina* are in the **Foucauld** and **Tazi** hotels, but the *Nouvelle Ville* has plenty of bars. The best-known is the **Renaissance**, which has a roof-top terrace. The **Café les Negociants** is another popular drinking-hole. Two popular bars on the Avenue Mohammed V are the **Ambassadeurs** at number 6 and the **Regent** at number 34. If you do opt for a drink in a de-luxe hotel like the **Mamounia** or **Tichka**, expect to pay from 45 dh for a whisky.

Nightclubs

All the tourist hotels have discos. One of the busiest is the **Temple de la Musique** in the PLM Hotel N'Fis on the Avenue de France. **Diamant Noir, Café Jet d'Eau, Star House, Regent** and the **Restaurant Fassia** nightclubs are 'in' places. The nightclub in the **Hotel es-Saadi** has a good cabaret, belly-dancing, etc.

Casino

One writer has described the **Grand Casino de Mamounia**, next to the Mamounia Hotel, as tacky, but having played in the casinos at Monte Carlo, Juan les Pins, Las Vegas, Cairo and Macau, I would say that it is reasonable, if your intention is to gamble. Games range from

American roulette to *chemin-de-fer*, craps and blackjack, with private salons available for poker. There are 129 slot-machines with a 200,000 dh jackpot (won recently by a Spanish woman on a group tour). Package tourists are the main visitors. There is no entrance fee and you do not require your passport (unless you need to change more money). Restaurant-bar. Grand Mamounia-style décor. Opens 8 p.m. and closes when the last customer leaves.

Spectacles   Although usually packed with tourists, two resorts outside Marrakesh are recommended for colourful dinner-spectacles.

Chez Ali will collect you from your hotel for a fabulous mini-*fantasia* staged in an open-air restaurant in the Palmerie.

Oasis, 9 km from Marrakesh on the Casablanca road, serves excellent Moroccan food in elegant, comfortable surroundings. The architecture and lifestyle of each province of Morocco is reflected in the complex. Accommodation in twenty rooms, plus six suites. Meals 300 dh; spectacle at 11 p.m.

Fantasia   The *Fantasia* may seem stage-managed for tourists, but it is very professional and offers a chance to see local folklore. A typical *fantasia* featuring tribal food, music and dancing, culminating in the thrilling charge of Berber cavaliers, is held several evenings a week in Marrakesh and is booked through the larger hotels. About 250 dh per person.

Festivals   Morocco's best dance-groups perform at the **Festival of Folklore** held in June in the el-Badi Palace. For times and prices, check with the Tourist Office or a travel agent. The **Festival of Classical Music** in mid-June attracts many music-lovers, mainly French. Performances are held in the floodlit courtyard of the Bahia Palace. The official *Fantasia* is staged outside the ramparts in July. Enquiries from RAM and the Tourist Office.

Sports   There is an eighteen-hole golfcourse 4 km down the Tizi N'Tishka road. Most tourist hotels have tennis-courts as well as swimming-pools. There are seventeen public swimming-pools in Marrakesh.

Shopping   Marrakesh, like Fez, is a great crafts centre where unusual souvenirs and beautiful *objets d'art* tempt you wherever you walk. If you are in a hurry or do not wish to bargain, visit the **Direction de l'Artisanat**, Place Djemaa el Fna, or the **Artisanal Centre**, Avenue Mohammed V, near the Koutoubia, where Najibi Mohamed Bel Abbess makes attractive silverware.

Caravane (8 Rue Zniket Rahba Kedima), near the Djemaa el Fna, sells Berber jewellery and carpets. Carpets are an attractive proposition, the most renowned come from the Chichaoua region of the High Atlas.

Leatherware and metalwork are also good buys. On one visit to Marrakesh I spent three days bargaining for a finely chiselled brass tray. I offered a price as I passed the shop one morning, and checked to see what the trader thought when I returned that way in the afternoon. On the second day, I stopped for mint-tea and we discussed everything except the tray. On the final afternoon, obviously impressed by my patience, he accepted my offer. Returning to my hotel, trailed by a boy bearing the huge object wrapped in newspaper, I was certain everyone in the street knew what I had paid.

Useful information

Tourist Offices, APOTM (local tour operators), 170 Avenue Mohammed V; ONMT, Place Abd el-Moumen Ben Ali, tel. 430258.
RAM, Hotel Atlas Asni, tel. 430939.
InterRent-Europcar, 63 Boulevard Zerktouni, tel. 431228.
Pharmacies, 166 and 120 Avenue Mohammed V.
Banks, on the Avenue Mohammed V and off the Djemaa el Fna.
Police, tel. 19.
PTT, Avenue Mohammed V. Telephone and post office open daily including weekends until 9 p.m.

Moving on

There are regular domestic flights to all major towns from Marrakesh-Menara **Airport** (5 km) and international departures to Paris, London, Geneva, Lyon, Brussels and Madrid. The **railway station** is off Avenue Hassan II. Seven departures a day to Casablanca for other connections. The direct night-train to Tangier leaves at 8.15 p.m. CTM and other **buses** leave from outside Bab Doukkala. Frequent services to major towns. Local buses leave from the Djemaa el Fna. There are *grand-taxi* ranks on the Djemaa el Fna and at Bab er-Rob, fare from Djemaa el Fna to Ourika 10 dh. Taxi-hire to Ourigane, from 200 dh. *Petits-taxis* charge from 5 dh per place within Marrakesh; ranks are on Djemaa el Fna and Avenue Mohammed V. **Horse-drawn carriages** can be hired near Djemaa el Fna, from 120 dh (tourist price). Outside Bab Doukkala from 20 dh (local price) but drivers are likely to refuse tourists a place. Negotiate a price per hour when bargaining.

There are many **car-hire** companies in Gueliz and agents at hotel desks. Parking police are active on the Djemaa el Fna. *Gardien des voitures* elsewhere. **Bicycles** are ideal in Marrakesh and can be hired from the Foucauld, PLM Toubkal, el-Andalus, es-Saadi and Agdal hotels, from 30 dh a day.

The High Atlas

Silvan valleys cutting into the High Atlas make a cool escape from Marrakesh especially during June–August. The most popular excursion from the city, to Ourika and Oukaimeden, can be made in a day although there is overnight accommodation. From Bab el-Jedid the road crosses the Haouz Plains which are covered with wild flowers in spring.

Ourika Valley

Once the controllers of the water supply to Marrakesh, Berbers in the Ourika Valley are subject to occasional floods. An abnormal thaw in 1987 hurled their houses about like matchboxes, also destroying many villas owned by wealthy Marrakshis.

The tiny hamlet of **Setti Fatma** is 22 km from where the road forks to Oukaimeden. A boy will lead you over stepping stones in the stream to the *koubba* of Setti Fatma, a greatly venerated female *marabout* commemorated in a huge four-day *moussem* in August. It is a pleasant spot for a picnic, but bring it up from Marrakesh: only walnuts and soft drinks are sold locally.

A motorable road ends at Setti Fatma, but you can trek from here to the small Berber village of **Tacheddirt** (10 km) with simple but clean accommodation in a Club Alpine Français hut. Guides and mules will present themselves in Setti Fatma; what you pay, as usual, will depend on how good you have become at bargaining.

Where to stay

In summer the Ourika Valley is crowded with local visitors, so accommodation is scarce. There are two charming hotels on the road from Marrakesh; Setti Fatma itself caters more for backpackers and campers.

Hotel-Restaurant Amnougour, 49 km Marrakesh; tel. 4304502. Twenty-three clean, light and airy rooms (numbers 18 and 19 are especially pleasant), with good beds; you go to sleep to the sound of the Oued Ourika rushing by in the valley. Recommended.

Hotel Ourika (****B), beyond the Amnougour; tel. 4433993. A very quiet place, rather like something you might find in Bavaria – including German guests. Thirty-seven beds and a licensed bar-restaurant. Parking. Small pool. View.

Hotel Azrou, on the river bank in Setti Fatma. Cheap and uncomfortable beds. Lovely view. Basic meals.

Where to eat

There are a number of pleasant restaurants on the road up the Ourika Valley. The **Kasbah de Ourika**, an old house that belonged to the Glaoui, is good for lunch; 80 dh menu. French management. Good view. Other places along the river are **Le Lion de l'Ourika** and the **Auberge Marquis**, with a large Moorish-style dining room – lunch groups. The **Auberge Ramontchko** is another possibility.

Shopping

The Musée d'Aghbalou, 47 km from Marrakesh, sells a mixture of genuine antiques and modern artefacts. Good carpets, rifles and ceramics. Pleasant owner. Credit cards accepted. A very worthwhile stop where there is no hassle to buy.

Oukaimeden

On a clear day the drive up to Oukaimeden is an invigorating experience, with views of Berber villages in the valleys. Occasionally you must halt for a shepherd bringing sheep down from the mountains – in summer they are taken up to cooler pastures. At 2,600 m the terraced orchards of walnuts and almonds cease and shortly afterwards you enter the white world of Oukaimeden, known to Berbers as 'the meeting place of the winds'.

What to do

Skiing

The world's second-highest ski-lift ascends to the peak of Djebel Oukaimeden (3,273 m). Ten rides cost 20 dh. Early morning is the best skiing time; the six runs become wet in the afternoon. You can hire equipment at a shop next to the Hôtel de l'Angour. Moroccan ski-instructors charge 40 dh an hour for lessons. Only 2½ hours' drive from Marrakesh, beware of arriving in the snow still wearing summer clothes, as I did. Adding injury to insult, the ski-lift also hit me on the head; I still had the lump five days later in the Sahara.

Trekking

If you plan to climb Djebel Oukaimeden, seek advice at the large CAF hut in Oukaimeden. French-run, it sleeps 160, has hot water and a bar-restaurant. From the peak you can descend in about 2½ hours to the CAF but on the Tacheddirt side of the pass.

A map in the CAF hut indicates the location of prehistoric **stone-carvings** at Oukaimeden. They overlook the dam at the road-barrier, but you may need a guide to point them out. The ink-blue dam is reported to have good **fishing**.

Where to stay

Oukaimeden has one hideous ski-lodge and two hotels where booking is essential.

Hotel Imlil (★★★B); tel. 459132. Cosy, Alpine-type chalet with eighty-one beds. Bar-restaurant and nightclub for *après-ski* life.

Hôtel de l'Angour (★★B); tel. 459005. Better known as *'Chez Juju'* after Madame Juvien, its warm, blonde proprietress who came to Morocco in 1947 from Brittany. Thirty-seven beds and a busy, friendly bar-restaurant. Within walking distance of the ski-lifts.

Amizmiz

Amizmiz, 50 km from Marrakesh, is another possible day-trip. Following the S507, you will pass the Barrage Cavagnac, renamed the Oued N'Fis dam, the first reservoir built by the French in 1935. Beyond here is the **Hôtel de France**, with basic rooms opening on to a walled garden (from 30 dh a night). On the river bank beside a crumbling *kasbah*, Amizmiz is an important market town for Berber farmers. A Tuesday *souq* sells pottery and carpets. Many of the acrobats somersaulting in the Djemaa el Fna and other squares in Morocco come from Amizmiz. Frequent bus-service to Marrakesh.

From Marrakesh there are two passes across the High Atlas to the southern oases. The most obvious if your destination is Zagora is the Tizi N'Tishka and on to Ouarzazate, but if you want to visit Tinmal, you must take the Tizi N'Test.

The Tizi N'Test Pass

Used as a caravan route and military corridor since the eleventh century, the Tizi N'Test (2,092 m) was opened to traffic in 1928. A sign at the exit from Marrakesh indicates whether or not the pass is open. The initial stretch of road to Ourigane is no problem, but snow and landslides frequently block the upper section in winter. There is less traffic than on the Tizi N'Tishka, but the descent from the peak can be treacherous in bad conditions. With a stop at the Tinmal Mosque, the crossing between Marrakesh and the Route P32 takes five to six hours.

From Marrakesh the road runs through olive groves up to **Tahanaout** (34 km). A striking Berber village overlooking the Oued Gheghala Valley, it has an important *zaouia* to Moulay Brahim. There is an annual pilgrimage for women who cannot bear children. Tuesday *souq*.

Asni   Surrounded by some of the tallest peaks in the Atlas, Asni (47 km) fancies itself as the 'Chamonix of Morocco'. A tiny settlement at 1,165 m, it offers peace and panoramic views. It is also a base for walking in the Toubkal National Park. Asni's one hotel, the Grand Hôtel du Toubkal, has a good reputation for food, but on my visit, although the hotel was open, I could find no one in charge. I walked in, removed a key, inspected a room and departed.

Grand Hôtel du Toubkal (***A); tel. 3. Clean, fresh rooms. Pool, solarium, garden. Ornate Moorish-style dining-room. Panoramic terrace for drinks. Parking.

Imlil   Imlil, 17 km from Asni, off the main road, is a small mountain hamlet which acts as base-camp for climbing Djebel Toubkal. I was told by local guides that the ascent of the mountain (4,167 m) requires only ordinary climbing knowledge in summer, but considerable alpine experience is essential between December and March. A CAF hut caters almost exclusively to climbers and trekkers. Maps, porters and donkeys are available. Other chalets charge about 50 dh a night. There are one or two café-restaurants. If you have no interest in outdoor pursuits, you can skip Imlil without loss.

Ourigane   Ourigane, 16 km south of Asni on the Tizi N'Test road, is less pretty than the Ourika Valley, but is a good half-way stop on the pass. There are two hotels on a wooded mountainside.

La Roseraie (****A); tel. 432094. Rooms and suites set around a large swimming-pool. Specializes in health and riding holidays. Very expensive.

Au Sanglier Qui Fume; tel. 9. Charming, wisteria-covered auberge, with fourteen clean, comfortable rooms by a stream. Built in 1930 as a soup-stop for timber trucks crossing the Tizi N'Test, it is managed by an elegant French woman. Rustic bar-restaurant with an open fire. Excellent home-cooking. Central heating, pool, parking, *pétanque*, fishing, walking and mule-treks. Ideal for independent travellers.

From Ourigane, the road climbs to Tinmal through the N'Fis river gorge, a fairytale world of *pisé* villages and orchards. This is Goundafi country, the fiefdom of feudal warriors who were constantly at war with the sultan and the Glaoui. Most of the local *kasbahs* belong to them. Ijoujak is a pretty village at the entrance to the valley; 2 km beyond Ijoujak turn right at a water tank to see the once-grand Goundafi *kasbah* of Talaat N'Yacoub, built in the early 1900s.

Tinmal   Three km further along the *piste* you will see the great brick-coloured Tinmal *r'bat* on the opposite bank. This alone is worth the journey over the Tizi N'Test, and as it is the only mosque open to non-believers in

Morocco, do not miss the occasion to see inside. The broken bridge across the river looks daunting, but children are available to help and the mosque is only a fifteen-minute up-hill scramble.

History

Built in 1121, the *r'bat*, or fortress-mosque, of Tinmal was the headquarters of Ibn Tumert, a religious zealot who preached against lapses from the Islamic code. Safely ensconced on this hill-top site, he launched armed punishment raids against any tribes who disobeyed. The Almoravid sultans in Marrakesh were unable to control his loyal disciples and in 1146, led by Abd el-Moumen, they swarmed down from the Atlas, ushering in the Almohad dynasty.

Except for a *gardien*, the *r'bat* is deserted. Its roof has gone and weeds grow in the courtyard, but the walls, arches and *mihrab* are well preserved. The *darf w ktarf* decoration in the prayer-chamber is probably the work of the same architect who built the Koutoubia. The position of the minaret, partly over and behind the *mihrab*, is unorthodox. A stairway up to the top opens on to a stunning view of the village of Tinmal against the Atlas.

Idni, the next hamlet, lies at the foot of the summit of the Tizi N'Test. A French-owned hotel has closed, but the **Café Igdet** is not without charm, and the owner, Mohammed, is very likeable. Asked how many rooms, he looked in and counted: *'Cinq ou six.'* And *combien*? That depends on whether or not there is a carpet. *Sans tapis*? *'Dix dirham'*, he replied, pressing me to stay for mint-tea.

The final 18 km to the top of the Tizi N'Test is effortless driving. There is a good view of Djebel Toubkal above, and the Souss below from a look-out beneath the TV relay station. The 1,600 m descent drops you down to the valley floor. Remember that ascending traffic has the right of way. A splendid tarmac road leads to the P32 junction to Taroudannt, 51 km west (see p. 216), or Taliouine, 67 km east.

Taliouine

A straggling roadside town, halfway between Taroudannt and Ouarzazate, Taliouine is bypassed by most travellers. The town itself has nothing to offer, but I found the site, near a large palm oasis, and with an old *kasbah* and an excellent hotel, wonderful for a night after driving over the Tizi N'Test. There is a Monday *souq* but otherwise little to buy apart from **saffron**. October is the ideal month to visit Taliouine, when the surrounding fields are carpeted in indigo-coloured saffron flowers. The town is the centre of the world's biggest saffron-growing area. More than 370 hectares, divided into 3,000 plots, are owned or worked by local farmers, who do quite well, thank you – a mature farm can produce 6 kilos of saffron a year worth some 30,000 dh. Itinerant workers from all over the Deep South come to cut the saffron crop in October or November. Saffron-flavoured tea is a popular local beverage; the precious herb sells for about 8 dh a gram.

What to see

The **Glaoui *Kasbah*** looks impressive from a distance; up close, you quickly see it is in an advanced stage of collapse. In the West an evacuation order might be placed on it, but being in Morocco, it is inhabited by fourteen poor families of the ex-servants of the Glaoui, including the *maître d'hôtel* at the Ibn Tumert hotel. The architectural moulding is different to that of other *kasbahs* in the Deep South. Four square towers feature shell motifs cut out of the plaster above the windows.

Where to stay

From Taliouine to Ouarzazate it is an easy run on a tarmac road via Tazenakht.

Taliouine has one of the best hotels in Morocco, owned by the PLM (Paris, Lyon, Marseilles) chain, but it is little used by groups rushing east or west.

Hotel Ibn Tumert (****B), BP 105 Taliouine; tel. 30. At the Ouarzazate exit, turn right behind the *kasbah.* Clean, quiet, comfortable rooms. Pleasant staff. Excellent licensed restaurant. Pool. Parking. The hotel shop has a huge variety of souvenirs and necessities, including super tampons – the man held up the packet to show me.

Auberge Souktana, Ouarzazate exit. Cheap, basic hotel run on a limited budget by a pleasant Moroccan, Ahmed Jadid, and his French wife, Michelle. Candlelight, home cooking. Quiet, if owner's children are not crying. Guided mule-treks to Djebel Sirouq, 120 dh per person per week.

From Taliouine to Ouarzazate it is an easy run on a tarmac road via Tazenakht.

The Tizi N'Tishka Pass

The P31 across the Tizi N'Tishka pass (2,260 m) to Ouarzazate is a splendid road with frequent switchbacks, often three S-bends together, and many blind corners. The road is not too steep, but in winter there are frequent landslides and rock falls. When snow or slides block the pass during December to March a dramatic 'brief' in the local paper advises prospective travellers. Use your horn to warn cars, timber-trucks, children and shepherds you are coming. Unfortunately this also alerts hustlers selling walnuts and rocks. They wait on the worst bends, and as you slow down they step out like matadors, holding the object like a missile about to be thrown through your windscreen. If you become nervous and stop, you are unlikely to get away without buying something. I soon learnt to swerve, making them jump out of the way, and also making them very angry.

Allowing for detours to Telouet and Ait Benhaddou (see p. 196), you can cross the Tizi N'Tishka in a day's drive from Marrakesh, reaching Ouarzazate (197 km) in time for an aperitif.

As well as the attraction of the great Glaoui *kasbah* at Telouet, the drive over the 'Tishka' is a marvellous nature lesson. 23 kilometres from Marrakesh, the gums are replaced by ash and walnut trees give way to woods of oak, juniper and pines, before even alpine vegetation ceases as the road climbs through barren scree. The peak itself is bleak and windswept, then the scenery changes abruptly on the southern flank – the village of Amerzgane is a harbinger of the spectacular '*kasbah* country' of the Deep South. By now you will be shedding your

Telouet

jacket. The crumbling Glaoui *kasbah* of Telouet is the main attraction on the Tizi N'Tishka route, a 20-km detour on a lonely, winding road. Beyond a forlorn village chickens, dogs and children scatter as you draw up, then they all converge on you. *'Donnez-moi un bon-bon'*, or *'Donnez-moi un cigarette pour Papa'*, is the plaintive cry of the Atlas. Having neither sweets nor cigarettes at the time, I gave one child a gold 25-centime piece which she turned over in her hand and then stuck in her nose. The few poor families living in the vicinity are the offspring of relatives of the Glaoui.

The ghostly Telouet *kasbah* was the headquarters of the Glaoui brothers: Madani (1866–1918) and Thami (1879–1956) were powerful local *caids*. In 1893 when a severe snowstorm struck a huge *harka* led by Sultan Moulay Hassan coming over the 'Tishka' from the Tafilalet, the brothers provided a banquet for the sultan's 3,000 men. They were rewarded with various ranks and Thami el-Glaoui was made Pasha of Marrakesh. By 1912 when the French arrived, the Glaoui were the undisputed 'Lords of the Atlas' and sub-Sahara. The French Protectorate entrusted Thami el-Glaoui with responsibility for crushing nationalist opposition in the south. Cruel but charismatic, he became a legendary figure in Europe. He visited Paris on several occasions and in 1953, at the personal invitation of Sir Winston Churchill, he attended the coronation of Queen Elizabeth II.

A *gardien* will unlock the massive double door of the *kasbah* and show you a portion of the shadowy labyrinth where, it is said, no single person ever knew the entire way round. Part-stone, part-*pisé* and rotting wood, it is a disturbing place, decorated in keeping with a Moroccan pasha's idea of *la belle époque*. Some rooms also display very fine craftsmanship. The Ministry of Culture plans to restore Telouet and other significant *kasbah-ksour* in the southern oases.

The southern oases

Ouarzazate

Ouarzazate's splendid name, conjuring up images of *kasbahs*, oases and caravans, is misleading. The town is a comfortable base for local sightseeing, but it is a new administrative centre, functional rather than attractive. The local economy depends on tourism and the film industry, both attracted by its dry climate and exotic environs – the films shot at the Ait Benhedda *kasbah* include *Lawrence of Arabia*, *Jesus of Nazareth* and *Jewel on the Nile*. The film studios, 3 km west of town, can be visited between 8 a.m. and 8 p.m.

What to see

The only attraction in Ouarzazate is **Taourirt Kasbah**, the great Glaoui *kasbah* that used to lord it over the southern caravan routes. An enormous domain, it once housed the extended family of Thami el-

Glaoui (he never lived there himself) plus hundreds of servants, builders and craftsmen. The massive edifice has fallen into decline, but it remains a fine example of a local *kasbah*. A small section of the crumbling complex may be visited from 9 a.m. to 12 noon and 3 to 6 p.m.; closed Sundays.

Where to stay

Ouarzazate is booked solid with package tours during the peak season. It lacks middle-range hotels.

Hotel Riad Salam (****A), Avenue Mohammed V; tel. 882206. A well-run hotel with mock-*kasbah* architecture. Clean, comfortable rooms with excellent beds. Mosquitoes and the *muezzin* disturb sleep. Swimming pool. Parking.

Hotel Le Zat (****A); tel. 882521. Quiet location on a ridge overlooking the dam on the eastern end of Ouarzazate, within walking distance from the *kasbah*-complex. Sixty comfortable rooms. Pool.

Hotel Bélère (****A), 22 Avenue Prince Moulay Rachid; tel. 882803. 263-room tourist hotel.

Hotel Tichka Salam (***A), Avenue Mohammed V; tel. 882206. In a shady street next to the Riad Salam, it is run by the same company. Smaller, but equally comfortable.

La Gazelle (**B), Avenue Mohammed V, near Place 3 Mars; tel. 882151. Owned by charming Madame Fillon. Thirty clean, pleasant rooms, all facing a garden. Bar-restaurant. Small pool. Parking. Long walk to town centre. Recommended.

Hotel Royal, 24 Avenue Mohammed V; tel. 882258. Basic, but clean and cool, with thirty-two rooms, from 62 dh for a double with shower. Public WC. Town centre.

Hôtel de la Vallée, 1 km south on Zagora exit. Simple new hotel run by pleasant young men. Terrace overlooking a small oasis. Rooms clean, but claustrophobic. All have basin and bidet. Hot water. 60 dh double. Restaurant. Happy atmosphere. Good for young travellers.

Where to eat

Avoid the big hotels. I had a delightful lunch at **La Gazelle** – a simple cheese omelette, runny in the centre, and a clean, crisp tomato and onion salad. With no groups, it is a very *sympatique* place to eat. **Chez Dimitri** on the Avenue Mohammed V is a colourful restaurant run by an ex-legionnaire, reportedly a millionaire and something of a local cult figure. His chef comes from Milan. The menu, mainly Italian cuisine, costs from 50 dh. Good food, good service, great fun. Licensed.

The **Restaurant Ouarzazate** and **La Kasbah** café-grill, both in the complex opposite the Glaoui *kasbah*, look attractive, but I did not eat there as the terrace was filled with French from the nearby Club Mediterranée. Moroccan menu from 70 dh. Unlicensed. Reservations essential.

What to do

Ouarzazate is not noted for shopping other than tourist-type souvenirs. The **Co-operative des Tissues**, a quasi-artisanal centre on the crossroads to Zagora, sells carpets and pottery. Open 8.30 a.m. to 12 noon and 1 to 6 p.m. weekdays; 8.30 a.m. to 12 noon Saturdays.

Useful information

Banks, a pharmacy, shops and the Tourist Office are all located on the Avenue Mohammed V. Other agents and rent-a-car are on the Place 3 Mars. Supermarket opposite Dimitri's.

Moving on

Ouarzazate **Airport** is five minutes from the town centre: daily connections to Casablanca, Marrakesh, Agadir and er-Rachidia; also direct flights from Paris. The CTM **bus** terminal is outside the Tourist Office, Avenue Mohammed V. Regular service to Marrakesh, about six or seven hours. Daily service to Zagora and twice-daily to Tinerhir. There are also private bus services. *Grands-taxis* leave from the Place Mouhadine.

Excursions from Ouarzazate

From Ouarzazate you can visit some of the spectacular local *kasbahs*. You may have seen the *kasbahs* in Tangier, Rabat and Essaouira, but in the Deep South they are more than just fortifications, housing a complete community within the fort. The greatest of the Glaoui *kasbahs* is Telouet, but local *caids* have left this part of Morocco studded with their feudal domains.

A typical *kasbah* consists of a series of stepped, battlemented towers, surrounding a lofty central *agadir* which was used as a store-house as well as the ultimate retreat. The lack of rain allowed towers to be built of *pisé*, several storeys in height, without any eaves; split palm-trunks were used for roofing beams. The windows tend to be small and defensive. Having visited Saada and other *pisé*-built towns in North Yemen, I was struck by the similarity of the architecture. The basic layout of the houses is the same, although the Yemenite house is not, strictly speaking, a *kasbah*. The ancestors of the Alaouites came from Saudi Arabia, so perhaps others came from neighbouring Yemen.

The *kasbah* was a fragile defence against attack in that it dissolved like gelatine if a stream was diverted around its base – one can imagine tower after tower collapsing in slow motion.

Ait Benhaddou

Ait Benhaddou, 22 km west of Ouarzazate on the P31, then 10 km from the signpost, is one of the most spectacular sights in Morocco. Ranged like tiers of milk chocolates on a bank of the Oued Asif Mellah, it is never without visitors, but you can wait until they leave. Walk down the path from the café-hotel. For 3 dh a mule will carry you across the river to the opposite shore, where children lead you up to the *kasbah*. A formidable stronghold, it was not built for gracious Western living, but as a refuge from the harsh outdoor life at night. Most people have now left in search of work, but it is still inhabited by half a dozen families scratching a living from farming and tourism. You can climb up to the top, but the best view is from the café-hotel opposite.

Ait Benhaddou has several basic hotels:

Café-Restaurant La Kasbah. Dormitory-type rooms. Moroccan-style clean. Bar-restaurant. Splendid terrace overlooking Ait Benhaddou. Avoid midday tour-groups. With the right company, fun for a night.

Al Baraka Auberge-Restaurant, on the road beyond La Kasbah. Four rooms, dusty but pleasant enough. 40 dh double, shared facilities, cold water. Three-course meals 40 dh. Unlicensed. Occasional folkloric events.

Kasbah of Tamdaght

Five km beyond Ait Benhaddou, about twenty minutes' walk, is another *kasbah* which is worth seeing. The bridge over the river has collapsed so tourist coaches cannot get through.

Kasbah of Tifoultoute

This former lofty Glaoui *kasbah* is about twenty minutes' drive on a good road west of Ouarzazate, signposted Agdz-Zagora. The decorative brickwork on the old tower may date from the seventeenth century, but the *kasbah* was restored in the 1960s. Something of an entertainment complex for package-tours staying in Ouarzazate, it is best visited in the early morning, or at dusk.

You can eat very well at the *kasbah* (tel. 2813), which is managed by Abdou and Dominique, his French wife. Traditional Moroccan food. Licensed. Each evening tourists are bused out from Ouarzazate for a display of rousing Berber dancing. Breakfast was delicious (20 dh) and a *gardien* let me out of the great, walled courtyard with a huge set of keys. Recommended.

Tagrout

Tagrout, or what locals call the *Kasbah des Cigognes* is about thirty minutes' walk from the Hôtel de la Vallée at the southern exit of Ouarzazate. My *faux-guide* said it dated from the seventeenth century. It is certainly very old, and very beautiful, although in an advanced state of decay. And, yes, storks do nest in its battlements.

The road to Zagora

If you have chosen to see Tinmal on the Tizi N'Test road, you can shorten your journey to Zagora by turning off the P32 at Tazenakht on to the S510 cross-country road to Agdz. Although exceedingly rough, the journey across the base of Djebel Anaour is enjoyable. At times barren plain or sandy *piste*, the landscape is broken by splendid *ksour* nestling in the oases. The biggest settlement, Ait Semgane-n-el-Grara, has sustenance in an emergency. Four-wheel drive is recommended, but I managed in the Renault 4. Fill up with petrol, water and anything you may need in **Tazenakht**, which sells good carpets and has a basic hotel, the last before Agdz. After turning off the road to Foum Zguid (see p. 200), the tarmac ends beyond the cobalt mines at Bou Azzer after which there are no road signs. Without a compass, I drove east into the rising sun, wondering whether or not I had been foolish to tackle such a lonely road. Twenty km from Tazenakht, I pulled up for an old man who half-raised a hand and then dropped it. Speaking only Berber, he indicated that he had no more idea of the way than me. We stopped several times to pick wild-flowers and for him to pray, and finally we reached the tarmac again. In Agdz, men said he was the *marabout* from Taroudannt making the pilgrimage to Tamegroute, south of Zagora. 'He is so happy,' they said. 'When you stopped, he had been walking for six days.' 'We will go together to Tamegroute,' I told them.

Agdz

Agdz consists of one long street lined with ox-blood-red arcades of shops which ends in a small square overlooked by a military-style *kasbah*. The town has some of the best pottery – old honey-jars and butter urns – in Morocco. There are several café-grills, a supermarket and two basic hotels.

Hôtel Café-Restaurant de Draa. Seventeen clean, simple rooms with good beds and hot water. Cheap. Friendly management.

Camping La Palmerie, 1 km down the dusty road past the irrigation pump. Clean, pleasant enough site with a little shade. Showers and simple meals.

The excellent direct road from Ouarzazate to Zagora, Route P31, takes you up and over the Anti-Atlas through the Tizi N'Tinift pass – where the entire south lies at your feet. The road then clings to the right bank of the Oued Draa, which drains the Anti-Atlas.

The Draa Valley

The river normally dries up in the Sahara, but after exceptional rain it occasionally reaches the Atlantic near Tan-Tan. When I drove down the valley the el-Mansour dam was open and the Draa was in full spate. The caramel-coloured *ksour* lining the river banks like medieval castles along the Rhine, the shiny green date-palms and the shimmering turquoise river made it one of the most magical journeys in Morocco.

The Draa and its dependent oases have been the subject of tribal disputes for centuries. In the sixteenth century a Berber family from Tamegroute rose to become the Saadian dynasty. Following their collapse, the powerful Ait Aitta Berbers ruled the valley until 1934. Thami el-Glaoui, in cahoots with the French, then dominated the region from the High Atlas to the Draa. Since Independence, the population of 80,000 – Berbers and Arabs, with pockets of Jewish converts – has lived in peace. Farming and commerce are the main activities and tourism will inevitably provide more employment.

A few kilometres beyond Agdz is your first view of the stunning river valley, a sharply defined belt of water lined with palms. On several occasions Mohammed, the *marabout*, and I stood in wondrous silence on spectacular look-outs – but never for long, as every look-out had a boy selling a basket of dates. The **Ksar of Tamenougalt**, on the opposite river bank, is one of the best in the Draa.

South of here there is an almost unbroken line of *ksour*, among the most impressive in Morocco. Their ramparts, crenellated roofs and tapering towers surround a jumble of courtyards, passages (with blind exits to confuse invaders) and houses. More like stables than places of human habitation, chickens and goats wander unrestricted through the family living quarters.

Tinzouline

Tinzouline, forty minutes' drive from Zagora, has a splendid clump of *ksour* that seem to grow out of the ground, rather than being built upon it; in the rare event of rain, they would all melt back into the landscape. About 6 km before Zagora, on your left is **Malal**, another curious mud-built village, entered through the triple-arched, diamond-patterned Bab el Kasbah. Tribal elders meet under the spreading tamarisk tree as no doubt tribal elders have done since time immemorial.

Zagora

Surrounded by palms, with an avenue of ox-blood-red shops, Zagora is like a ruby set in an emerald ring. The town is a popular tourist destination from Ouarzazate (94 km), but the locals are more relaxed and you might even consider staying several days. Everything of significance – the PTT, bank, shops, cheap hotels, café-restaurants, pharmacy and mechanics – is on or behind the Avenue Mohammed V. It ends at a dusty roundabout in front of the *caid*'s office, where a faded sign reads *'Tombuctoo, 52 jours'* and an arrow points south to the Sahara.

The palmery

The most interesting thing to do in Zagora is to visit the palmery. A four-wheel drive is advisable for the sandy tracks and frequent mud patches created by leaking irrigation channels. Take a guide, otherwise you may spend most of your time trying to find your way out. In spring, the female palms are fertilized by an official pollinator who scrambles up the trunks as nimbly as a rat. How long had he been doing this job, I asked. *Cinquante ans.* And how old was he? *Soixante*, he told me. My attention was caught by a boy with a sparrow crushed in his palm. I gave him a dirham, and popped the bird, too young to fly, into my camera-bag. An hour later, on the opposite side of the oasis the boy appeared with another sparrow, which I bought for a biro – a bird in the hand being now worth two in the great Zagora palmery!

Where to stay

Zagora has several very good hotels – you often find things in Morocco where least expected. Booking is advised throughout the year. All hotels have group-tours, although most stay at the de-luxe Hotel-Club Reda, and all have mosquitoes from the palmery.

Hotel Tinsouline (★★★★B); tel. 847252. In the town centre. A well-run hotel with ninety clean, cool, quiet, rather small rooms, overlooking the palmery. Nice swimming-pool. Good, licensed restaurant with pleasant service. Four-course menu from 80 dh. Parking. Recommended.

La Fibule du Draa (★★A); tel. 847318. About fifteen minutes' walk from the town centre in the Amazrou palmery, M'Hamid exit. Twenty-seven large rooms with Moroccan décor, all with private facilities. Clean and calm, with a pretty garden pool. Very popular. The restaurant serves good *tajines*. Recommended.

Hotel-Restaurant Asmaa (★★B). M'Hamid exit. Fourteen clean, comfortable rooms, all with shower. Kasbah-style architecture; hideous *nouveau-Maroc* décor. Pleasant garden. The restaurant has a reputation for outstanding Moroccan food.

Hotel Oued Draa (★A), Avenue Mohammed V; tel. 10. Fourteen rooms above a courtyard. Back rooms quieter, but poorly ventilated. Clean, with showers and WC. Traditional Moroccan restaurant below. Meals from 25 dh. Bar.

Hôtel la Palmerie (*A), Avenue Mohammed V; tel. 847008. Twenty clean, basic rooms with WC and shower, and probably very hot in summer. Restaurant-bar. Nice *patron*. On the edge of town near the sign to Timbuktu.

Camel trips and desert excursions are arranged by most hotels in Zagora.

Shopping

Souvenirs and artefacts shops are found outside the Hotel Tinsouline. The **Maison du Berbère** has a good choice of carpets but prices are high because of tour groups. The *lithams*, or turbans worn by tribesmen, are now made in pink, yellow, red and green as well as the traditional black, because of tourist demand. Zagora holds two weekly *souqs*, on Wednesday and Sunday.

Excursions from Zagora

From Zagora you can visit Tamegroute and Tinfou. Beyond here, the wistful outpost of M'Hamid is the end of the road for all save ghostly caravans to Timbuktu.

Tamegroute

The pot-holed road to Tamegroute (22 km) passes Amazrou, which once had a large colony of Jews, like Beni Hayoum and Beni Sbih, further south. Tamegroute is a small village with a greatly revered *zaouia*, founded in the seventeenth century by Abou Abdallah Mohammed Naciri. The Naciri brotherhood was very influential in the Draa, acting as ombudsmen as well as missionaries in the disputes among the caravanniers. I left the *marabout* in front of the mosque. Taking his swag he gently kissed my hand and walked, ever so slowly, towards the gate. Non-Muslims may visit the courtyard and, peering into the *zaouia*, I saw him kneeling in front of the mausoleum.

Within the complex is a celebrated **library** of early Islamic books, many written on gazelle skin. The gracious custodian will show you a history of Islam from the eleventh century – Sunni doctrine, he stresses, not Shi'ia – a fifteenth-century street map of Alexandria, a sixteenth-century work on astronomy and a seventeenth-century volume on the medical uses of plants. Islamic scholars travel to the library from all over the world. There is no local accommodation other than the *zaouia*. There are primitive pottery kilns at the southern exit of Tamegroute.

Tinfou

The desert proper begins at Tinfou, about fifteen minutes' drive. Basic rooms are available at the **Auberge Repos-Sable**, run by two artists of repute. Their paintings cover the walls and sand covers everything else. Friendly ambience. Meals. 30 dh a night.

Zagora to Foum Zguid

This road is deserted apart from trucks that depart from Zagora on market days, between noon and 2 p.m. Take all provisions for the dusty, bumpy, five- to seven-hour trek – the route of the 'Marathon des Sables', which was won in 1989 by a twenty-six-year-old Moroccan who had never seen the desert. Between them, the sixty-six courageous competitors drank 25,000 litres of mineral water supplied by back-up trucks. There are no facilities.

East from Ouarzazate

Driving across arid *hammada* from Ouarzazate on Route P32, I saw a boy with five camels, still in shaggy winter coats, against the Atlas snow-line. It was one of those instant images that pop up in Morocco. **Skoura** is surrounded by *kasbahs*. The biggest, **Amridil**, is 4 km from the centre of town. Its imposing appearance is relieved by extravagant decoration, some deeply moulded, others *trompe l'œil*, the patterns always angular like the scenery. Skoura itself is a dusty administrative centre with a basic hotel and an uninspiring Thursday *souq*. Skoura–Kelaa des M'Gouna is 50 km.

Kelaa des M'Gouna

Kelaa des M'Gouna is a small, tree-shaded town where every shop, including the mechanics, sells *Eau de rose*. Pink Persian roses are grown exclusively for distilling *attar* in the local Rose Water Distillerie during April and early May. I have no idea of the cost of rose-water as my guide bought some for me when I was filling the car with petrol. 'It cost me 125 dh, but as you are my friend, my brother – *soyez bienvenue à Kelaa* – I will give it to you for 100 dh,' he said, sticking the box beneath the dashboard. Festival of Roses (May).

Where to stay

There is only one hotel, which may be empty or booked by a group-tour, but most travellers do not stay overnight.

Les Roses du Dades (****B); tel. 883807. Turn left at the main junction in the town centre. Modern and bland, the hotel is nevertheless quiet and comfortable. Swimming-pool, stables. Restaurant-bar. Recommended.

What to do

An excursion leaves from the hotel at 9 a.m. – on horseback you visit potteries, an ancient Glaoui *kasbah*, and have lunch in a traditional Moroccan house. 350 dh including guide.

The **Bureau des Guides et Accompagnateurs**, opposite the Café Rendezvous des Amis, provides information on local treks, mule-rides and trips to the *kasbah* at the entrance to the M'Goun gorge.

Vallée des Roses

Local people in Kelaa des M'Gouna recommended the Vallée des Roses detour, which rejoins the P32 before Boumalne du Dades. The rough road which leads off behind the hotel gets worse with every kilometre and after one staggering clump of *kasbahs* signs of human habitation vanish. In spring, however, thousands of roses bloom in the gorges and it is a superb sight. After about an hour the road veers south and drops on to the tarmac again. Kelaa des M'Gouna–Boumalne du Dades 23 km.

Boumalne du Dades

Endeavour to reach Boumalne du Dades by mid-afternoon as the Dades Gorge looks its best before sunset. Boumalne itself is a dull, garrison-type town, with one main street of white and yellow shops ascending the hill.

Where to stay

The hotels are built on the plateau above the commercial area. Cheap eating-places surround the mosque. The hill-top **Chems** is said to be the best restaurant.

Hotel Madayeq (****B); tel. 834031. Attractive but bland package-tour hotel, with 100 rooms and orange fibre-glass chairs by the swimming-pool. Terrace and bar-restaurant.

Hotel-Restaurant Salam. A new hotel opposite the Madayeq. Twelve rooms with hot showers, from 50 dh. Meals.

Hôtel-Restaurant Vallée des Oiseaux; tel. 834138. A motel-type establishment near the Shell station, with twelve rooms, six with showers. Clean and comfortable. Restaurant.

Hotel Tamlalte, 15 km from Boumalne. Better than usual basic hotel. Eleven rooms and one hot water shower. Improvements to the décor would do wonders. Clean and calm, but soft beds. Meals and refreshments.

Dades Gorge

The Dades Gorge is an impressive short detour into the High Atlas from Boumalne. In a four-wheel drive vehicle, you can make the 'Todra loop' and rejoin the P32 at Tinerhir, but most travellers are

Ait Oudinar

content to drive as far as Ait Oudinar (24 km). Outside Boumalne take the road marked 'Meserhir'. The *kasbahs* built by the Ait Aitta along the river valley are dwarfed by the tumbled rock formations that change colour every hour. There are some splendid picnic spots and I imagine climbing in the gorge is a thrilling experience. Buses from Boumalne to Ait Oudinar.

Ait Oudinar has one hotel and a good camp site.

Auberge Gorge du Dades. A basic hotel by the Dades of twelve clean rooms with basins and three hot showers. There is electricity for five hours each evening. Delicious Berber cooking. Friendly owner. A charming spot for the night. Mule excursions into the gorge from 100 dh with a guide.

Tinerhir

The section of the P32 to Tinerhir is uninspiring, but the town itself has a dusty, raffish atmosphere that is appealing. Flanked by a long arcade of shops, the main square contains everything of importance: a bank, the PTT bus terminal and *grand-taxi* rank. A few palms shade tribesmen as they exchange greetings, holding each other's hand in the long, intimate grasp of peoples living on the edge of the Sahara. A *souq* behind the Hotel Todra consists largely of workshops banging out wrought-iron objects.

A Glaoui *kasbah* built on the hill above the town once glowered over the palmery inhabited by the Ait Aitta; today it is a sad graffiti-covered ruin.

What to see

The best plan is to arrive in Tinerhir at dusk, stay overnight, visit the Todra Gorge early and the palmery later. Both can be seen in a day.

The view from the hill of the vast Tinerhir oasis is one of the great sights of the south. A visit to the **palmery**, one of the biggest in southern Morocco, is worthwhile and you can hire a mule if you do not wish to walk. The majority of the villages belong to the Ait Aitta, though whether actually *ksour* or *kasbahs* is hard to say. Most have tapered, crenellated towers and the walls of the houses are cut in a zig-zag pattern, just as though the builder has spontaneously slashed the *pisé*. Desultory slashes become extraordinary patterns on the walls of the great Ait Amitane *kasbah* 6 km north of Tinerhir.

Each *ksar* controls a section of the palmery and is responsible for the maintenance of the irrigation canals. Try to see the oasis before mid-day when people stop for a siesta; if it is late in the day wear a long-sleeve shirt and trousers against the mosquitoes.

Where to stay

As a base-camp for the Todra Gorge, Tinerhir is a popular over-night stop for package-tours, so booking is advisable.

Hotel Sargho (★★★★B); tel. 834181. A member of the Kasbah Tours hotel chain, the Sargho has 62 plain but comfortable rooms. The swimming-pool is the only one in town. Bar-restaurant. Parking. Quiet with superb views. Ten minutes' walk from the town centre.

Hotel Todra (★★B); tel. 834249. A clean, pleasant, older-style hotel on the Place Principale. Thirty-one rooms, most with showers. Kitsch décor, but congenial ambience. Restaurant.

Where to eat

You will neither starve nor rave about the choice of food in Tinerhir. I had a reasonable dinner at the **Hotel Sargho**, Austrians in a mini-bus spoke highly of **La Kasbah**, an attractive, air-conditioned restaurant serving good portions of local food from 50 dh, while some French people suggested the **Kafer Restaurant Sada** for good, cheap couscous.

Todra Gorge

Many travellers like to spend a night in the Todra Gorge. At 7 a.m., I counted thirty tourists cleaning their teeth in the Oued Todra – a French Landrover expedition had negotiated, with some difficulty, the loop from Dades (two vehicles had broken chassis). Visiting the gorge from Tinerhir is no problem as you can negotiate the cost of a place in a *grand-taxi* or hitch a ride on a Berber truck. In a good four-wheel drive you can carry on to Imilchil and exit on to the P24 north of Beni-Mellal – eight or nine hours of tough driving.

Outside Tinerhir, the tarmac road climbs a ridge overlooking a strip of lush cultivation in the valley. Beyond the 'Source of the Sacred Fish' the *piste* enters the gorge proper, flanked by towering cliffs. It ends at the river, which is usually just a trickle across the gravel bed.

Where to stay

Accommodation is limited to three hotels built under the precipice.

Hotel el Mansour has palms growing through the roof. Quiet, as group-tours stay at the other two. Five very basic rooms, shared WC. Simple Berber-style meals.

Hôtel des Roches. Ten rooms. Shared outside washbasins and WCs. Very cheap.

Hotel Yasmina. A popular hotel since 1932. Outside facilities. Meals. Cheap.

The hotels organize mule-rides up the gorge and expensive expeditions to the *Fête des Fiancés* at Imilchil in September.

There are two **camp sites**, Le Lac and Camping Atlas, in the lush palmery at the 'Source of the Sacred Fish'. Small café-hotel.

The Tafilalet

From **Tinejdad**, 40 km east of Tinerhir, you soon enter the pre-Saharan province of the Tafilalet, which covers 60,000 km. You can either carry on to the capital, er-Rachidia, on the P32, or cut across to Erfoud on Route 3451 (90 km), which is poorly served by public transport if the number of hitch-hikers is an indication. In London there would have been a queue, but here everyone stood under the shade of the last gum-tree. All raised a hand as I passed but I stopped for a more enterprising couple who had walked further along the road and were standing in the sun.

The scenery between Tinejdad and Erfoud is flat and dusty with mini whirlwinds chasing each other across the plains. The odd blue-bellied lizard scuttles across the road as if its life depends on it. **Jorf**, a large, crowded town living half-in, half-out of long yellow arcades, would make an ideal set for a Western movie and even in this out-of-the-way place, you can have Kodak developed, a 'Photo-Copie' made and a 'Tailleur aux Jeunesse' will run up a suit while you wait. There is also petrol. Jorf to Erfoud is a 30-minute drive.

Erfoud, Rissani and the dune outcrop near Merzouga form the sandy heart of the Tafilalet, the most remote oasis complex in Morocco, sustained by the rivers Ziz (Arabic for gazelle) and the Gueris, which rise in the High Atlas. It is a harsh region where dates and tourism provide a small income for some but the population of about 80,000 is falling, as people drift away in search of work. Itinerants return to harvest the dates from half a million palm trees, but times are bad – headless palms, especially in Rissani, indicate the effects of a long drought. The Tafilalet has none of the exotic desert charm of Zagora. Trapped in the car by a sand-storm, I found the *landscape brooding, almost menacing.*

History   The Tafilalet has been likened to a miniature Mesopotamia. Homeland of the ruling Alaouite dynasty, for thousands of years it was one of the most prosperous regions of the Sahara, profiting from the caravan trade in slaves, gold and ivory from the sub-kingdoms of Niger and Mali. Almost obliterated by sand, the ruins of the ancient capital of Sijilmassa lie on the outskirts of Rissani. On many occasions local tribesmen revolted against a central authority beyond the Atlas, and when the Saadian dynasty was in disarray, a *marabout* movement gained strength in the Tafilalet and seized Marrakesh, which was subsequently taken by Moulay Rachid (1666–72), a member of the Alaouite family of *shorfas* from the Tafilalet. Many local Filali are distant relatives of the Alaouite family in Rabat.

The venerated founder of the Idrissid dynasty, Moulay Idriss I, arrived in Morocco through the Tafilalet. A majority of the people are Arab, although the indigenous natives are Berbers of the various Ait

Aitta clans. Both dark and light-skinned people inhabit the *ksour* but inter-marriage is not practised and sexual license is prohibited. Marriages are arranged by the parents and girls are often betrothed at the age of fifteen.

The date industry

Date-palms were probably brought to Morocco by the Arabs between the seventh and twelfth centuries and became the economic mainstay of the southern oases. An annual caravan used to transport dates and indigo to Timbuktu. Today the number of palms in the Tafilalet is estimated at 500,000. The harvest varies from palm to palm: one tree may yield 10–20 kilos of dates, while another in a more favourable position may produce 70–80 kilos. Felling a palm is illegal without authority and picking dates before the designated harvest is also a punishable offence. A farmer's wealth is measured in date-palms; the average holding is thirty trees.

Morocco has about thirty-five different types of date, which are graded according to sweetness, dryness and texture. As with apples, what you enjoy depends very much on individual taste. Sweet, honey-like dates include *melhoul, boufegour* and *bousekni*. An entire camel-load of dates cost $3 at the turn of the century; today, a kilo from the Draa or the Tafilalet costs at least 10 dh. The average annual consumption in the Deep South is about 200–300 pounds of dates per head.

In October, nomads from miles around pitch their tents on the perimeter of Erfoud hoping for work as date-pickers. Men stamp the dates into packs with their bare feet. Seeing the date harvest may put you off eating dates for life.

er-Rachidia

At the junction of the P32 and the P21 to Midelt and Meknes, er-Rachidia is also known as *Ksar es-Souq*, after a fort built by the Foreign Legion at the turn of the century. The town is an important market centre for local Berber farmers and pastoral nomads. It is based on one long broad avenue, the Mohammed V, which reminded me of a town in the inland Riverina of New South Wales where I grew up; there was equally little to do. There is a Sunday *souq*.

Where to stay

The town has about 400 beds. Booking is advisable in case a group tour is in town.

Hotel Rissani (****B); tel. 572186. On the south side of the Ziz river bridge. Very clean. Good, big beds. Garden. Pool. Views. Parking. Recommended.

Hotel Oasis (**A), Rue Abou Abdallah; tel. 572519. Forty-six rooms with bath. Clean and pleasant. Bar-restaurant. Town centre, near the market and mosque.

The Ziz Valley

From er-Rachidia the Oued Ziz winds through a rugged landscape. *Ksour* on both banks owe their existence to irrigation channels, some of which are hundreds of years old. The bus-trip from er-Rachidia through the valley to Erfoud takes two hours; it will be longer by car as you will want to stop. It is a fascinating journey, especially during the October date harvest. If you forget to fill up with petrol in er-Rachidia, you may stop longer than intended.

Source Bleu Meski

Twenty-two km south of er-Rachidia, off the P21 to the right, is the Source Bleu. A tank around the spring, built by the Foreign Legion, makes a delightful palm-shaded swimming pool in the barren *hammada*. I would have loved to plunge in but hustlers drove me away. There is a camp site with the only guaranteed flushing WC in Morocco – it is built over the spring.

Erfoud

Erfoud is a hot, dusty town built by the French in the 1930s to administer the Tafilalet. The tamarisks and eucalypts have grown taller, but Erfoud has changed little and, as in many frontier towns, you are often saved from potential boredom by who you meet. I was walking down the main street when I heard my name: 'Christine! Christine! You must be the writer driving the white Renault 4. You are four months late,' cried a handsome youth, shaking my hand enthusiastically – he worked in a hotel I had contacted.

What to see

You can walk around Erfoud in thirty minutes and have seen all there is. The bank and the PTT are on the Avenue Mohammed V and there is a daily *souq* in the market square. The main *souq*, under tents, is on Sunday. A visit to the **Marmar Marble Factory**, near the Hotel Salam, is recommended. Here marble inset with fossilised shells is cut and polished for export and slabs are made into ashtrays, paperweights and table-tops. The fossils come from a ridge 90 km from Erfoud which archaeologists date from the Devonian period, 350 million years ago.

A 3-km uphill walk from behind the main square in Erfoud takes you to **Bordj Est**, a fort built by the French now occupied by the Moroccan army. There is a panorama of the oasis. Date Festival (October).

Where to stay

Erfoud is desperately short of hotels. Bookings are essential but the cheap establishments will take guests on a first-come basis. The best place is the Auberge-Kasbah Derkaoua, 23 km of sandy *piste* from Erfoud.

Auberge-Kasbah Derkaoua, BP 64. French-owned. Twelve small, but comfortable rooms, plus hot-water bottles for winter. Small pool, garden, absolute peace and quiet. Stunning dining-room, excellent service, French-Moroccan cuisine. Licensed. Highly recommended.

Hotel Salam (****A), Route de Rissani; tel. 576424. Almost always booked up with tour-groups. Small rooms are kept spotless by housemaids fighting wind-blown sand. Do not leave your window open. Plain pool area. Bar-restaurant. Good breakfast. Parking. Fifteen minutes' walk to the town centre.

Hotel Tafilalet (***B), Avenue Moulay Ismail; tel. 576036/6535. Overpriced and unattractive hotel with twenty rooms, all with bathroom. Soft beds. Bar-restaurant. Popular with Landrover expeditions. Near town centre.

Hôtel les Palmiers, 36 Avenue Mohammed V. Fifteen airless and very basic rooms all with hot-water showers. Friendly manager says hotel is air-conditioned in summer.

There is an exposed, stony **camp site**. Not recommended.

Where to eat   Eating in Erfoud is limited. There are several cheap café-restaurants on the Avenue Mohammed V: try **Café-Restaurant Les Fleurs** and **Café du Sud**. The **Hotel-Restaurant Ziz**, at the end of Avenue Hassan II, serves reasonable food, but more important, it is licensed to sell beer and wine. Ask to see the store-room: it's an eye-opener in a place like Erfoud.

Moving on   **Grands-taxis** to er-Rachidia and to Rissani 5 dh. A three- or four-hour trip to Merzouga by Landrover taxi costs 300 dh; enquiries at Hotel Tafilalet. The CTM **bus station** is on the Avenue Mohammed V.

Rissani   The journey to Rissani (22 km) on a good road takes about forty minutes. About half-way you enter the oasis, a dusty, melancholic place with many dead palms. The town centre, a collection of *kasbahs*, barracks and other ox-blood-red fortifications, surrounds a vibrant market square shaded by tamarisks. Most travellers stay in Erfoud and I found nowhere to recommend here.

The souq   That this once wealthy capital of the Tafilalet has shrunk in status to a three-times weekly *souq* (Sunday, Monday, Thursday) is sad, but you can sense Rissani must have been a great terminal on the desert trade route. Laid out under the trees are piles of salt, fossils, rocks, onyx objects and pink *roses du sable*, or 'sand roses', formed of eroded sand crystals. Nomads wander about buying ropes, rugs, sandals, knives and charcoal. A few chickens and rabbits are also sold. Larger animals are sold behind the *souq* – camels, goats and a few sheep. The car park holds 300 donkeys.

Sijilmassa   Scattered stones are all that remains of the legendary city of Sijilmassa, west of Rissani. Founded in AD 757, Sijilmassa was the wealthy capital of the Tafilalet from the twelfth century until its destruction in the fifteenth century.

Mausoleum   About 2 km south-east of Rissani is the mausoleum and *zaouia* of Moulay Ali Cherif, the father of the Alaouite dynasty. Entry to the mausoleum is forbidden, but behind it you will see the huge **Ksar d'Abbar** enclosed by long walls. Dating from 1800, it accommodated various members of the extensive Alaouite family. A triple enclosure topped with gun emplacements probably acted as the royal treasury. Other ksour around Rissani and environs include the *ksar* of Oualad Abdelhalim, which was built in 1900 by Sultan Moulay Hassan's elder brother, the governor of the Tafilalet.

Shopping   Shops surrounding the market square sell attractive *objets d'art* as well as trash. Years ago, I bought an old musket in Rissani fashioned from bits of wood, inlaid camel-bone and motor-car for £15 – today you pay £50 for something similar. Silver jewellery, an occasional lovely *fibula*, sabres, powder-boxes, incense burners, candlesticks and woven baskets are other good buys. A French tour-guide told me si. considered Rissani the best place to buy carpets in Morocco.

Other shops line the Avenue Moulay Ali Cherif. In **Nomad Artefacts** Mahjoubi Hassan told me his father had been a caravannier taking soap, tea and carpets from Erfoud, Zagora and Goulimine to Timbuktu, the caravan of thirty or forty camels changing at each stop. According to Hassan, the last caravan passed through Rissani only two years ago. Finally cross with my questions, he stood up and cracked a carpet like a whip. Was I sure I did not want to buy anything? No? 'Then have *harira* with my mother and me at seven o'clock,' he said. 'And be sure to mention my name in your book.'

Merzouga

Many travellers come to Morocco to climb not the Atlas mountains, but the great Erg Chebbi sand mountain at Merzouga. Dawn over the dune, at about 6 a.m., is one of the great sights of the south. Where the tar ends and the sand *piste* begins follow the telephone poles into Merzouga, a small hamlet with a Saturday *souq*. If you have no car, you can always find a seat in a Landrover taxi. On market days there are trucks from Rissani.

Erg Chebbi

The dune is a vast pyramid of sand blown up over the centuries on the black plain. You half expect Wilfred Thesiger to come plodding over the peak with an entourage of wild-haired Bedouin boys, or Peter O'Toole, robes flying, to come charging down on a white Arab mare. People who wish to climb the dune usually bed down on one of the local café roofs. A place between the snoring sleeping-bags costs from 50 dh, including a *tajine* dinner. The **Café des Amis** is popular with young travellers; older people may prefer the **Hôtel des Palmiers**. Most rooms are dormitory-style as Merzouga is short of accommodation and never without tourists. Independent travellers who want to see Erg Chebbi in style should stay overnight at the **Auberge-Kasbah Derkaoua**, between Erfoud and Merzouga (see p. 206).

Figuig Province

Figuig is one of the loneliest provinces in Morocco, whose 100,000 inhabitants practise pastoral nomadism and date-farming. A speciality is *taem figuigi*, couscous made with rancid butter and dates. The P32 tarmac road from er-Rachidia to Bouarfa crosses an arid plain. South of Bouarfa it becomes the P19 to Figuig Oasis, a road on which you will not meet another Western traveller.

Figuig Oasis

The town is an administrative centre, garrison and border-crossing to Algeria (8 km). A bank, shops and bus-terminal are found on the Boulevard Hassan II. The Hotel el-Meliasse has large rooms with showers from 50 dh. The town is surrounded by *ksour*, and if you have not visited the *ksour* country of southern Morocco, a 30-km tour around the palmery is recommended. At Ksar el-Hamman women bathe in warm springs with their robes billowing out around them.

You can buy leatherwork, silver jewellery and carpets woven by the Ait Serhrouchen tribe. The nearest tourist-type facilities are in er-Rachidia (405 km).

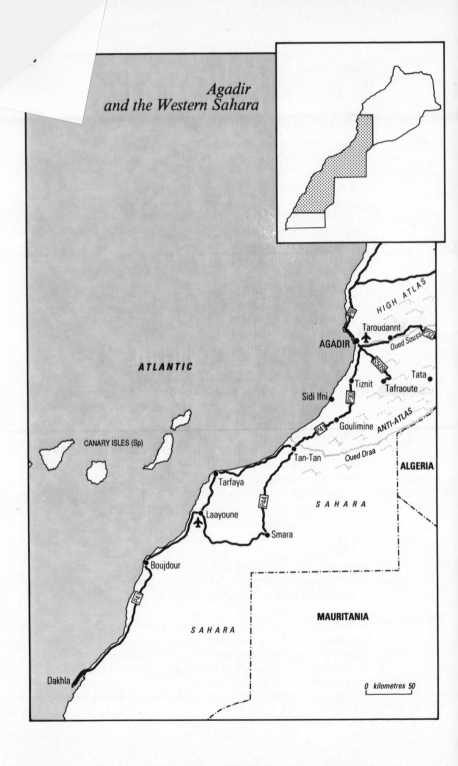

Agadir
and the Western Sahara

HIGH ATLAS

Taroudannt

AGADIR

Oued Souss

Tata

Tiznit   Tafraoute

Sidi Ifni

Goulimine   ANTI-ATLAS

Tan-Tan   Oued Draa

ALGERIA

ATLANTIC

CANARY ISLES (Sp)

Tarfaya

SAHARA

Laayoune

Smara

Boujdour

SAHARA

MAURITANIA

Dakhla

0   kilometres   50

Agadir and the Western Sahara

Introduction

The Souss Valley, sheltered by the High Atlas and the Anti-Atlas, and the vast expanse of Western Sahara share the best and worst of Morocco's climate. The Souss is almost semi-tropical; the Sahara is dry and swept by the relentless wind, the *chagi*. Cutting a swathe through the Anti-Atlas from Agadir to Taroudannt, the Souss is a fertile, self-contained region. It is largely peopled by Berbers of the Chleuh tribe, who are racially pure and vigorously independent. While excellent roads link it to Agadir, the region maintains an individual character. You will feel more relaxed in the Souss. There is little hard-sell and no hostility if you won't buy.

Agadir, on the Atlantic at the mouth of the Souss, was purpose-built for package-tourism. Morocco's leading beach resort, it now accounts for 40 per cent of the total earnings from tourism. The town has everything for the modern tourist and is an excellent base for the independent traveller, preferably with a car.

From here you can head south to Goulimine and on to Tan-Tan in the Western Sahara. Further south, the journey is often more colourful than the destination, but it is an indescribable joy to be the only foreigner. All there is in what the Spanish called the Rio de Oro is the ocean creaming on to white beaches, with excellent fishing. It helps to like seafood.

Agadir

If older travellers identify with Tangier, today's generation of tourists associates Morocco with Agadir, although many of its 500,000 visitors each year are middle-aged blue-collar workers – German, Swedish and British in that order. Americans are conspicuously absent from the rows of deck-chairs facing the Atlantic. While Agadir offers excellent opportunities to explore the Souss, most of these tourists cling to their hotel, where their needs are understood. Staff speak their language, the kitchen serves familiar meals and they can read the tabloids flown in by Royal Air Maroc.

Unlike Marrakesh, or Fez, Agadir takes care of its tourists. Behind a strict policy of *laissez-faire* is a sensible governor and a powerful hotel lobby. No one wants to scare the goose that lays the golden egg. The beach is swept at dawn and patrolled by mounted police, so tons of flesh can tan horribly in peace.

Before you hold forth, as an independent traveller, about how awful Agadir is, drive up to the headland. The *medina* here once enjoyed the best view on the Atlantic coast; now the odd flight of steps to nowhere indicates you are walking on a mass grave. At 11.42 p.m. on 20 February 1960 a fifteen-second tremor flattened the town; 12,000 people were buried in their houses, which eventually had to be levelled. Present-day Agadir is no classy dame, but her rise from the ashes is the miracle of modern Morocco. You may miss her dearly in the Western Sahara.

History

Portuguese interests in Agadir date from 1505. The colony was attacked several times by the Saadian ruler Mohammed ech Sheikh, who captured the fort in 1541 and started a domino movement of Portuguese withdrawals from their Atlantic ports in Morocco. Agadir profited from sugar-cane, cotton and date exports until it was conquered by Moulay Ismail in 1687. Internecine rivalries after his death led to Sultan Sidi Mohammed Ibn Abdullah's blockade of the port. He moved the Jewish merchant community to the rival port of Mogador (now Essaouira). Cheaply-produced sugar from the West Indies also contributed to Agadir's decline. In 1819 the town was hardly inhabited, but resettled by traders and fishermen under French administration it developed into one of the world's biggest sardine-fishing ports. Fishing, light industry and tourism are the present-day activities.

Main areas

Arriving in Agadir, you will find it has not exactly knitted together since the earthquake, but what you have is a clean, bland, well-planned town. You can find your way about easily with a street map – free from the SCIT on the Boulevard Mohammed V, or from Holiday Services, Rue Hassan II.

The town is divided into five zones, all well-signposted: residential, port, industrial, commercial and tourist. The 'Secteur Touristique et Balnéaire' is sandwiched between the beach and the very long Boulevard Mohammed V, which runs from the port to the Royal Palace. Most of the big hotel complexes are found here and on the Boulevard de 20 Août. All new buildings must comply with anti-earthquake regulations. New architecture is an eclectic mix of Spanish and Greek, with green Moorish tiles. If you parachuted into Agadir, you might be anywhere in the Mediterranean.

What to see

There is little to spark an interest in Agadir. You have a good view from the headland. The **kasbah** built c. 1540 has recently been restored. An inscription over the entrance notes that the Danes had trading interests here in 1746. There is mild curiosity in buildings which withstood the earthquake. French-built, they include the Office

National de Pêche and a row of shops, including the Hotel Miramar, at the port end of the Boulevard Mohammed V.

Nouvelle Ville

Outside the Tourist Zone, Agadir is functional rather than picturesque. It was built with a similar urgency to parts of post-war London. The town centre surrounding a large, grey concrete administrative block known as Immeuble A is of an ugliness without parallel in Morocco. The PTT is located opposite, together with most of the shops and banks. Where to stay

Where to stay

Agadir has around 20,000 beds, but you must have a reservation. Most hotels are booked for package-tours; middle-range hotels are scarce, and cheap hotels are occupied by local holidaymakers or travelling salesmen.

Hotel Medina Palace (*****A), Boulevard du 20 Août; tel. 845353. Large deluxe tourist hotel. Moorish style. Swimming pool heated in winter. Tennis.

Hotel Sahara (****A), Boulevard Mohammed V; tel. 840660. 554 beds. All amenities. Popular with British tourists. Parking.

Club Salam (****A), Boulevard Mohammed V; tel. 840840. 420 beds. All amenities. Well-managed. Friendly staff.

Hotel Oumnia (***B), Quartier des Dunes; tel. 840351. 360 beds. On the beach. All amenities. Facilities unremarkable, but pleasant atmosphere.

Hotel Miramar (***A), Boulevard Mohammed V; tel. 840770. 24 beds. Near the port and main beach. Rear rooms quiet. Good restaurant.

Hotel Paris (**B), 571 Avenue Kennedy; tel. 822694. 21 rooms around a courtyard. Convenient for the bus station and Artisans' Centre, but a long walk to the beach.

There are a number of studios and self-catering flats in Agadir. Ask the SCIT for a list.

Residence Tafoukt, Boulevard de 20 Août; tel. 20875. 210 beds. Convenient for the beach. Shop, bar, pool and parking.

There is a **camp site** at the port end of Boulevard Mohammed V. Showers, shops and 24-hour international call-box. Direct beach access. Quiet though unattractive site.

Where to eat

You will eat neither well nor authentically in Agadir, where most holidaymakers are on *demi-pension*. Outside the hotels, restaurant menus are posted in German, English, French and Italian. In a medium price range **Le Jardin d'Eau** (French), the **Miramar** (Italian), **La Tonkinese** (Asian) and **Darkoum** (Moroccan) are not bad. Avoid the pretentious **Restaurant du Port** which serves poorly cooked fish at silly prices. The stalls on the right before you enter the port serve the best seafood in Agadir, recognized by the smoking chargrills and crowds of locals. If having lunch here, try to arrive by 12.30 (they stay open until 11 p.m. in summer and 7 p.m. in winter). Delicious plates of fresh prawns, *calamares* and sardines cost from 20 dh; the service is slick and tourists are treated with a special courtesy. As you might expect, they are not licensed. Other cheap, local-style restaurants are found around the Place Lahan Tamri. Food shopping in Talborj is a quarter of the price of somewhere like the Moussem Super Market in the *Secteur Touristique*.

What to do

Nightlife

Agadir's tepid nightlife is limited to discotheques in its large hotels. Two of the best are **Tan Tan** in the Hotel Almohades, and the **Byblos**, part of the Dunes d'Or Hotel. Entrance and the drinks are similar to European prices. Some establishments, like the Hotel Bahia, have a 'happy hour'.

A Berber evening in **Temsia**, a small village 30 km from Agadir, is highly recommended. Held in an illuminated eighteenth-century fort, it begins with a superb dinner of chicken, or fish *tajine* and homemade *tangoun*, prepared by Berber women cooks. The cost of 150 dh includes entertainment provided by Berber musicians – they were led by an eighty-six-year-old dancer married to a twenty-one-year-old girl on my visit, but he may have expired by now. The tour offers a glimpse of genuine local folklore. You will need a sweater unless you join in the dancing. Contact **Sahara Tours**, Avenue General Kettani, tel. 821565.

Shopping

Agadir has several possibilities for shopping: local shops, the Artisans' Centre, or a weekend *souq*. The hassle from traders is negligible compared to the 'three pirates' – Tangier, Fez and Marrakesh.

Traders around Immeuble A gently urge you to come in, but their goods are shoddy. Several shops sell postcards of Agadir before the earthquake: you may get a handful in lieu of change. The Artisans' Centre offers a limited choice. The best shopping is in the weekend *souq*. A jolly, genuine *souq*, despite being built in the late 1960s, it has a selection of attractive ethnic bric-à-brac: bellows, oil-lamps, cartridge holders, jewellery. Take your time bargaining. Even go away and return as people are packing up at 6 p.m. A good stall for 'Saharan items' is opposite the gate off the Rue Moussa Ibn Noussair.

Sports

Agadir is the activities centre of Morocco. Water-sports include wind-surfing, sailing and para-gliding. There is a new marina. Swimming is safe and there is good surfing at Taharzoute (18 km). There are more than 200 tennis courts, two golfcourses and nearby equestrian centres.

Useful information

Royal Air Maroc, Avenue General Kettani, tel. 823145.

InterRent-Europcar, Boulevard Mohammed V, tel. 823003.

British Consulate, Rue des Administration Publiques, tel. 827741.

ONMT, Avenue du Prince Héritier Sidi Mohammed, tel. 822894.

American Express, Voyages Schwarz, Boulevard Hassan II.

Banks, Avenue des FAR.

PTT, top end of Avenue Sidi Mohammed.

Newspapers are sold in hotel bookshops and in shops on Avenue Hassan II.

Moving on

International and domestic flights leave from Agadir **Airport**, 4 km south. Local **buses** to Tarhazoute, Inezgane and the airport leave from the Place Salam. This is also the *grand-taxi* rank. *Petits-taxis* are plentiful. Mopeds and motorbikes for hire near the Hotel Almohades.

Tarhazoute

If you dislike crowds, drive, hitch or catch a bus to the swathe of empty sand at Tarhazoute (18 km). It has a beachfront camp site and seafood restaurant. The haunt of hippies during the 1970s, the town itself is scruffy and peopled with hustlers pushing cannabis.

The Souss

Immouzer des Ida Outanane

The Ida Outanane are a confederation of Berber tribes living in this western aspect of the High Atlas above Cap Rhir. Turn right at Iamraht. The drive to Immouzer (25 km) is picturesque, but is marred by Moroccans selling fossils and other diggings from the Atlas. They practise the same frightening ploy as the crystal sellers on the Tizi N'Tishka, stepping out on the bends and forcing you to slow down. Some became quite aggressive when they saw I was alone.

Built on a mountain-top, Immouzer des Ida Outanane is a small town with a Thursday *souq* which attracts coaches from Agadir. The local honey is famous; marijuana honey is an irresistible present to take home. Honey Festival (August).

Auberge des Cascades (★★★B), tel. 16. A delightful spot with mature garden. Pool. Bar-restaurant.

The **Immouzer Tinkert Cascades** are 4 km walk from the village. The rich mineral content of the water has calcified rocks, even surrounding plants. There is a blue grotto for swimming. Crowded at weekends.

Inezgane

Urbanization and industrial growth in Agadir will eventually engulf Inezgane, 13 km to the south. The town is a busy regional centre with a big Tuesday *souq* but is otherwise of little interest. South-bound travellers change buses here. It is a staging point for *grands-taxis* with inland connections to Taroudannt and Marrakesh. The **Pergolas** restaurant, under French management, serves an excellent lunch.

Massa Lagoon

To reach Massa Lagoon, take the Tiznit road and turn right, 6 km beyond the village of Tiferghal, marked Tassila. A rough *piste* continues past the village to the lagoon, formed where the Oued Massa ends in marshes. Surrounded by dunes, the estuary is famous for birdwatching. You can count up to twenty different species during the migratory period. There is a beautiful camp site at **Sidi R'bat**, further along the beach, which also has clean, basic rooms. Sidi R'bat has two claims to fame: the beach is said to be where the whale disgorged Jonah, and it is where the Arab warrior Oqba Ibn Nafi is supposed to have ridden his horse into the ocean after conquering Morocco. A return-

Taroudannt

trip from Agadir takes a day.

You can also see Taroudannt in a day, but endeavour to stay. It has several good hotels and is only really animated after dusk. There are two roads from Agadir. Avoid the shorter P32, which is congested with market trucks. The slightly longer Route 2 is less stressful, but neither is particularly scenic except for occasional hazy glimpses of the High Atlas.

History

Taroudannt lies at the head of the fertile Souss Valley between the Anti-Atlas and the High Atlas. It was the Saadian capital in the sixteenth century before the Saadi sultans transferred rule to Marrakesh. This is why Taroudannt is sometimes called an imperial city. With the blockade of Agadir it was unable to export its products and fell into decline. Ignored by the French, it shrank to nothing more than a market town for the Souss, which is how it remains today. Lying off the tourist circuit, it is one of the most charming towns in Morocco.

What to see

Taroudannt has no great monuments like Rabat or Marrakesh. Its unique man-made attraction is the red **ramparts** enclosing the *medina* in a hot embrace. They seem to run off in all directions when you arrive at the roundabout from Agadir. The walls date mainly from the eighteenth century and have been greatly restored.

Taroudannt has two main squares within its dark, ox-blood-red *medina*. Lined with *café-terraces*, the Place Assarag is the social centre. The most direct access to the *souqs* is beside the Banque Marocaine. It is easy to find your way about in the *medina*, but should you become lost, there is always a tout to show you the way out and attempt to sell you a carpet.

The *souq* is full of eye-catching shops. Taroudannt is chief town of the Chleuh Berbers, who are talented craftsmen. You can buy carpets, *babouches* and other typical Moroccan items. There are many jewellery and antiques shops. Number 122 in the *Souq* **des Bijoux** is one to look at. Beware of fakes. If you go into **Ali Baba's Cave**, you will not come out without buying something.

Shop 3 in the Spice Market is a traditional Berber **herbalist,** stacked with jars of cure-alls: cocoons to be pounded and drunk against diarrhoea; garlic as a cure for intestinal cancer; cloves to press on an aching tooth; gum-Arabic for tachycardia; powdered cowrie-shells and lemon-juice to dab on acne. As I sifted through the mumbo-jumbo, a customer bought 250 grams of ginger-root – to make his wife work harder in bed, he said. Among blocks of indigo and incense, bulb-eyed chameleons cling to tiny sticks as if their lives depend on it. If not used as fly-catchers, they are dried and burned against the 'evil-eye'.

Taroudannt has two weekly markets – on Thursday and Sunday – when Berber farmers bring in produce to sell. The same hand held up to warn against taking a photograph is just as likely to proffer an olive or a date.

Miss the tanneries near Bab Khemis if you have seen them in Fez or

Marrakesh. Do not buy local wildlife pelts.

Where to stay

Like the raffishly personable Tan-Tan in the Western Sahara, somehow Taroudannt has that magical thing called style. Having one of Morocco's best hotels has something to do with it. Many people go to Taroudannt just to stay at the Gazelle d'Or, but the two other hotels – the Salam and Taroudannt – are equally good for different reasons. **Hôtel la Gazelle d'Or** (*****A); tel. 852039. Built in 1930 as a hunting lodge by a French nobleman. 32 rustic bungalows with open fires set in lush gardens. Tennis, riding, *hammam* and Olympic-size swimming-pool. Décor is 'Pasha' and *nouveau-riche*. Tie *de rigueur* for dinner. Charming management. Utter peace. Advance reservations essential in winter and during the 'Turtle Dove-Shooting Season': May–July.

Hotel Salam (****A); tel. 852312. 143 rooms and thirty-four suites. Ancient palace with exotic décor and a loyal following. Excellent Moroccan food. Courtyard pool. All amenities. Avoid lunch-time groups.

Hotel Taroudannt (*A), Place Assarag; tel. 852416. French-run hotel of great character with fifty-three beds. Bar like a Marseilles movie-set. Room-keys from the barman.

Where to eat

The best places to eat are local cafés, not always easy to find. Try the **Restaurant de la Place**. The **Hotel Taroudannt** serves reasonable meals. Dining *al-fresco* is a pleasant experience at the **Hotel Salam**.

Tata

A new tarmac road has been built from Taroudannt to Tata (200 km). A dusky-pink town surrounded by irrigated palms and gardens, Tata is a thoroughly Berber place. The dry surrounding hills are studded with *ksour*. **Tiggane** and **Agadir-Lehne** are recommended. Hikers will find Tata makes a good base. It is still rarely visited by tourists. Bank, PTT, café-grills.

Where to stay

Relais des Sables, Avenue des FAR; tel. 802301. Sixty rooms, pool, licensed restaurant.

Hôtel la Renaissance (**B), 96 Avenue des FAR; tel. 802042. Clean, friendly and comfortable.

Beyond Tata you really need a four-wheel drive. The road linking it with Foum Zguid degenerates into a rough *piste* after Kasbah el-Joua and there are several checkpoints.

The Western Sahara

If you are without transport, the entire journey through south-west Morocco can be made by bus, or *grand-taxi*, although you will have to change several times en route. RAM flies daily from Casablanca to Agadir, Laayoune and three times a week to Dakhla. The Compagnie Moroccan Maritime operates a shipping service between Agadir and

Laayoune. Unless you travel at least one way by road, however, there is no point in going to the Deep South, as the road, the towns and the people you pass are its attraction.

Before you make a circuit of the Western Sahara, be clear what it holds in store. Outside Agadir there is no tourist development as such – few decent hotels and no restaurants. At times basic comforts, too, are missing. Even the omnipresent pharmacies peter out. There is no WC between Tan-Tan and Laayoune (over 400 km). If you ask where the WC is in a local café (and even these are few and far between) the owner will politely tell you to use the desert.

The beauty of driving in the Western Sahara is the superb tarmac road taking you through the desert. Except for occasional loose edges and pot-holes, the surface is good and you can average 110 km per hour. Four-wheel drive is unnecessary unless you expect to shoot off on desert *pistes* – not advisable without local knowledge. The main danger is encountering wind-blown sand on the road where least expected. Hitting a dune is a jarring experience, while colliding with a camel can terminate your holiday. Remember, therefore, that ships in the desert have right of way. It is also important to plan your journey carefully so you do not drive into the sun. This usually means an early departure when travelling south, but with the rising sun behind you on the return leg, you can leave whenever you like.

Petrol costs less in the Western Sahara than in the rest of Morocco, often $10 a tank less. Ensure your tank is full before leaving places such as Goulimine, Laayoune and Dakhla, but you will never be more than 200 km from a pump. Check the spare tyre is in good condition and carry water. Should you have a problem on the main road, it is never long before a fish truck or a *grand-taxi* stops and its driver and passengers get out to help. Out of sight of the tarmac is another story. And if you are finicky about food, stock up on tinned commodities in Agadir. You can find mineral water and basic fill-you-ins en route.

A recommended circuit starting from Agadir, to Tiznit, Goulimine, Tan-Tan, back to Goulimine, Sidi Ifni and Tafraoute, ending in Agadir, takes about eight to ten days (1,000 km).

To head for Tiznit out of Agadir follow the Boulevard Mohammed V towards Inezgane. At the edge of the city is a road sign that spells the magic of far-away places: Goulimine 196, Laayoune 642, Dakhla 1,339, Nouakchott 2,055, Dakar 2,580. The road to Tiznit is good, though uninteresting – about 2¼ hours direct.

Tiznit   If Tiznit is your first fortified town, you will not be disappointed. Planted on the hot plains between Agadir and the desert, it evokes strong images of Morocco's past yet its walls are not as old as you might imagine. Extending for more than 5 km and originally topped with thirty-six towers, they were constructed by Sultan Moulay Hassan between 1883 and 1885.

History   The subsequent history of Tiznit is linked with the charismatic personality of Ahmed el-Hiba, a Blue Man from the Western Sahara who declared himself Sultan of Tiznit in 1912. After swearing to rid Morocco of infidels, he led a huge *harka* of Blue Men – some sources say 12,000 – over the Atlas to Marrakesh, but he was out-gunned and politically out-manoeuvred by French and loyalist forces and was obliged to retreat to Taroudannt. Ultimately conceding defeat, he died in 1919.

What to see

The **Grand Mosque** where el-Hiba was proclaimed sultan is reached by following the Rue de l'Hôpital through the *medina*. The mosque's curious minaret, similar to those in Timbuktu, is pierced by a series of perches to assist the ascent of the dead to Paradise.

The **Lalla Tiznit spring**, or *Source Bleu*, is 100 m further on. Tiznit is said to be named after Lalla Tiznit, apparently a lady of ill-repute, who caused a spring to gush forth miraculously when she renounced her wicked ways. The state of the spring, especially during summer, does not encourage you to bathe. Beyond here is **Bab Targua**, one of the nine gates in Tiznit's walls, with access on to the ramparts.

El-Hiba's father, Sheikh Ma el-Ainin of Smara, is buried in Tiznit.

Shopping

Shopping in Tiznit is better than in Agadir, but you must bargain well, as traders are used to day-trippers. Small shops around the *mechouar* sell decorated swords and silver jewellery – necklaces, rings, earrings, *fibulas* and 'Hands of Fatima'. Tiznit is the start of the 'Blue belt' and you are likely to see some of these striking nomads in the *souq*. There is a busy Thursday *souq* on the Tafraoute road selling vegetables, fruit, nuts and olives from the Anti-Atlas. You can walk there in ten minutes from the first roundabout.

Where to stay

The cheapest hotels in Tiznit, around the *mechouar*, tend to be hot in summer and always noisy from the bustle of shoppers and traffic.

Hôtel de Paris (unclassified), Avenue Hassan II; tel. 2865. Near the roundabout. Large, clean rooms with excellent beds and private bathrooms. Good restaurant. Recommended.

Tiznit (***A), Rue Bir Inzaran; tel. 862411. On the roundabout. Comfortable, although the front rooms are noisy. Small swimming-pool and disco – the Anzli Club – both something of an anachronism in Tiznit.

Moving on

CTM **buses** to Tata, Goulimine and Sidi Ifni leave from Bab Oulad Jarrar. *Grands-taxis* are found outside the *mechouar* or along the road past the roundabout, and Landrover taxis for Tafraoute on the Tafraoute road beyond the Hotel Tiznit.

North-west of Tiznit is the Sidi Moussa d'Aglou beach (17 km) – reached by *grand-taxi* if you have no transport. The boisterous surf makes swimming dangerous, but looks beautiful. Around the headland is a curious semi-troglodyte fishing village. There are camping facilities, but skip Sidi Moussa d'Aglou if you plan to visit the Plage

Goulimine Province

Blanche near Goulimine. The café-restaurant serves good fish *tajine*.

A rugged mix of mountain, plain and desert, Goulimine Province has the true Saharan climate. Cereals and legumes are grown where larger streams – the Oued Draa and the Ksabi – permit irrigation, but most of the population of 159,000 are pastoral nomads practising trans-humance between the Anti-Atlas and the Atlantic.

The town of Goulimine lies 120 km south of Tiznit on a good, direct route through **Bou Izakarn**, at the foot of the Anti-Atlas. A garrison town, it has a basic hotel, the Anti-Atlas. An important road junction between the Souss and the Anti-Atlas, Bou Izakarn is the place to negotiate a *grand-taxi* for Amtoudi and Ifrane de l'Anti-Atlas. Goulimine is 41 km (see pp. 231-2 for the alternative route to Goulimine via Sidi Ifni).

Blue Men
The legendary Blue Men of the Western Sahara, without whom it would lose much of its appeal, are encountered in markets all over the Souss, but they are at home, as it were, from Goulimine south to Mauritania: their peripatetic lifestyle ignores frontiers. 'Deny me the freedom of movement and you deny me the right to breathe' is an old saying among the tribes. Their name comes from their fascination with the colour blue, either light blue or deep indigo; the Mauritanian nomad even stains his skin with indigo which is never washed off. The long blue robe is called a *khont* and wound turban-like around their aquiline features is a strip of blue or black cotton cloth known as a *litham*.

The Blue Men can be roughly divided into three groups: Tekna, Reguibat and Moor; the Moors are a mixture of Berber, Arab and African negro. Goulimine is home-base for the Tekna. The town lies on the northern fringe of their territory between the Oued Noun in the north, the Seguiet el-Hamra in the south, and the Draa *hammada* stretching west to the Atlantic. Ethnologists attribute their origin to the Sanhaja Berbers and Maaqils, a Yemeni tribe which migrated to Morocco in the thirteenth century. They are sub-divided into sixteen local tribes who live by herding camels and sheep and trading. They also own the oases.

The Reguibat conform even more closely to the classic Saharan nomad. A subdivision of the Sanhaja group, their name comes from a *marabout* in the Touat area – Sidi Ahmed R'Gubi. Their domain is essentially the desert and, accustomed to roaming in the wilderness, they guard their independence passionately, caring even less for bureaucracy than the Tekna. Resourceful and frugal, they count their wealth in camels and carpets.

The Moors, distinguished by their education and knowledge of classic Arabic, are more Arabized than the other two. The Imraguens are fishermen of similar mixed Berber and negro stock. A subgroup of the Ouled Delim tribe, the Chnagla are also nomad-fishermen whose crude camp sites are passed on the journey down the coast. The Blue Men all speak *Hananya*, a language close to literary Arabic, but with expressions lifted from the Berber dialect of the Souss.

In character the Blue Man resembles the Arab Bedouin nomad,

being equally independent and resourceful but also vain and aloof, considering himself a cut above sedentary mortals; indeed the descendants of the Lemtuna long ago founded the Almoravid dynasty in Marrakesh.

Every urban family counts at least one relative in the *bled* looking after the herds, but as the demand for Western goods increases, the traditional lifestyle is changing. Younger, educated Blue Men are settling down in commerce or the civil service, or moving away in search of work. Tourism is one solution to the local employment problem and many sedentary Moroccans now dress up as Blue Men in order to attract tourists visiting the Saturday camel market.

Goulimine

An ancient caravanserai between Morocco and Timbuktu, today Goulimine is an important administrative and market centre. Coming down through the Mighert pass from Tiznit, you will see it spread out on the plain, a mixture of stone-coloured houses and pink arcaded shops. The large edifice on your right is a flour mill; the ONMT is the red building further along on your left. Its tourism officer, Sheikh Ma el-Ainin Mohamed Laghdaf, is one of the hundreds of grandsons of the great Saharan Blue Man Sheikh Ma el-Ainin. The only official guide in Goulimine is a grizzled Blue Man aged eighty-nine who fought with nationalist forces in the Spanish Civil War. He waits at the Salam Hotel.

The Avenue Mohammed V takes you past the post office and the evocatively named 'Rendezvous aux Hommes Bleus' garage. Head downhill to the Place Hassan II, overlooked by *café-terraces*.

Goulimine's *souq* is quiet during the week, but on Friday, the day before the camel market, it is crowded with Blue Men doing their shopping. If you cannot resist a schoolboyish urge to dress up like one of them, you can buy all the right gear in Shop 80–81 **Dbish El Houcine**, where an entire Blue Man outfit – robe, trousers and **litham** – costs under $20. Ask someone to show you how to tie the **litham**. El-Hiba was called the 'Blue Sultan', as he was never known to take his **litham** off. Before buying cloth, open it up and check it is clean; many rolls are stained from the trader and customer chatting over coffee.

What to see

Goulimine's Saturday **camel market** is one of Morocco's best known *souqs*. Excursions from Agadir depart early, with the first sleepy-eyed tourists arriving around 9 a.m. You can stay Friday night at the Salaam Hotel, see the *souq*, and leave before they arrive. Without a car, take a *petit-taxi*, or walk – just follow the locals walking south; it takes thirty minutes from the Salam.

Although the *souq* has become a tourist attraction, it has not been ruined, and apart from a few energetic traders who spread out swords, jewellery and other bric-à-brac on their blue robes, it has probably altered little since the last century. An important weekly event for the nomads, it is held in a large, rocky site off the road to Tan-Tan. One section is reserved for vegetable produce, another for animals; some have spent several days on the hoof, arriving only at dawn on the day of the *souq*.

You are likely to see fifty to eighty camels (as many as 1,000 beasts converge on Goulimine during the huge *souq* held in conjunction with the *moussem*). Tribesmen draw back the camels' lips to examine their teeth – an indication of age. Young animals between six and eight months old are sold quickly. A bunch of grass tied around an animal's neck shows new ownership. Camels for transportation are becoming obsolete as motorways creep into the desert. Most brought to Goulimine are sold for breeding and meat. You may wish to avoid the butchers' shops. A pair of hairy legs – camel, goat or cow – at the entrance shows the day's 'special'.

The main *souq* sells produce from the Anti-Atlas. There are piles of white turnips, onions and apples. Blue Women also sell raffia mats. The people sliding their feet along the mats are feeling for knots. Bargaining is brisk and a buyer soon walks off with a rolled mat under one arm.

Where to stay

The dispute over the Western Sahara has inhibited investment in a local hotel industry. At present, the only place I can recommend in Goulimine is the Hotel Salam. Even if you don't stay at the Salam, check the bar. The last bar before the Sahara, it is packed with Blue Men whose regal composure is affected by the consumption of large quantities of Flag Pils. Salam staff cope well with the problems of running a hotel in a frontier town and travellers are assured a warm welcome. Bookings are essential on Friday night.

Hotel Salam (**B), Route de Tan-Tan; tel. 872057. Fifty-four beds. Bar and restaurant.

Awful second choices are the L'Ere Nouvelle and the Bir En Zarane. Cheap cafés are found on the Place Hassan.

What to do

The famous *guedra* danced by the Blue Women is staged for tourists at the Salam at lunch-time and on Saturday evening. The hotels Mauritania and L'Ere Nouvelle have similar performances at 12 noon and 9 p.m. Recommended.

Excursions from Goulimine

If you have time before the Saturday market, drive to one of the small oases around Goulimine. **Ait Boukha** (17 km) is the most picturesque. Locals enthuse about d'Abainou, a hot spring (15 km) but the site is dirty and the small hotel profoundly melancholy.

The **Plage Blanche** (60 km), off the road to Sidi Ifni, is one of the most beautiful beaches in the Maghreb, with good swimming and miles of white sandy beach. Take water and a picnic.

Ifrane de l'Anti-Atlas (60 km) is a Berber settlement surrounded by circular walled villages. Christian and Jewish communities lived there in the twelfth century. Few tourists visit Ifrane de l'Anti-Atlas so you will be the object of curiosity, especially among children asking for *stilos*. There are several attractive walks among the irrigated palm-groves. The **Anti Atlas Hotel** has clean rooms around a small garden, and there are rooms above the **Café de la Paix**, the best place to eat.

Amtoudi

You are in for a rough but fascinating ride if you visit Amtoudi (100 km). Its twelfth-century *agadir*, built on a lofty pinnacle hundreds of feet above a gorge, is one of the most spectacular in the Atlas. An *agadir* is a fortified village store-house or a subterranean cave used by the Berber tribes to hide grain and other essentials for survival.

From Goulimine, take the asphalt road towards Tata and beyond the palm-oasis of Taghagjit turn left at the sign for Amtoudi. No petrol stations.

Several jeep-loads of tourists sometimes come from Agadir for the day, ascend the pinnacle by donkey, eat at the Auberge Amtoudi and leave – actually a splendid excursion. The trek up to the *agadir* and back takes about two hours in the company of a local guide. Its walls are in remarkably good repair and the tribe who lived here clearly had everything necessary for a long siege. The view is excellent. Remember your jacket.

Amtoudi's only facilities are at the Auberge: a clean lavatory and washing area, excellent meals, but no accommodation. The owner, Haj Ouhela, Amtoudi's entrepreneur, is building a 56-room hotel in co-operation with Holiday Service of Agadir. After lunch you may care to walk up the gorge. Camping is permitted in the *wadi* but do not become a news item about a foreigner being swept away in a flash flood.

Tan-Tan Province

The province of Tan-Tan is mainly desert and stony hill-plateaux. Vegetation consists of short, hardy scrub and cactus-like euphorbias. The scarcity of water makes sedentary living difficult and most people, both Berber and Arab, are pastoral nomads. Cereals are cultivated where there is moisture, but it is a losing battle against drought and locusts. People are extremely poor, but their dignity reveals nothing of their hard life. No one is really hungry, however. The Atlantic teems with fish and Tan-Tan is one of Morocco's major fishing ports. Sardine exports exceed 130,000 tonnes.

There are no facilities between Goulimine and Tan-Tan (125 km) so fill up with petrol at the 'Rendezvous des Hommes Bleus' garage. The road is good, but subject to flash floods when streams draining the Anti-Atlas overflow. There is a wonderful panorama from the plateau half-way to Tan-Tan. Crossing the valley is the Oued Draa, which marked the limit of French military power. The police checkpoint here is the first of many in the Western Sahara.

Tan-Tan

A curious arch formed by kissing camels spans the entrance to Tan-Tan. Although this smacks of Agadir-style tourism, you are likely to be the only visitor. Tan-Tan was included in the military zone of the Western Sahara for more than a decade. It still lives in a timewarp which is part of its charm. The entire town looks like a movie set for a Spanish Western. Everything is painted a uniform mustard and blue

– shops, houses, the mosque, even the *petits-taxis*. The population of some 52,000 are nomad traders living half in and half out of the desert. They also wear blue.

Tan-Tan is only eight or nine hours' drive from Agadir, but it has better weather. When Agadir experiences cool December days, Tan-Tan basks in sunshine, although the ocean is chilly; the annual average temperature is 19–20°C (66–68°F).

What to see   There is something vaguely exciting about Tan-Tan, which cocks a snook at the surrounding Sahara. The sandy Place Tan-Tan, now a car park, was a halt for caravans until a few years ago. Explore the town on foot. You don't need a map – there isn't one. And there are no *faux-guides*. You leave these in Goulimine. Walk along the Avenue Mohammed V to the Place Laayoune, slowly. No one hurries in Tan-Tan. Overlooked by café-hotels and enclosing the *petit-taxi* tank, this is the centre of town.

The **medina** leads off the Place Laayoune. Its small, shuttered shops close in the afternoon, but open at 4 p.m.; in summer they stay open until late at night. The major shopping centre for Saharan nomads, Tan-Tan sells tents, camel halters, ropes, rugs, bullets, sandals and skewers for *brochettes*. An occasional shop has an item of jewellery pawned by a Blue Woman.

Tan-Tan has a Sunday *souq* and an immense **moussem** is staged in late May or early June (no one seems to know). The occasion pays homage to Sidi Ma el-Ainin, with prayers at his shrine and the sacrifice of a she-camel. There is a huge camel market and in the evening women dance the *guedra* in tribal tents.

Where to stay   Tan-Tan has about twenty-five hotels, most unsuited to Western travellers. People talk of the **Royal** with a bar and pool, but it is quite likely to be full of army personnel and hence closed to visitors. The **Hotel Dakar** on the Place Tan-Tan and the quieter **Amgala** on the Avenue de la Jeunesse (around the corner) cost from 60 dh for a double room with a shower. As Tan-Tan's 'premier hotels' they are often full, and if obliged to stay at one of the other establishments, you may dream of Agadir.

Where to eat   The **Hotel Dakar** restaurant has the best reputation in Tan-Tan. Simple café-snacks are in the Rue du Commerce. The hotels **Sahara** and **Chahrazade** have *café-terraces*, while the shaded **Le Jardin**, above the Place Laayoune, is a stylish spot for coffee and cakes.

An enquiry about drink reveals that Tan-Tan is a dry town. You could try asking about black market Scotch – the hills are alive with contrabandists – but you will probably have to wait till Laayoune (400 km) to buy an alcoholic drink.

Moving on   **Buses** and **grands-taxis** for Goulimine and Laayoune leave from the Place Tan-Tan.

Tan-Tan   Tan-Tan town is 25 km inland from Tan-Tan Plage. The beach is
Plage   uninspiring compared to the Plage Blanche, but it offers pleasant

swimming. Do not venture too far out, however; there are no lifesavers and if you get caught in the undertow it's 'Hello America!' Lifesavers, touts and other adjuncts to tourism will no doubt come with the completion of the Hotel Ayoub, a four-star hotel with tennis courts, shops and a conference centre. Shabby villas already line the beach. Plans for Tan-Tan Plage include essential services, a post office and mosque, but happily the old town is too far away to be ruined by nouveau-Moorish architecture. If open, one or two cafés can supply limp salad and seafood lunch. Avoid the adjacent port. You have a good view from the road to Tarfaya.

Tan-Tan is a logical place to retrace your steps to Agadir but it is worth driving a further 10–20 km along the road to Tarfaya, where the Saharan plateau looks as if it has been snipped off with a pair of dressmaking scissors. Unable to get down the jagged cliffs, fishermen perch on the wind-buffeted edge of the 40-m drop. A helper stands poised to cut off anything big – the alternative for the fisherman is a high dive into the Atlantic.

South from Tan-Tan

Where the Oued Draa enters the Atlantic is a lovely spot to park and walk down to the lagoon. Cafés and sports facilities planned for the tourist development of Tan-Tan are likely to spoil it. The mouth of the Oued Chibka is another picturesque stop. Also striving to reach the ocean is the Oued el-Ouar, which ends just before the beach. No facilities.

Akhfenir

Akhfenir, roughly two-thirds of the way to Tarfaya, is a string of roadside cafés selling seafood. Whether you eat in the **Café France**, **Café Tanger** or **Café Marché Vert**, the cost is the same and none will bankrupt you. Akhfenir also has a mechanic and petrol station.

With the minaret of Tarfaya on the horizon, you then drive parallel to a long stretch of beach. It is the most accessible place on the Atlantic coast but close scrutiny reveals it is strewn with detritus of passing ships. Ocean reefs, fog and desert sand storms have claimed many vessels venturing too near this treacherous coastline, as the rusting hulks at Cape Juby testify. Beach fishing is excellent.

Tarfaya

At Cape Juby the road swings inland for Laayoune but continue straight on for Tarfaya, whose outlying houses are half-buried under sand dunes. Death by asphyxiation is a likely prognosis for the small settlement, whose women spend half their lives sweeping their thresholds clear of sand. After the *chagi*, some families have to be dug out of their homes. The Spanish withdrew from Tarfaya in 1958, leaving peeling remnants of Spanish occupation – a church, barracks, beachfront villas – and little else. An enquiry in French now elicits a response in Spanish, spoken fluently by many locals. The town itself is tiny, with a score of shuttered shops clustered around the mosque. Most of the inhabitants – estimated at 7,000 – combine a little commerce with fishing. Tarfaya lies on the main migration route for large pelagic species of fish including swordfish and tuna. Fishermen sell their catch along with a few onions and other vegetables on a corner near the mosque. Basically Tarfaya resembles a sleepy dog which awakes, stretches and barks only once a week – at Friday prayers.

History   Tarfaya began life as a small trading post founded by a Saharan adventurer named Donald Mackenzie. In 1895 Mackenzie sold 'Port Victoria' to the sultan for £50,000 and it was subsequently used to supply building materials and weapons to Sheikh Ma el-Ainin in Smara. The Berlin Conference of 1885 gave Tarfaya to Spain, but like the rest of the Rio de Oro, it did not interest Madrid. It was offered to France in the early 1900s, but the offer was withdrawn when the town was found to have value as a stop on the 'Aéropostale Service'. Tarfaya relives this claim to fame each October when competitors stop during the 'Rallye Aérien' from Toulouse to Tarfaya, Saint Louis and Dakar, Senegal. They are billeted in tents, as Tarfaya has no accommodation.

Pilots such as **Saint-Exupéry** have left vivid descriptions of flying over this empty shoulder of south-west Morocco, of moments during a storm when the desert appeared to levitate as hundreds of tonnes of sand were sucked into the air. Flying blind through this reddish hell, or buffeted by wind in the thin blue air above it, the airstrip at Cape Juby was a friendly landmark.

At present there are no facilities of any kind in Tarfaya. Like Tan-Tan and Laayoune, its long-term prospects for tourism investment depend on the outcome of the United Nations referendum to determine the status of the Western Sahara.

The road between Tarfaya and Laayoune (100 km) is one of the best stretches of the Atlantic Highway – you can reach Laayoune in an

Tah   hour. At Tah, 35 km from Tarfaya, you pass a monument marking two significant events in Moroccan history: the visit to the Western Sahara by Sultan Hassan I in 1885, and the 'Green March' rally by King Hassan II in 1975. Tah marks the so-called 'dissuasion line', where by arrangement with Spain the marchers turned back.

Rio de Oro   If you have travelled this far south, you are one of the few tourists to visit the Western Sahara. Its first contact with Europe was in 1405, when a French vessel landed at Boujdour to waylay a Tekna caravan. By the fifteenth century, the Portuguese and Spanish were trading in slaves and gold discovered at the mouth of the river at Dakhla – the origin of the region's misleading name 'Rio de Oro'. In 1884, when Portuguese and Spanish interests clashed, Madrid declared a protectorate over some 112,000 square miles of south-west Morocco. Until 1914 Dakhla and Tarfaya were significant settlements. The inhospitable hinterland subsequently became a sanctuary for tribal resistance to the French and Spanish protectorates, led by Sheikh Ma el-Ainin, the sultan's official representative in the south.

Sheikh Ma el-Ainin and his sons, notably el-Hiba, planned their campaigns from his capital at Smara. They remained at the forefront of resistance to colonial rule until 1934. From 1934 until 1946, the

'Spanish Sahara' was administered as an adjunct to the Spanish zone of northern Morocco centred in Tetouan. With no apparent potential, south-west Morocco was ignored by Madrid and conveniently forgotten by the rest of the world. Prior to 1975, there were only two schools in the Western Sahara and twenty-four telephone subscribers, giving local Saharoui no option but to continue fishing and pastoral nomadism. Spain's attitude changed abruptly when rich phosphate deposits were discovered in Bou Craa. Billions of pesetas were subsequently pumped into the phosphates industry. The underlying theme of the Saharoui independence struggle comes from a dream of enjoying a per capita income from phosphates comparable to the oil-wealth that transformed the Arabian Gulf states.

The Saharoui

Most Saharoui, commonly known as the 'Ahel es-Sahel' (people of the Atlantic littoral), remain nomads, still relying on the camel for sustenance, transport and as a unit of exchange. Trading in skins, salt and dates is also second nature and many tribes, notably the Tekna in Goulimine and Laayoune, also own shops. The figure for the indigenous population of the Western Sahara is sensitive, as it is vital to the referendum. An official Spanish estimate in 1974 was around 74,000; the figure of 120,000 claimed by Rabat now includes many workers from other areas in Morocco.

Tall, lean and with a preoccupied air, your average Saharoui man wears a blue robe – the *derraa* – which has a large embroidered pocket on the chest. His scarf, or *shesh*, may be blue or white and he wears traditional nail sandals. I found a certain resemblance between Saharoui and Sudanese women. Tending to obesity, they share the same flat-footed gait, although unlike in Sudan, they are mercifully uncircumcised. The Saharoui woman's robe, a *melfha*, is similar to the Indian sari. Blue, black or white are popular colours among older women, patterned yellow, red and green are trendy with the young generation of students.

Laayoune Province

One of five provinces in the Western Sahara, Laayoune is 36,000 sq km of pebble plain, limestone plateaux and dunes. It has a harsh climate, though without the enervating humidity of the central Atlantic coast. Rain barely settles the dust. When the *chagi* blows it is time to remain indoors, or if you are a nomad to wrap your *litham* around your face and stand, like the herd, with your back to the wind.

Laayoune

The best view of Laayoune is on the road from Tarfaya. Park beyond the large military garrison on the right. Do not photograph it, or your arrival in Laayoune may be delayed.

Not yet thirty years old, Laayoune sits on a ridge on the other side of the Pont du Marché Vert. Built by the Spanish, it has been the focus of massive spending by Rabat since 1976. Almost everything is new – roads, schools, houses, hospital, mosque and a sports stadium seating 30,000. From where, one wonders, will the spectators come? I was reminded of Abu Dhabi during the oil-boom: Laayoune, too, is modern, characterless and invaded by cheeky sand drifts. The population of 130,000 is a mix of Saharoui traders and many Moroccan entrepreneurs from the north, attracted by generous wages and government-sponsored projects.

What to see

The old Spanish settlement in what is now 'Lower Laayoune' overlooks the riverbed of the Seguiat el-Hamra. It has become a depository for rubbish from the market by the cathedral, which is now closed. The curious, white domed houses, like stalkless mushrooms, were built on the principle that curves deflect the sun.

The new town, 'Upper Laayoune', has twin centres linked by the Boulevard de la Mecque. At one end is the *mechouar* flanked by four bizarre monuments like hollow space-capsules topped with coronets which can be floodlit should the king arrive unexpectedly at night. The large building is the **Palais des Congress**, while the modern glass pavilion, the Hall of the Green March, exhibits memorabilia of this event. The **Moulay Abdelaziz Mosque** is the spiritual, commercial and entertainment centre of Laayoune. Surrounded by shops and the Artisans' Centre, the mosque overlooks the Colline des Oiseaux, a cliff which has been landscaped to provide the first public park in the Western Sahara. There are fountains, gardens and cages of very expensive tropical birds. Nothing has been overlooked to keep the birds content. They are fed on bananas and nuts and have blinds to pull around their cages in a sand storm. Effectively it is better to be a bird in Laayoune.

Shopping

The **Artisans' Centre** is one of the most pleasing in Morocco. Denied an education under the Spanish, men and women are now learning crafts and skills with a furious enthusiasm. You can buy camel saddles, pipe holders and nomad bags. Close scrutiny reveals some are lined with chewing-gum wrappers and the drums are empty tins of powdered milk covered with camel-skin. Such souvenirs are a wistful testament to the lack of funds, but hats off to local ingenuity.

The Central Market, still known as the *Souq* **el-Jma'al** (camel market) sells foodstuffs. Modest shops along the Avenue Hassan II sell other requirements. Laayoune is also where to get your hair done. A surfeit of beauty salons is inherited from Laayoune's day as headquarters of the Tercios regiment and attendant ladies.

Where to stay

It is a surprise, after the long drive south, to find two four-star hotels in Laayoune. There are no good middle-range hotels.

Hotel Parador (★★★★★A), Rue Okba Ben Nafia; tel. 894500. Revamped Spanish *parador* with sixty-five beds, managed by Club Mediterranée. Large, comfortable rooms. Pool. It is the best place to stay in Laayoune and the only de-luxe hotel south of Agadir.

Hotel Massira (★★★★A), Avenue de la Mecque; tel. 894225. Also managed by Club Mediterranée. 150 beds. All amenities. Both hotels may be full of Club-Med guests, or they may be empty.

Hotel Nagjir (★★★★A), Place Dchira; tel. 894168. Clean and comfortable hotel. Over-rated but the management is trying hard. Centre of the New Town. Only nightclub in 100,000 sq km.

Hotel el-Alya, 93 Rue Kadi el-Glaoui; tel. 894144. Basic but clean. Medium priced.

Hotel Lakoura, Avenue Hassan II, tel. 893378/9. Depressing area near the central market. Uninspiring but clean and suitable for one or two nights.

Where to eat There is little choice of where to eat in Laayoune. The **el-Alya** restaurant is probably the best value, but check the chef is there. If he cooks for a lunchtime package-tour from the Canary Islands, he might take the evening off. Food at the **Parador** and **Massira** is not the usual Club-Med standard. Try the **Café Amal** (Place Dechira), **al-Sud** (near the stadium), or **Café Tafoukat**, by the market.

Moving on There is a RAM office at 7 Place Bir Anzarane (tel. 84071). The **airport** is five minutes from the town centre. The **bus station** and ***grand-taxi*** rank is near Souq Makhah, at the end of Avenue Hassan II. The CTM bus to Marrakesh leaves at 4 p.m.; 200 dh. The fare to Tan-Tan is 50 dh. Laayoune to Tan-Tan by *grand-taxi* costs 350 dh with six passengers.

Excursions from Laayoune There is limited information – usually verbal – on local attractions at the ONMT, located at the foot of the Colline aux Oiseaux. The tourism officer reminded me of an Arab oil sheikh convinced he will strike it rich. Tourism, as enjoyed in Fez, or Marrakesh, is seen as Laayoune's divine right, but while a visit there makes an unusual day-trip from the Canary Islands, Laayoune's pull over Morocco's traditional resorts is feeble.

Sand dunes The main attractions are the great dunes thrown up by the Sahara, 12 km south of Laayoune. Huge barriers to stop sand encroaching on to the road meet with little success and a fleet of bulldozers stands ready like snowploughs in a northern winter. The best spot to see the dunes is behind the power plant, where the plateau ends abruptly – rather like the Great Rift Valley – on a sea of sand. You can park here and slide down to the dunes, but keep your shoes as the initial descent is tough. Films such as *Ishtar*, starring Dustin Hoffman and Isabelle Adjani, have been shot against this backdrop.

Lemsyed Oasis The tourist office extols '*la fraicheur de son climate, l'eau douce et les palmiers*' of Lemsyed Oasis (18 km), but it is a small plot of ragged palms not worth visiting. A crumbling Spanish fort, now occupied by the Moroccan Southern Infantry, lies across the *wadi*.

Laayoune Plage Laayoune Plage is about 25 km south of town, near the phosphate terminal. The beach lies beyond a melancholic village invaded by sand. It is polluted and pebbly but swimming is safe. A lagoon has a small flock of resident flamingoes. Take a picnic.

Bou Craa A roller-coaster, sand-covered tarmac leads to the phosphate mines at Bou Craa (120 km). You need permission (hard to obtain) to enter. Outside the compound there are no facilities.

Smara

Smara is not worth the long drive from Laayoune (240 km) and decidedly not the 1,000 km loop from Tan-Tan. It has historic interest for French or Moroccan scholars, but little else. Most of the celebrated town built by Sheikh Ma el-Ainin in 1884–5 lies in ruins.

A scholarly Blue Man who knew the Qur'an by heart at the age of eight, Sheikh Ma el-Ainin planned to build a great town on the caravan routes between Morocco and Mauritania. From the black laterite *kasbah* of Smara, he harangued local tribes into resistance against the French and Spanish. His huge mosque, planned as the biggest in the Sahara, was based on the Mezquita in Cordoba. At night with the desert wind whipping through its arches it is eerie. The white *zaouia* is glimpsed above the walls of his library, stripped of books by the departing Spanish. Surrounded by black *hammada*, Smara is the last resort. Two awful hotels face each other at the crossroads. The entire town lies within a military zone.

South from Laayoune

Outside Laayoune you wave goodbye to familiar facilities and you need a valid reason for wanting to travel further south. The logical place to go is Dakhla, on the Mauritanian border, but it is 536 km (a five- or six-hour drive) from Laayoune, itself 642 km from Agadir. It is possible to catch a *grand-taxi* to Dakhla from Laayoune.

If you cannot resist the temptation to travel south of Laayoune, drive as far as the terrible Café Lemsid (70 km). Beyond the phosphate port fed by a 120-km conveyor belt from Bou Craa, the road surface is poor and driving needs your full attention to avoid pot holes. While traffic is light, *grands-taxis* recklessly driven by Blue Men are likely to shear off your wing-mirrors. Disappointingly, the road veers inland and no matter how much you may want to swim, do not attempt to cross without a four-wheel drive. The ocean is always further than it looks.

The **Café Lemsid** looks like a giant sweet that has fallen off a truck. Caramel and raspberry red, it sits by the road surrounded by the detritus of local civilization: burst tyres, perished fan-belts, broken fish-traps, and empty port-a-gas cylinders. A blanket is stuffed in a hole in the wall to keep out the *chagi*. To nomads, however, this is the supermarket of the Sahara. Among useful items stacked in no particular order behind its counter are boxes of Gunpowder tea, flour, candles, packets of 'Tide', balls of string and tinned sardines. Fresh fish is delivered daily from Boujdour, so that even in this God-forsaken place you can sit down at a broken table for lunch. A lame, fish-eating chicken hops about for scraps. No one would eat it, I decided; it was much too horrible. When a car drew up outside, I expected it to disgorge a host of Fellini film extras – dwarfs, fat ladies, transvestites and dancing bears – but they were merely crushed taxi passengers glad of the chance to stretch their legs on the journey north to Agadir.

Boujdour

The port-town of Boujdour is almost half-way to Dakhla. Its most prominent building is a lighthouse built by the Portuguese in the fifteenth century and restored in 1965. A one-street town leads down to the fishing port, on which Boujdour pins its future. Present fishing methods using lines from small boats cannot differ much from 500 years ago, when the Italian navigator Cadamostro spoke of immense banks of sardines, anchovy, mullet and squid. Today the Atlantic to Cape Blanc is fished by a dozen nations, notably Russia, Canada and Japan. Estimates show the waters off the Western Sahara can support an annual catch of 2 million tonnes or more. A desalination plant and freezing works may improve Morocco's chances of sharing this harvest from the benevolent Atlantic.

Boujdour at present has no accommodation. The menu at **Rashida's** café-grill not unnaturally features fish *tajine*.

Boujdour to Dakhla

South of Boujdour is a long beach where Chnagla fishermen collect crabs and shellfish on the reefs. Great middens of shells, some over 3 km long, indicate they have been doing so for a considerable time.

About 145 km south of Boujdour, the road veers inland. **Skaymat** is a fly-spot settlement, but beyond here you reach the coast again. Seventy km before Dakhla there is a splendid beach flanked by cliffs. This was the frontier between Morocco and Mauritania from 1977 to 1979, until Mauritania relinquished its share of the former 'Spanish Sahara'.

Dakhla

Dakhla lies at the end of a long peninsula which encloses a series of sandy bays. It has enormous tourist potential – swimming, fishing, wind-surfing and sand yachting are all possibilities – but whether it becomes the 'Tijuana of Morocco' depends on the referendum on Western Sahara (see p. 29). The *souqs* cater mainly to the 'garrison man', as Barnaby Rogerson neatly puts it. Aftershave and elaborate penknives hold little attraction for Milady Traveller. The *hammam* is named after the 'Green March' (women 10 a.m. to 5 p.m. and men 6 to 8 p.m.).

Where to stay

Hotel Doums (★★★A), Avenue el Walaa; tel. 8908045. Twenty-nine rooms. New. Licensed restaurant.

What to do

Dakhla is a military zone. There is little to do at night. Soldiers kill time playing draughts. Local fishing is legendary (see above). The town hosts an annual *Concourse de Pêche*, when a few keen anglers fly in for three days' fishing. Local skiffs are available for hire. There are also jeeps.

Beyond Dakhla

The tarmac ends outside Dakhla, but you can continue to the border on a *piste*. You will drink plenty of tea at the checkpoints while your passport is scrutinized – usually upside down – and details of your life are tossed about in Arabic. Where is your husband? Dead, I answered. Children? Dead. All dead, I found an effective reply. You leave the Atlantic behind for a good four- or five-hour drive to al'Gargarat. From down here Agadir seems like paradise.

With some experience of driving in the Deep South you will possibly enjoy the return trip better. Leaving Laayoune by 9 a.m. takes you to Goulimine by dusk, including a stop in Tan-Tan. Leave Goulimine early, before 10 a.m., for Sidi Ifni, en route to Tiznit.

Sidi Ifni

Do not allow locals to dissuade you from driving to Tiznit via Sidi Ifni. Winding around the Atlantic cliffs, this is one of the most beautiful roads in Morocco and the 62 km should not take more than two hours. Scenery is pastoral, with shepherds herding flocks among the *argan* trees. From the highest point you have a view of the Oued Ifni, which slows to a trickle during summer and never quite reaches the ocean. *Souq el Arba de Mesti* (37 km) has a Wednesday *souq*.

History

Sidi Ifni was a peaceful fishing village when Spaniards from the Canary Islands landed in 1445 and established a base-camp there. They called it Sidi Ifni after a local *marabout*, Santa Cruz de Mar Pequeña. In 1524 the colony was attacked by Saadians supported by tribesmen from the Western Sahara. Not until the Spanish occupation of the Sahara in 1934 was Sidi Ifni colonized again. Some 8,000 civilians and 25,000 troops and their families settled in the tiny enclave covering only 2,500 sq km. They built churches, hotels, a theatre and casino, but streets were left unpaved and there was no lighting. Madrid returned this curious little place to Morocco in 1969, when the Moroccan government cut off all land communications.

What to see

A white-washed town on a cliff-top, Sidi Ifni looks exactly like a Spanish village of the 1960s. The old **Plaza de España** remains the social centre for the evening *paseo*, when Moroccans circumambulate a blocked fountain plunged in overgrown gardens. A closed Catholic church and a locked-up Spanish consulate complete the picture. A baroque stairway leads down to the beach from a crumbling *mirador*.

Sidi Ifni exudes a strong feeling of *déjà-vu*. In El Orogeria, the watch-mender lamented the departure of the Spanish: Moroccans are apparently even worse time-keepers. In the barber's, others remembered Spanish National Day, when officers and wives stepped out a smart *paso-doble* in the Hotel Baamrane.

There is a small shopping centre and a Sunday *souq* near the airport, where goats graze on weeds in the concrete runway. I drove along it believing it was a road until flagged down by a soldier. Beyond is a new block of apartments, indicating Sidi Ifni is changing.

Where to stay

There are no de-luxe hotels.

Hotel Bellevue (★A), 9 Place Hassan II; tel. 875072. Clean. Request a room with ocean view. Bar and restaurant with mixed menu.

Other hotels are the **Beau Rivage**, which has basic rooms, a terrace and a colourful bar-restaurant, and the **Hotel Baamrane**, situated on the beach. Once elegant, the Baamrane is now dilapidated and the housekeeper had gone shopping, taking the master-key, so I could not see a room. Bar and parking.

The road to Tiznit

The coast road north of Sidi Ifni reminded me of the tiny Canary Island called La Palma. Groves of cactus sprout from higgledy-piggledy stone walls dividing small farmhouses with large water-jars under the eaves. Everything is cactus-green and Atlantic blue. **Mirhleft**,

232

thirty minutes' drive from Sidi Ifni, is a small village with simple holiday cottages to rent along a striking blue bay. The **Tafkout** and **Farah** are basic hotels. There are excellent nearby beaches. At Gourizim you turn inland for Tiznit. The drive is especially impressive on the way back from Laayoune: only after being in the desert can you appreciate the colour green. The green hills are left behind as you descend on to the dry plain at Tiznit. Sidi Ifni to Tiznit takes about one hour.

The Anti-Atlas

Tiznit to Tafraoute (144 km) is one of those magical journeys encountered in Morocco. You must leave Tiznit by 2 p.m. in order to arrive in time for sunset. Winter lighting-up time is 6 p.m. and the road is not safe to drive at night. Reckon on three or four hours for the journey.

Outside Tiznit you begin a roller-coaster ride over the folding foothills of the Anti-Atlas. The road follows a stream through a succession of gorges where goats stand in the trees nibbling *argan* nuts. About 20 km from Tiznit is a stream where children excitedly wait for tourists. It is a favourite ploy to direct you into a rut and then expect a handsome reward for pushing you out. Unless the stream is in spate, when you might require four-wheel drive, ignore the cries of: 'Les enfants vous sauvent, madame, monsieur . . .' Windows locked, drive across and keep going.

Tirhmi (61 km) overlooks the valley where el-Hiba sought sanctuary from the French. It sells the last petrol before Tafraoute. Now you start the hairpin bends up the Col du Kerdous. At 1,100 m the four-star Hotel Kerdous will one day offer seventy-two rooms, swimming, solarium and splendid view. **Tahala**, 111 km from Tafraoute, is a town of faded ox-blood-red houses ranged on a mountain ridge. The only accommodation is the odd, sometimes very odd, room above a café. The final 30 km to Tafraoute is winding mountain driving. Sound your horn to alert women, children and donkeys carrying loads of wood. Proof of the hazards are several trucks in the *wadis*.

Tafraoute

Nestling in the Anti-Atlas, Tafraoute lies in a fertile valley planted with date-palms and olives, but above all with almond trees. The region grows the best almonds in Morocco, and is especially picturesque in mid-February under dusky pink blossom (Almond Festival). Members of the Ammeln tribe who live in Tafraoute and the adjacent valleys lead a curious lifestyle, possibly as a result of a severe famine in the last century. Possessing similar business acumen to Jews, they are found running shops all over Morocco and overseas. Left in Tafraoute, their wives, children and elderly relatives, one of whom takes care of the almond trees, manage quite well. In fact with regular remittances from husbands in Casablanca, Agadir or Fez, they effectively enjoy a higher standard of living than other Berbers in the Atlas. The men return frequently behind the wheel of a Mercedes. When this shiny status symbol is paid off, they begin building a sumptuous villa in which to retire: you will see many of these half-completed houses as you walk about the valleys.

What to see

You can cross Tafraoute in a five-minute stroll – you only need a guide if you want to see the rock-drawings. The official guide is a gentle octogenarian who spent thirty years cooking for the French. He attributes the great age of many Tafraoutis to the lack of pollution and food additives and to the apricots and almonds in their diet.

The central square is lined by the Banque Populaire, the PTT, a garage, L'Etoile du Sud Restaurant and an arcade of souvenir shops. Shops in the market sell earthenware dishes, incense burners and small charcoal stoves. A grocer also sells *argan* paste. Ask if you may try a spoonful – it has a curious taste. Wednesday *souq*.

Where to stay

Investment in the hotel industry in Tafraoute would be a good bet, as it is short of beds.

Hôtel les Amandiers (****B), tel. 800008. 120 beds. Large, clean hotel on a rock pinnacle five minutes' walk from town.; Parking. Bar and restaurant. Sleep spoilt by dog-fights. Parking.

The hotels **Tanger** and **Redouane** are two basic hotels near the market. The cost of rooms rises and falls according to demand – from 20 dh. There is an over-priced camp site.

Where to eat

Tafraoute has few restaurants. The **Café A'Day** serves tasty Berber meals. A great raconteur, its chef, Ibrahim Arkarkour, takes a special interest in foreigners. The **Hotel Tanger** serves cheap nourishing *tajines* and soup. A three-course menu with drink at the theatrical **Restaurant l'Etoile du Sud** costs 38 dh. Avoid eating either here or at Les Amandiers at noon, when groups arrive from Agadir.

Excursions from Tafraoute

The pure air and peaceful ambience of Tafraoute and environs make it a delightful place to stay for a couple of days. Hikers can spend several weeks without retracing their steps. All the valleys are beautiful from afar and different up close, some noted for rock-drawings, or decorated mosques, others for *souqs* and ingenious irrigation systems. Several interesting villages lie within a short walk of Tafraoute, others require transport. A spectacular view of Tafraoute is obtained by climbing the rock behind the Amandiers Hotel. A comparison with Petra is not far wrong – the rocks are jumbled together in the same strange manner and the sunset has few equals.

Agard Oudad

Agard Oudad, the 'finger' in Berber, is the pinnacle of rock featured on most of the postcards, an easy 3-km walk from Tafraoute. At the road sign, follow the track across to the village built at the base of the huge granite outcrop. Early morning, or about 4 p.m. is the best time for photography. The curious rock-paintings 1 km further on are the work of the Belgian artist-exhibitionist Jean Veran.

Tazagha

Planted with date-palms and almond trees, this tiny settlement is minutes' walk from the Amandiers. Take a guide to point out rock-drawings of gazelles. You can extend this walk by including a visit to **Adai** (3 km), whose houses clustered around the mosque are an interesting example of Tafraouti architecture. Returning to Tafraoute along the main road takes 15–20 minutes.

Ammeln Valleys

An all-day hike from Tafraoute takes you through the Ammeln Valleys, the 'Valleys of Almonds' – take a left turn at a road fork 8 km along the road to Agadir. Of some twenty-seven villages set beneath the rocky spurs of Djebel el-Kest (2,374 m), **Oumesnat** is especially interesting: its houses seem to sprout from the rocks. From here you can walk through another twenty villages as far as **Ait Taleb,** then loop back to Adai and rejoin the main road. Every village has a tiny shop selling mineral water, fruit and bread, but you would be wise to take a picnic with you. Ordinary walking shoes are satisfactory unless you plan to climb up to the higher villages, stuck like wasps' nests in the crags. Rarely visited by tourists, their timid inhabitants only come down for the *souq*. Trekking in this part of Morocco is certain to become popular and you could make enquiries about hiring a donkey to carry your gear.

Souq Tleta de Teserirt

The Teserirt road climbs the Anti-Atlas above Agard Oudab. On Fridays the market is crowded with men and women in dark *djellabahs,* each seated behind a pile of dates, olives, oranges or onions. A close look reveals everything is handmade: clothing, shoes, and bags: there is no plastic to blow away.

Tafraoute to Agadir

The drive over the Ida Ou Gnifif pass takes roughly four or five hours on a reasonable road. At the major fork outside Tafraoute turn left; right takes you on a magical mystery tour of the Anti-Atlas. The landscape is dotted with *ksour* and when you stop, the only sound is the hoarse cry of a Berber working his mule. The main crops are cereals and almonds. Over the pass you drop into a gorge. Across the stream is the café-restaurant Vallée Madao, which has clean Wcs and snacks. At the end of the long valley is a spectacular *ksar* crowning a hill. Watch for squirrels and pot-holes on the road to **Ait Baha,** a scruffy roadside town, which marked the old border between the tribal territory of the Anti-Atlas and the Souss. It has a basic hotel, well-stocked shops and garages. You have a stunning view of the High Atlas from the Agadir exit.

A superb highway runs to Biougra (33 km from Agadir) when you are down on the plain again. **Ait Melloul** is an important market centre and road junction. Bus and taxi passengers may have to change here or in Inezgane.

Inezgane

Near Agadir Airport, Inezgane is a convenient place to stay if you are flying home. It has a good range of hotels.

Where to stay | **Hotel Club Hacienda** (★★★★A), Route Oued Souss; tel. 830176. 100 beds. Bar, nightclub, tennis, riding, swimming-pool.
Hôtel les Pyramides (★★★B), Route de la Pepinière; tel. 834705. If you cannot obtain accommodation at the Hacienda. Fifty beds. Bar, swimming-pool.
Hotel la Pergola (★★A) 8 km, Route d'Inezgane; tel. 830841. Bungalow-style hotel with forty beds. The restaurant has a good reputation. Bar. Parking.

Useful Reading

Morocco File, Amnesty International, London, 1989.

The Traveller's Guide to Morocco, Christopher Kininmonth, Jonathan Cape, 1972.

Morocco, Barnaby Rogerson, Cadogan Guides, 1989.

Journey into Barbary, Wyndham Lewis, Penguin, 1983.

The Rough Guide to Morocco, Mark Ellingham and Shaun McVeigh, Routledge & Kegan Paul, 1988.

Casablanca, Jean Michel Zurfluh, Soden, Casablanca, 1988.

Morocco, Shirley Kay, Namara Publications, 1980.

Atlas Mountains, Robin G. Collomb, West Col, 1987.

The Rogue's Guide to Tangier, Bert and Mabel Winter, Tangier, 1986.

Lords of the Atlas, Gavin Maxwell, Century, 1983.

The Kasbahs of Morocco, Rom Landav, Faber & Faber, 1969.

Morocco That Was, Walter Harris, 1921.

Islamic Monuments in Morocco, Richard Parker, Baraka Press, Virginia, 1981.

In Morocco, Edith Wharton, Century, 1920.

The Voices of Marrakesh, Elias Canetti, Marion Boyars, 1978.

A Year in Marrakesh, Peter Mayne, Eland Books, 1953.

The Sand Child, Tahar Ben Jalloun, Quartet, 1988.

Points in Time, Paul Bowles, Arena, 1982.

Index

Visitor's Guides

Tour & Explore with MPC Visitor's Guides

Britain:
Cornwall & Isles of
  Scilly
Cotswolds
Devon
East Anglia
Guernsey, Alderney
  & Sark
Hampshire & Isle of
  Wight
Jersey
Kent
Lake District
Scotland: Lowlands
Somerset, Dorset &
  Wiltshire
North Wales &
  Snowdonia
North York Moors,
  York & Coast
Northumbria
Northern Ireland
Peak District
Sussex
Treasure Houses of
  England
Yorkshire Dales &
  North Pennines

France:
Alps & Jura
Brittany
Corsica

Dordogne
Loire
Massif Central
Normandy
Normany Landing
  Beaches
Norh-East France
Provence & Côte
  d'Azur

Germany:
Bavaria
Black Forest
Rhine & Mosel
Southern Germany
Northern Germany

Italy:
Florence & Tuscany
Italian Lakes
Northern Italy
Sardinia
Southern Italy

Spain:
Costa Brava to Costa
  Blanca
Mallorca, Menorca,
  Ibiza & Formentera
Northern & Central
  Spain
Southern Spain &
  Costa del Sol
Tenerife

USA:
California
Florida
Orlando & Central
  Florida
Athens &
  Peloponnese
Austria
Austria: Tyrol &
  Vorarlberg
Crete
Cyprus
Denmark
Egypt
Goa
Switzerland
Turkey

World Traveller
The larger format
Visitor's Guides

Canada
Czechoslovakia
France
Greece
Holland
Hungary
Iceland & Greenland
Norway
Portugal
Sweden
USA

A complete catalogue of all our travel guides
is available on request